CALIFORNIA REWRITTEN

Also by John Freeman

Prose
The Tyranny of Email
How to Read a Novelist
Dictionary of the Undoing

Poetry
Maps
The Park
Wind, Trees

As Editor
Tales of Two Cities
Tales of Two Americas
Tales of Two Planets
The Penguin Book of the Modern American Short Story
There's a Revolution Outside, My Love (with Tracy K. Smith)
Sacramento Noir

CALIFORNIA REWRITTEN

A JOURNEY THROUGH THE GOLDEN STATE'S NEW LITERATURE

JOHN FREEMAN

HEYDAY

Berkeley, California

Copyright © 2025 by John Freeman

All rights reserved. Except for brief passages quoted in a review, no portion of this work may be reproduced or transmitted in any form or by any means, electronic or mechanical, including photocopying and recording, or by any information storage or retrieval system, or be used in training generative artificial intelligence (AI) technologies or developing machine-learning language models, without permission in writing from Heyday.

Library of Congress Cataloging-in-Publication Data

Names: Freeman, John, 1974- author
Title: California rewritten : a journey through the Golden State's new literature / John Freeman.
Description: Berkeley, California : Heyday, 2025.
Identifiers: LCCN 2025019084 (print) | LCCN 2025019085 (ebook) | ISBN 9781597146920 hardcover | ISBN 9781597146937 epub
Subjects: LCSH: American literature--California--History and criticism | Literature and society--California | California--In literature | LCGFT: Literary criticism | Essays
Classification: LCC PS283.C2 F74 2025 (print) | LCC PS283.C2 (ebook) | DDC 810.9/9794--dc23/eng/20250509
LC record available at https://lccn.loc.gov/2025019084
LC ebook record available at https://lccn.loc.gov/2025019085

Cover Design: Archie Ferguson
Interior Design/Typesetting: *the*BookDesigners

Published by Heyday
P.O. Box 9145, Berkeley, California 94709
(510) 549-3564
heydaybooks.com

Printed in East Peoria, Illinois, by Versa Press, Inc.

10 9 8 7 6 5 4 3 2 1

*This book is for Blaise Zerega,
and everyone else at* Alta *magazine, for saying yes.*

CONTENTS

Introduction: Anywhere but Here 1

I. EARLY MYTHS 11
Bad Indians, by Deborah A. Miranda 13
Butcher's Crossing, by John Williams 21
How Much of These Hills Is Gold, by C Pam Zhang 31
The Woman Warrior, by Maxine Hong Kingston 39
A Paradise Built in Hell, by Rebecca Solnit 47

II. ARRIVALS AND MIGRATIONS 53
Devil in a Blue Dress, by Walter Mosley 55
A Place at the Nayarit, by Natalia Molina 61
The Distance Between Us, by Reyna Grande 67
America Is Not the Heart, by Elaine Castillo 75
Solito, by Javier Zamora 81

III. BUILDING CITIES 91
Clark and Division, by Naomi Hirahara 93
I Hotel, by Karen Tei Yamashita 99
Southland, by Nina Revoyr 105
There There, by Tommy Orange 111
The Swimmers, by Julie Otsuka 117

IV. OF LANDSCAPE AND LOVE 123
Under the Feet of Jesus, by Helena María Viramontes 125
The Consequences, by Manuel Muñoz 131

V. LAW AND ORDER 139
Bad Mexicans, by Kelly Lytle Hernández 141
The Dark Hours, by Michael Connelly 149
Your House Will Pay, by Steph Cha. 157

VI. HOW WE SOUND 161
The Sellout, by Paul Beatty 163
Gordo, by Jaime Cortez 169
The Gangster of Love, by Jessica Hagedorn 173
Less, by Andrew Sean Greer 179
Colored Television, by Danzy Senna 183

VII. THE STATE OF POETRY 191
On City Lights at Ferlinghetti's 100th. 193
Postcolonial Love Poem, by Natalie Diaz. 201
On Ada Limón 207
On Gary Snyder. 215
On Kay Ryan 225

VIII. EXPLODING FANTASIAS 229
Interior Chinatown, by Charles Yu 231
Citizen, by Claudia Rankine 237
Voyage of the Sable Venus, Robin Coste Lewis 247
Barbarian Days, by William Finnegan 253

IX. THE SUBURBS. 261
Holy Land, by D. J. Waldie 263
Mean, by Myriam Gurba 271
Elsewhere, California, by Dana Johnson 277
The Barbarian Nurseries, by Héctor Tobar. 283

X. DIGITAL DYS/UTOPIAS 287
The Gold Coast, by Kim Stanley Robinson 289
The Every, by Dave Eggers. 295
The Candy House, by Jennifer Egan 305

XI. RUPTURES 311
Stay True, by Hua Hsu 313
Telephone, by Percival Everett 319
Goodbye, Vitamin, by Rachel Khong 323
The Wrong End of the Telescope, by Rabih Alameddine. 329
Gold Fame Citrus, by Claire Vaye Watkins 335
Dead in Long Beach, California, by Venita Blackburn 343

XII. WHO IS A CITIZEN?. 347
The Mars Room, by Rachel Kushner 349
The Sympathizer, by Viet Thanh Nguyen 357
The Other Americans, by Laila Lalami. 365
The Backyard Bird Chronicles, by Amy Tan. 371

Acknowledgments. 379
Appendix. 381
   99 More Essential California Books 381
   Recommended Reading from California Authors. 385
Permissions. 389
About the Author. 391
A Note on Type. 393

CALIFORNIA REWRITTEN

INTRODUCTION

Anywhere but Here

I began my life as a reader by escaping. I read to be anywhere but here—here being a suburb of Sacramento, California. Its tidy planned streets all named after Civil War battlefields. Each house a palm tree. Sprinklers set to water-conservation levels. When my parents drove off to work, I climbed atop our baking shingle roof and squinted through the pages of Charlotte Brontë, George Orwell, and Alice Walker. The further a book took me from the Central Valley, the better. Nevil Shute's *On the Beach* clobbered me, simply because Australia was so far away it might as well have been Narnia.

In reading this way, I wasn't rebellious. I was actually mimicking the trajectory of all my English classes. For a public school student, I was very lucky. My classes were small. They used a curriculum of such rigor and classical design that I might as well have been at Eton. We began my first year with *Gilgamesh* and ended with the Cavalier poets. Second year we read Plato to understand the design of Gustave Flaubert and Jane Austen. In my third year of high school, I wrote a twenty-five-page paper on the influence of Hinduism on Ralph Waldo Emerson's theology. By senior year, we'd read all of Shakespeare's plays but one.

What we didn't read were Californians.

Sure, John Steinbeck snuck in; we took half a semester to read *The Grapes of Wrath* and then another week to watch the maudlin movie made of it. But in a state that had projected its studio-lot image across the globe, the literary absence felt peculiar.

This was California in the late 1980s and early 1990s. A state stolen from Indigenous people, bought from the Mexicans after a war, built by immigrants, and narrated by all kinds had long since developed a serious literature of people from all backgrounds. It was in its third twentieth-century flowering, actually. The voices of the pre-statehood settlers like Bret Harte and Samuel Clemens gave way in the 1900s to three waves of overflowing talent—first in the early 1930s, when novelists such as Frank Norris overlapped with the earliest Asian American writers, chronicling their experiences in a state being carved from industry, then in the late 1940s to 1950s, a period bookended by two astonishing novels, Carlos Busan's *America Is in the Heart*, which follows his path from the Philippines to the canneries of Seattle and California, and Jose Antonio Villareal's *Poncho*, which kicked off an already burgeoning movement in Chicano letters. Then again in the 1970s, when radical artistic movements met social change and produced a statewide explosion across genres, from poetry to plays, among which the Beats were merely a part.

And here I was growing up in the middle of another boom period, yet we didn't read any of the leading lights, such as Maxine Hong Kingston, a groundbreaker with her memoir turned family myth, *The Woman Warrior*. Not far down the road was Gus Lee, author of *China Boy*, a vivid portrait of growing up in San Francisco's Chinatown in the 1950s, a period also brought to life in Amy Tan's first book, *The Joy Luck Club*. This was the middle of the AIDS crisis, too, but none of us were given Randy Shilts, who reported on the discovery and spread of HIV in one of the best nonfiction books ever written, *And the Band Played On*, even though its presumption of there being a patient zero later proved to be incorrect. Joan Didion grew up a few miles from my home, but no one thought to assign *Slouching Towards Bethlehem*. Let alone the Raymonds, Carver and Chandler; the fellow Berkeley High classmates, Ursula K. Le Guin and Philip K. Dick; or Octavia E. Butler, who predicted our climate and constitutional crises. We learned landscape writing from Emerson rather than from John Muir.

Of course, by the end of my high school's California-less survey of literature, I longed to go "back East," as we called the East Coast of America. The underlying message I had absorbed was that culture came from elsewhere. Critical thinking, ideas, anything serious. I was lucky in this response, to a small degree. At least in the literature I was being taught, most characters looked like me, shared my gender, my skin color, a series of assumptions. I didn't feel displaced by reading it; I simply sensed the world around me, which I already didn't think much of, losing yet more value. Even the places I loved going—the parks and cities of California, its big hot boring freeways that stretched on and on, the forests, the foothills, the tiny towns through the Central Valley—all of it had been deemed unliterary by my education. Still, looking back, I can only imagine how my nonwhite classmates felt.

California has always struggled to see itself. It's a myopia that begins with the name. Like many other conquered lands, the state also could have been called so many more accurate things. A number of these possible names lurk in our cities and rivers or perch atop our mountains and beaches. Take Malibu, where the Chumash people lived as far back as possibly 7,000 BCE, the name coming perhaps from their word Humaliwo, which means "where the surf sounds loudly." Or Milpitas, whose name comes from the Mexican Spanish for "cornfield." Perhaps a place as big as the Golden State shouldn't have been given one name but many? Napa, probably a corruption of a Wappo word that means "homeland," might have been the best. But it also might mean "bear," "fish," or "village," depending on who is doing the translating. Perhaps a state this big could have multiple meanings. But *California?*

The name comes from a novel—at least, that's the consensus. In all the history of states and countries, has there ever been a stranger, more official enshrinement of the interaction between the imagination and place? There are a few trick names of towns: Middlemarch; New Zealand, which may have been named after Eliot's book; and not to be outdone, the British have a seaside village in Devon called Westward Ho! (*with* the exclamation point). Still, when Spanish explorers began to sail around the coast of Baja and started calling the area California, after an island in a novel by Garci Rodriguez de Montalvo called *Las Sergas de Esplandián*, they leapt over the thousands of years of Indigenous history, not to mention more than one hundred tribes with their own literatures and languages—and doomed the state to a kind of futurity and fantasy.

California has been rewriting itself ever since, working against and with the winds of adventure, always trying to catch up with who actually lives here—or, in some cases, is arriving. Always describing how we live and often, as a result, what we fear. Frequently, this work is done by the recently arrived. When Bret Harte, the grandson of an Orthodox Jewish trader from Albany, turned up in 1854 and started telling the tales of miners arriving, he was not at the beginning of the state's literature but somewhere way in the middle or even its late silver age. To deal with how much had to be unremembered in order to make the place new, California spawned concepts that are with us today. Like nature. Like the wild. Jack London played to the latter concept, and how many children around the world grew up listening to its call?

I sometimes mourn the youth I would have had if I had appreciated sooner the landscape and culture I come from in California. I did go east, studied literature, and moved to New York, but I felt upon arrival as though something was missing. The idea that a tiny, several-mile-long island was the so-called center of the literary universe struck me as absurd. I went to book parties; not one of them had a firepit. Let alone a diverse cast of characters, as so many spaces in California do almost by simple demographic math. The physical elements of New York City were totally eclipsed by its concrete, too: You can smell the water around the island, but never feel it on your skin. I adore some of the city's bookstores, but I didn't find one that had figured out how to meld what was happening on the streets around it to the shelves inside it the way that City Lights, San Francisco's temple to political action and wide reading, does.

I also got tired of the insularity of it all. It took an absurdly long time for America's so-called center to see that a new wave of California literature was cresting at the turn of the twenty-first century. Literature of so many kinds and so many genres from so many different types of people—at the highest level—has been coming out of California and from Californians for decades now. In fact, if there's been an American moment in any genre this past century, it has had a California component. Dave Eggers's *A Heartbreaking Work of Staggering Genius*, made by California. Claudia Rankine's *Citizen*? Written while she taught in California. Maggie Nelson's *The Argonauts*, a breakthrough in conceiving gender, composed in California. Viet Thanh Nguyen's rewriting of a Vietnam War novel? Straight out of California. Rebecca Solnit introduced the concept of "mansplaining" in her great essay "Men Explain Things to Me," written in San Francisco.

The list goes on. Want a poem or two in the shape of a bullet that contains a universe? Kay Ryan writes them in Fairfax. She won a Pulitzer for them. As did Fairfield native Tracy K. Smith for her cosmic poetry in *Life on Mars*, as well as Frank Bidart for his epic body of work, and Adam Johnson, who proved you can imagine North Korea from San Francisco. In fact, more Californians have won Pulitzers in literature in the past decade than writers from any other region in America.

In an interview recently, the California writer Kathleen Alcott theorized that what makes California different is our sense of time. That when you can travel one hour in any direction and wind up in a desert or on a ski slope or against a rice field or within a small forest, time begins to mean something different to you. Because landscape, after all, is time. It's made by geologic time. California, as much any other place on earth, knows how sudden and dangerous a rupture in geologic time can be. We also, I think, are at the forefront of knowing what happens when humans try to yoke this vast, mysterious living thing called the Earth to human time. The fires that burn almost all year round, for example. The droughts. The sudden necessary migrations. The changes in crop patterns. Our literature has paid tribute to this already, from William T. Vollmann's epic nonfiction narrative, *Imperial*, to Claire Vaye Watkins's *Gold Fame Citrus*, still the best cli-fi novel to have emerged from a burning, troubled America since the astonishingly prognostic *Parable of the Sower*, by Octavia E. Butler.

I agree with all this, but I think something more fundamental to literature is happening in California that explains why so many of its writers are breaking new ground—why it is, I think, a literary mecca for a world in which only a precious few can choose to stay put. Writing, after all, like all art forms, is social; it draws its power from the sounds and concerns of people, from the histories they carry in their bodies. The novel, the essay, reporting, and poetry, which makes music from the sound of language, depend on how we translate what the body knows. Listening to it, stylizing it, seeing around its easier representations to more accurate narratives and better frames.

California, more than any other state in America, has begun to accept what is there, what is within its borders, and who calls it home.

I am not arguing that there is no racism in California, or white nationalist ideas. Read Mike Davis and Jon Wiener's *Set the Night on Fire: L.A. in the Sixties*, and you'll learn how white nationalism had a cozy bosom in this part of the country for almost a century. But what the state is, who came there, and who lives there now? It overwhelms an attempt to pretend whiteness as a norm.

Since I was in high school, books like *The Joy Luck Club* and *The Woman Warrior*, as well as Héctor Tobar's *Translation Nation*, have been read and taught to students by the hundreds of thousands. Books that acknowledge the depth and complexity of families and individuals who are, as I write these words, being berated and hectored by the president of the United States. Threatened with unlawful deportation. Things I had to learn of in museum exhibits, such as the incarceration of the Japanese during World War II, have been brought to life in books, such as Julie Otsuka's devastating *When the Emperor Was Divine*, also taught in schools now. Isabel Allende's novels are taught, in English and in Spanish, across California, as well as books by Reyna Grande, Victor Martinez, Luis J. Rodriguez, Javier Zamora, Victor Villaseñor, and Helena María Viramontes, something immensely important in a state where a third of the residents speak Spanish. Elsewhere the whitewash of culture has been significantly altered by books, as in Los Angeles. Walter Mosley retold the postwar history of Watts from the viewpoint of an African American private dick, Easy Rawlins, which begins when a white man walks into a bar owned by a Black man.

And now we're in the full throes of an era when the offspring of these writers are publishing. Cast your eye onto novelists like Elaine Castillo, whose debut novel, *America Is Not the Heart*, about a queer war veteran and her epic journey from the Philippines to Milpitas, proves that the banal suburbs are just as hospitable to the epic-scale novel as what we've come to expect from glamorous cities. Or turn your ear to Javier Zamora, America's young second coming of Rubén Darío, who walked to the United States alone as a child at age nine without his family and reconstructed that journey in his tremendous debut book of poems, *Unaccompanied*, and a follow-up memoir, *Solito*. Zamora was tutoring young students at Dave Eggers's 826 Valencia center when he wrote the first lines of his book of poetry.

CALIFORNIA REWRITTEN

Week to week, this big, glorious, contradictory state is coming to life on the page. Women in California prisons in the work of Rachel Kushner; Native people at a powwow in Oakland in the work of Tommy Orange; the new sounds of the Central Valley in the stories of Jaime Cortez, who grew up there, a child of documented immigrant farm laborers. Book by book, these novels and poetry and story collections are showing what bodies carry, by putting us—as readers—in them. Bodies are not simply born, the poet Natalie Diaz, from Needles, reminds us; they are built. But how? You cannot always see the gouges of tools. You have to imagine them—and in a state as trained in the eye, as saturated by light as California, this is crucial work.

I wrote many of these essays when all our bodies were ordered to stay still. During the pandemic, prompted by editors at *Alta* magazine, several friends and I got together to read books by and about Californians. It wasn't a celebratory time, but we had time—all of us did then—and what better way to pass it than by reading and then doing what we normally did, talking about those books, on a Zoom call. The idea was meant to be temporary: a stay against the insanity of forced stillness. How good it felt to escape, all the way back to the Gold Rush, which was no easy time either, as conjured to life so freshly by C Pam Zhang in her novel *How Much in These Hills Is Gold*, which boldly imagines a character between genders making their way in miner camps just as the restrictions against Chinese laborers have begun to fall hard on anyone foreign. The next month we talked to Walter Mosley about *Devil in a Blue Dress*, and several hundred people attended. Speaking from his studio on the beach in Los Angeles, he swiveled between his desk and the collection of paints he uses to make visual art, the history of his great city and its sprawling present unfolding in vibrant color.

Introduction

Months became years, and the California Book Club, as we were calling it, expanded from a few hundred members to twenty thousand. What began as a casual operation at *Alta* now involves a month-long exploration of each book, and the Zoom calls are exhilarating glimpses of the intensity with which stories about life in California are received—in part because they dramatize the lived experience of many readers. I'll never forget being halfway into the Zoom call about Naomi Hirahara's *Grand and Division*, a crime novel that unfolds in the wake of a Japanese American family's departure from one of the incarceration camps in Utah. The book's title proceeds from the address where the family in the book land, in Chicago. In the chat window of that call, one of the listeners said that not only had her family landed on that street corner too, but that, based on the description of the apartment in the book, it was probable they had lived in the same apartment as the characters in the book.

California is not a destination point but a kind of portal for remarkable journeys. I often wonder why my father, when I was growing up, never talked about his father's father—a man who lost everything and died poor. Maybe that's why my brothers and I only recently learned the true trajectory of that man's father, my great-grandfather, who'd been a baker in Grass Valley, back when the state was a few decades old and the Gold Rush had long since proved to be yet another hoax for most. Was he good to his neighbors? Did he respect people connected to the land? What tirednesses did *his* father, my great-great-grandfather, take to work every morning? What griefs? What about his wife, who'd died young, leaving him a widower with children? Not long ago I learned that this ancestor had also married his brother's widow in Canada. His family had moved there from

England, where he'd been born into the indentured poor. Hence my name. Freeman.

My grandfather was born in San Francisco in 1909, two and a half years after the earthquake and fire, on Church Street. I've seen photographs of the city from that time. What nerves are built by walking to school past rubble on that scale? What strengths? He never spoke of it. Nor did he speak of being poor, because by the time I met him he wasn't anymore. He'd built a different body around that long-ago body, the one he was born in. Was it built with fury? With love? With fear? Is that why he saved with such savage determination, why he planned? I'll never know, because we buried those stories with him in East Lawn Cemetery in Sacramento. I long for a novel that would imagine them for me.

EARLY MYTHS

BAD INDIANS

by Deborah A. Miranda

Every story is a kind of model. To function, it must have a shape, it has to have scale, and it has to have participants. A frame becomes so much more interesting once a person enters it, Kurt Vonnegut once said. I didn't appreciate the power of models until I moved to Sacramento in the mid-1980s—enthralled with a story that California pipes out across the country so regularly that it's hard to tell where it's coming from. The bland, sunny story of a place of outdoor activities and convertibles and feathered hair blowing in the wind. It was the 1980s, after all, and that's when my family reentered the frame.

That fall, I encountered another myth that California projects, not outwardly but within. That fall, little replicas of the missions began to appear everywhere around my school. Papier-mâché buildings modeled on the twenty-one religious outposts that Franciscan priests had established between 1769 and 1823. I was too old to participate, but around my school and neighborhood, hundreds of tiny renditions of this evangelical franchise backed by the Spanish Empire began popping up. These models, familiar to anyone who passed through California schools between then and very recently, were accompanied by largely imaginary reports on the lives of the Native Californians who'd passed through them. These "reports" reiterated a tale as fantastical as that of John Wayne's Westerns, also then playing on perpetual repeat. In the missions' case: of a benevolent church, bringing religion to a heathen coast, and peoples who were grateful for the chance to come into the fold.

In reality, the missionization of California's Native population was one of the country's most thorough and destructive genocides. In little more than half a century, the population of Indigenous people was reduced from a million to mere thousands through brutal neglect, abuse, disease, and outright murder. Like many evangelical systems in which a small group of untouchable people held all the power, missionization was also a sexual kleptocracy that wreaked untold damage through generations.

It is astounding how long this destructive and delusional fantasy of benign coexistence sold by "the mission project" has remained a core part of the California curriculum, even in spite of the 2016 move by state legislators to free educators from the need to include it in their curriculum. And yet many still do. Indeed, it is the last act of that genocide, as with scores of others: the erasure of the reality that the myth replaces. It is not as if the records of how the various tribes lived in what has become California do not exist—photographs, oral testimony, and more have been preserved. And of course, there are people who keep alive the stories and knowledge that were passed down to them—Indians like Deborah A. Miranda, who was born in Los Angeles and grew up in Washington, of mixed Mexican, European, and Native heritage. The tribe she's enrolled in, the Ohlone–Costanoan Esselen Nation in the Greater Monterey Bay area, has been battling the federal government for recognition for years.

Miranda's 2013 book, *Bad Indians: A Tribal Memoir*, is a desperately needed correction to centuries of historical sanitization and colonial myth-building. "What would these missions say, / if they could speak?" Miranda asks in a poem in the book. "What would I ask them, / if they would answer?" *Bad Indians* is an attempt to imagine that answer. To stop replicating narratives of omission and invention and to use the actual materials that exist to ask hard questions. To build a new lexicon around her own history, as well as that of California Indian people. To craft her own mission project in the form of a book.

Miranda's dialogic kit is rich and deep, and it uses archival aesthetics to create a story that is as full of information and lacunae as California history itself. Accepting that some parts of her family's past will never be retrievable gives Miranda the chance to enable readers to appreciate how much was destroyed in the history of contact between California's Native tribes and the Mexican and European settlers who came to establish the mission system. Redeploying some of the very same questions schoolchildren are asked to contemplate, the book tells the story of her family within a larger tale of California Indians over the past three hundred years, adopting the forms of poems and letters, brief memoirs, historical essays, investigations, worksheets, oral histories, found poems, field notes, pseudo-phrenological data, and special prayers. It is a dazzling array of storytelling modes.

In using these forms, which have been wielded against her own people, Miranda takes the power of descriptive categorization and replaces it with a rich tonal expression of regard. This tone is one of mutuality and of respect, so it has within it veins of irony and sarcasm too. There are notes of grief and of longing, even edges of wonder, flat-out wonder. Finally, and most important, there are many sounds of care in her voice, for Miranda knows that in attempting to re-create her past, she has begun a project that may take her the rest of her life. Indeed, outside this book, she has already dedicated time to making sure the Ohlone–Costanoan Esselen achieve recognition.

If Miranda were not so deft in weaving these many threads, *Bad Indians* would become a cacophony. Instead, moving at just the right pace between prose and poetry, between lyric forms and prosaic facts, Miranda has crafted a classic memoir. It is not just an act of retrieval; it is a meditation on memory and the spiritual act of living in honor of what could have happened, what almost certainly happened. Just at the point that the book has given us something heavy to carry, the form bears us aloft. Her novena to her ancestors is, in particular, a high point of this act of belief:

> Oh unholy pagans who refused to convert, oh
> pagans who converted, oh pagans who recanted,
> oh converts who survived, hear our supplication:
> make us in your image, grant us your pride.

Along the way, this memoir delivers, too, what life stories often provide: vivid portraits of people. Miranda moves elegantly between kith and kin, treating both with love and respect. She peels back layers of assumption around a trio of over-100-year-old women, women who were interviewed by one anthropologist, and imagines the stories they knew. She pauses on the historical record of a young girl who was assaulted at her mission and whose chronicle was carried forward a century in the body of a woman who spoke to a white anthropologist. On the page, we see a record of her account, written down in the hand of the man recording it. There it is, stark as day, as if it happened yesterday.

This collapsing of time suits one of the great projects of Miranda's book, which is to dream about how the past is in fact not past for many people in California and how it travels in waves. Miranda traces the echoes of the church's history of child abuse to what she suffered growing up; she follows the theft of land all the way to the vast numbers of homeless people today; she draws a line from the violence of forced conversion to the rediscovery of Indigenous rituals now, but also epidemics of suicide and drink. In this sense, Miranda's mission model is about one of the most realistic to have ever been created for what missionization meant to California Indians—it does what previous models did not: It traces the architecture of pain into the present.

Bad Indians also narrates how history isn't just simply an event that happens but a context and a place through which people travel and attempt to retrieve information. Situating her family within the history of the California missions and their unraveling and decadence, Miranda introduces us to her great-grandfather Tomás Santos Miranda, born 1877, the year Crazy Horse was killed and Sitting Bull escaped to Canada. At the time Tomás was born, California's Indian population had sunk from one million, pre-missionization, to just twenty thousand, thanks to disease, abuse, sickness, and sterilization. Of him, Miranda has one photo.

But suddenly, the official record of the state begins to capture parts of her family's existence. To see their names deep into the middle of this book is like seeing stars for the first time. "The young couple Tomás and Inés were counted in the 1905–06 Kelsey census in Sur," Miranda writes, "along with two children: my grandfather Thomas Anthony Miranda and his sister Carmen. The Mirandas were noted as 'Indians without land.'" The one photo of him, however, says something entirely different. Here is a man, large in effect, whose immensity of presence means that, in a photo with fourteen people in it, the eye goes directly to him. As Miranda says, he is dangerous, not because of what he is capable of but because of what he has seen.

The memoir as an existential family mystery: Here is another form that Miranda's book grows out of, in keeping with other highlights of the genre, such as Tracy K. Smith's recent *To Free the Captives: A Plea for the American Soul*, which begins with Smith finding her father's name in an Alabama census, nearly a century after it was taken. How many people have backtracked through their own family trails to run into a place where the trail goes cold? How many have felt that burst of sunlight when they see for the first time their family name amid the violence of an archive?

As we drift toward closer times, details proliferate. We meet Miranda's grandfather Tom, whose "life story is not just about being Californian," she writes, but of being a "California Indian after a great holocaust." He was a lumberjack, a cowboy, a racetrack money runner.

He died when she was fourteen, but left behind tapes—tapes made during family dinners, stolen moments, sometimes with her own father asking the questions. Spliced in there are Tom's own words about how he visited his grandfather on ten acres or so, where he would spearfish and dry salmon. He tells of David Jacks, an early-twentieth-century land speculator who bought up or outright took huge plots until he had amassed some sixty thousand acres and wondered why he was disliked. We hear of his work, women he knew, when Pearl Harbor was bombed, the incarceration of the Japanese. "There is something to me that doesn't fit. Who the hell was our president then? Seems it was a setup. It was a put-up job. The government can do some funny things."

The photos as we get nearer and nearer to the present grow brighter; the distance from us to them is closer. Smiles become sharper. Miranda isn't just a great storyteller; she looks at art and describes it brilliantly. This skill becomes one of the ways she disintermediates from her own life at a young age, due to trauma. We see her childhood as a tableau, a disturbing scene. By the time we get to Miranda's first memory, at age three, of her father pressing her mother up against a wall with force, the reality reel is liquid clear. But thanks to everything that has come before, we know all the forces that are pushing down on this family. By the time Miranda is six, her father has disappeared, off to prison. She grows up, suffers abuse, leaves a young marriage, and loops back to describe being a kid largely outside, her head turned by sagebrush manzanita, details coming back in orbitals, her father being sentenced to eight years when she is three. "I found books that provided names for the riches surrounding me. Field guides, children's encyclopedias. I started with birds, their songs the first thing I heard each morning."

This is not a book in which landscape rescues all, in which land has the innate and mystical power to heal, but it does do some of that. Seeing and describing the world allows Miranda to realize where language has failed her. "The more names I could put to a creature, the richer my loneliness became. I could not name the dysfunction around me—I didn't have words for alcoholism, depression, trauma—but I learned the language of naming to make sense of what I could."

With time, Miranda grows up and tries to make amends with her father, who goes back to Washington state to try to reconcile with her mother. She tries to figure out what is retrievable.

At some point, it becomes clear that she is making a container for the world she is living in right now. A model for a world she is actually inhabiting. Maybe a model isn't the right metaphor.

> Maybe, like a basket that has huge holes where pieces were ripped out and is crumbling to dust and can't be reclaimed, my tribe must reinvent ourselves—rather than try to copy what isn't there in the first place. We must think of ourselves as a mosaic, human beings constructed of multiple sources of beauty, pieces that alone are merely incomplete but which, when set into a new design together, complement the shards around us, bring wholeness to the world and ourselves.

Has there ever been a memoir that has respected this inherent multiplicity so beautifully? The one we see in a river, in a leaf, in a family? It is unlikely.

BUTCHER'S CROSSING

by John Williams

Growing up in the American West, especially if you're white, one inherits a set of myths so grave and insubstantial they can only be passed on in the dark. In gestures and overheard sounds, in the half-remembered plots of B movies. The pose of advertising pitch men, or the way a person stands when wearing a gun. You might think one could dodge this heritage, until you realize it's all around you. That to live in the West is to spend one's time unconsciously assembling a story in your head—like a melody that has been presented to you in parts. In this way, the myths of the West—when you live there—can feel as inevitable as the size of a sky or the heat of summer, the scarcity of water. Were they written down, no one would believe them. For to subject our myths to actual debate would shatter the projected nostalgia on which they depend. So for a long time the culture encouraged itself not to speak of them but rather to perform them and allow them to enact themselves upon us.

I learned all this on a ranch twenty miles east of Sacramento, where my uncle Carl lived. He and his brother operated a slaughterhouse, and occasionally there'd be up to a hundred head of cattle, fattening up.

Carl drove a long white Cadillac with cow horns on the hood, and a tiny green MG convertible, which backfired and leaked oil. Riding in that smaller car down two-lane roads at speed was like hanging outside the cockpit of a crop duster. Grit and hot air would blow across your face—the engine felt dangerously close. One of the shocks of arriving back to Carl's ranch after one of those buzzing jaunts was to walk through a gate to his inner sanctum, where a perfectly blue pool gazed at the sky unblinkingly. Carl was as tanned as a leather sofa, smoked cigars, and spent a lot of time in his swim trunks. He was kind to my brothers and me, and often dispatched us inside the house to get him another beer. One of the most intense memories of my childhood is running from the bright white light near Carl's pool into the cool dark of his house, passing his guns and the wood-paneled TV set, usually playing a Western on silent, and pulling a hand-chilling can of beer from a refrigerator stuffed with meat.

So much of what I know about the West I learned in that single brief pathway, out of the heat, through a living room, and into the artificial cool of a miniature ranch—the soles of my feet wet on one side, but dry by the time I was standing by the refrigerator. It would be two decades before I realized that most of what we did on those weekends was impossible: that the land on which we stood was practically inarable, that to put a temperature-controlled pool at the center of it a folly beyond words, that the access to water and food that seemed to never end in a house stuffed with domesticated objects of the West—tools, guns, animal heads staring out from their taxidermy in mute protest—was a way of enshrining a victory over the past.

This simultaneous flirtation with the past and declared victory over it is where the myths of the West begin. If I had to describe to you what these myths were, I would say they had to do with power and landscape and self-reliance. Growing up there, a white kid, as I was, you are taught that the land was empty, save for what was wild, before we got there. You might ask who is this "we," and the answer is of course, *us*. I might add that we were brave and tamed that landscape, and made it useful, which is to say it no longer was a landscape but a backdrop for our ambitions. It became a resource. It was not our goal to bring justice and order to the land, but these things came because we were there and we were good. We had honor and dignity. We were ennobled by the land's awful beauty, its sudden violences—but we remained its master.

Of course, while a small part of this was true—it is hard not to admire the determination of farmers wrestling with dry soil—the exaggerations and falsehoods of this larger mythos hid a far crueler, less flattering history. The westward expansion in the US—from the Lewis and Clark expedition, which told the government there was land, and huge amounts of it, to the War of 1812, to the Indian Removal Act of 1830—was a march toward empire that depended on sanctioned violence and blood-letting. Manifest Destiny, the concept coined by newspaper editor John O'Sullivan, a proponent of annexing Texas, called on early American citizens and settlers to claim their right to land from coast to coast. As a concept, it depended on the notion that white Americans were morally superior, that these white Americans had a mission to spread our institutions as far across the continent as possible, and that they had a divine destiny under God to do so.

This combination of righteousness and license created the conditions for one of the worst genocides in human history. Civilizations that were many thousands of years old—whose modes of knowledge were as complex as they were old—were wiped out or widely subdued in a brutal forty-year period. Even if settlers came in peace, the US government eventually came in force and removed or murdered Indigenous Americans. The gains were reinforced by the railroad and the Homestead Act of 1862, signed into law by Abraham Lincoln, which promised 160 acres of land to anyone who could prove they had lived for five years in one place and could show they'd made improvements on it. In many cases, this put homesteaders in direct contact with already displaced Native Americans, a form of neighborliness that was disastrous to them.

Genres emerge to turn myths into ritual—the romance spins a yarn about how love can be sealed in a pact, ending in a marriage; the crime story is a tale in which civilization has some kind of order, even its crimes. What is a Western, in the filmic sense, but a tale that slowly sands down the chaos and violence of genocide and turns it into a hardy parable of resilience, very often one in which white suffering is placed at the center of the story? Played or read over and over, these genres enumerate stages of belief, give fans or viewers or readers a sequence or ceremony with which to subdue reason. A way of living in a world that is cruel and turning away from that cruelty into fantasy. In this way, formality leads to familiarity, which feels, in part, like truth.

It is not by accident then that many Westerns take place in the period between 1860 and 1930, the window between the Homestead Act and the Great Depression and the Dust Bowl, which devastated the plains and the West—an almost perfect storm created by a drought and bad farming methods. That seventy-year period is when white settlers were at the frontier, and it's the behavior of that person that the Western as a genre seeks to atone for, mythologize, and ultimately expiate. There were Westerns as far back as the dawn of silent film, but they were very different than, say, the Westerns you might catch on a Sunday afternoon in Sacramento. In Edwin S. Porter's 1903 *The Great Train Robbery*, for instance, four gunmen hold up a train, blowing up compartments with dynamite, killing firemen, passengers, and anyone who tried to escape. They ride off on their horses proud and enriched, not as bad men who have done good, but as bad men who have gotten away with a crime. This early film—notable not just for its violence but for its use of cross-cutting and on-location shooting—predicted a genre as violent and lethal as the history of the West.

Instead, the Western became a genre notable for how it tamed the West's violence, made it into entertainment, smuggling in notions of decency and justice and honor along the way. The peak year of the Western was 1959, when some thirty different Western series were shown on network television *a day*. This was not long after Dwight Eisenhower authorized the Federal Aid Highway Act, essentially setting in motion the closing down of the American frontier in symbolic automotive terms. Immediately, though, a new frontier developed: the rest of the world, as the US began to make the military bases it had established around the world after World War II permanent, and moved toward an ongoing proxy war with Communism around the globe. Around this time, an American actor named Ronald Reagan was hosting a television series called *Death Valley Days*, which featured so-called true stories of the old American West. The show was sponsored by General Electric, the largest US military contractor.

The collision between Hollywood and its myths and the US imperial expansion and its need to declare new "frontiers" had long-lasting consequences for American culture. It gave birth to an era of American power and self-celebration so long and ecstatic that it managed to insulate the US from its own imperial demise for decades, even as the signs were all around it. With more than eight hundred bases in foreign countries, the US is the largest empire the world has ever known, by a long stretch. And yet it has long since been displaying an empire's catastrophic inability or refusal to take care of its citizens at home. Predictions that this would happen began almost as soon as postwar expansion did. Beat literature rose up in the late 1940s and early 1950s as a political response to internal and external imperial expansion. And in the late 1950s, one began to see the rise of the anti-Western—films by John Ford (*The Searchers*) John Sturges (*The Magnificent Seven*), and John Huston (*The Misfits*), which examined with a far colder eye what exactly had happened during westward expansion, what its legacy was, and what the contemporary West felt like.

Two American writers in particular have done a great deal of heavy lifting to demythologize the West and how it was won. One of them is Cormac McCarthy, who in *Blood Meridian* tells the tale of a child runaway who wound up joining the infamous Glanton gang of scalp hunters in Texas, who chased and murdered and tortured Indians as they tried to clear the land for Scotch-Irish settlers. The other is a writer who until 2007 was largely lost to time—John Williams. In the ensuing years, thanks largely to the *New York Review of Books* rereleasing of his 1960 novel, *Stoner*, Williams has gone on to a staggering posthumous afterlife. "William Stoner entered the University of Missouri as a freshman in the year 1910, at the age of nineteen," the novel begins, after which unfolds a tale of ordinariness that is absolutely devastating. How much pathos and drama Williams wrenches from this brief, humble life. *Stoner* is a tale of pain and grief and the accumulation of slights that make a person. For Stoner these slights begin early, disguised as boons. Williams's hero comes from poor farming stock. "At thirty his father looked fifty; stooped by labor, he gazed without hope at the arid patch of land that sustained the family from one year to the next. His mother regarded her life patiently, as if it were a long moment that she had to endure."

The family's one hope for advancement takes the form of sending Stoner to the University of Missouri agricultural school. This was in the era when US normal schools—colleges that taught practical skills—were beginning to also teach liberal arts. Away Stoner goes, quite aware of how much his family has risked, and he promptly falls in love with literature instead. Stoner emerges from school a man of literature and a teacher, estranged from his essential roots. He marries above his status to a brittle, unhappy woman, and begins a life in which he slowly turns himself into another person. And then has all the safeties of this new identity stripped away from him.

This journey holds a kind of resonance because it comes from very close to the bone. John Williams was born in Clarksville, Texas, in

1922 and was raised in Wichita Falls, the grandson of poor farmers who were almost wiped out by the hard conditions of early America. His parents moved frequently during the Great Depression until his father found a job as a janitor at a post office. Williams didn't find out until he was eight that his father was not his biological father and that his birth father had been murdered by hitchhikers. He was a minor student who, while growing up, fell in love with writing. He flunked out of junior college, married quickly, and then went off to the army, flying supply missions in the China-India-Burma theater of World War II. He was shot down at one point, flying low over the treetops in Burma, crashing in a jungle. Half of the plane's passengers were killed. Williams and three other survivors strapped supplies to their backs, used a compass to find the Burma Road, and walked to safety.

On returning to America, Williams eventually moved west to Denver, where he took a PhD, began to teach, and also began reading about the West as a place. Meticulously researched, unflinchingly told, *Butcher's Crossing* is Williams's response to the mixture of drivel and lies he encountered about the West. The novel begins on a dusty crossroads in Kansas. The town features little more than a butcher, a saloon, a brothel, and a brining pit where people coming back from buffalo hunts wash the meat and viscera off the hides they've gleaned. The year is 1870, and William Andrews, a twenty-three-year-old Harvard divinity student, has recently abandoned his sedate life in Boston to "find himself in the great wild West." Shortly after arriving in Butcher's Crossing by stagecoach, Andrews meets a guide named Miller, who convinces him that a great score exists out there, should they only possess the gumption to undertake it. Miller claims to know that a rare and not often seen herd of buffalo will be traveling through Colorado, and he convinces Andrews to finance the trip to go and kill them. All it will take is $600, or half of what Andrews is carrying with him. Miller's idea is one part adventure, two parts boondoggle. They will go out and engage with nature and the masculine side of themselves, and make a little money on buffalo hides along the way.

Of course, things don't work out exactly that way. Miller leaves with Andrews's money, and for a time it seems possible he will not come back. Meantime, rather than contemplating a life in nature, Andrews wiles away the hours in a dingy hotel, flirting with a sex worker named Francine; she tries to unburden Andrews of his virginity, but he balks. As Miller's absence stretches, Andrews puffs himself up on notions of nature that one can sense—even this early in the novel—are going to be brutally dashed. "Always, when his gaze lifted from the town, it went westward toward the river, and beyond. . . . He thought of the times when, as a boy, he had stood on the rocky coast of Massachusetts Bay, and looked eastward across the gray Atlantic until his mind was choked and dizzied at the immensity he gazed upon. Older now, he looked upon another immensity in another horizon."

Eventually, Miller returns, and with two others they begin a trek into the Rockies in search of buffalo. Williams takes pains not to romanticize the trip. Hardly high adventure, it proceeds as a series of near misses and beddings downs. They wake, drink bitter coffee, eat salted beans, trek for ten or twelve hours, then bed down and wake up and do it again, numbed by the repetition not into the trance state Andrews has anticipated but a simple creatureliness that has its own pleasures. Williams's prose observes the landscape with a clean, unfiltered lens—simply describing what it is should be enough—man's glory or vanity need not be inserted. Reading his descriptions of the gullies and mountain fastnesses, the high plains with buffalo grass, it's hard not to think of Albert Bierstadt's landscapes from the late 1860s—how hard they worked to sell their wares, the awesome mountain peaks seen from high lake shores, the skies oddly blue, shafts of nearly heavenly light illuminating the spectacle as if to remind viewers where the true glory lay.

For every landscape description that feints at this idealized mode of viewing nature, there are dozens of others in *Butcher's*

Crossing that make clear the hard realities of cloven-footed travel over rocky terrain. The group does not pace their resources well and soon runs dangerously low on water. At one point, the men must soak rags in a stream and shove their arms down the mouths of their oxen to wash the beasts' swollen tongues. Astride a horse, Andrews feels alternately dizzy and cold, as thirsty as the oxen that lumber all around him. Andrews hardly possesses the strength for this sort of work, and passes out from the labor. He's even outworked by Miller's one-handed alcoholic assistant, who mocks and judges him with the peculiar mixture of shame and righteousness one finds in hard-drinking evangelists.

Finally, they find a herd, and over the next forty pages, *Butcher's Crossing* lends another meaning to its title. There's no way to describe what the men do other than butchery. The buffalo are big, slow, and stupid, and once circled, all there is to do is shoot one, wait for the blood to finish running from its nose, then move on to the next, and the next, and the next. The killing becomes monotonous—in three hours, Miller kills seventy of them simply by squeezing his trigger. And then the grisly, mechanical work of pulling off their skins begins—complete with all the false starts, quivering viscera, and growing disgust one would expect when a herd of majestic animals has been reduced by repeating rifle to a pile of coin.

This is one of the truest passages one will ever read in all of American literature. By simply attending to the details of how the West was cleared—not won—Williams lays waste to the attitudinal mythology that still clings to the mud flaps of all the unnecessarily large pickups you will find out West today. Not surprisingly, Andrews returns from this journey a changed man, hardly ennobled. The market for skins has collapsed, so the wastage of what was sublime is doubly felt. He is also suddenly aware that all the tans and skins he has grown used to wearing as symbols of western attitude have come from the hide of a living animal.

When I was a child, that was something that occurred to me, as well—because I mostly didn't grow up in a house with animal skins or heads or ephemera on the wall. As the long white hood of my uncle's Cadillac carved its way down the smaller Central Valley highways, I used to look at the horns up front and wonder whether he would drive the car still if it were adorned with parts of a human skull.

HOW MUCH OF THESE HILLS IS GOLD

by C Pam Zhang

How the Gold Rush hasn't been the subject of better novels is a question worth putting to West Coast literature. To grow up in California in the 1980s was to encounter this period in history books as one of heroism and hucksterism, as if three hundred thousand people coming to a territory in search of gold over five years—that would be 120 million in today's population—wasn't more than a rush. These were not tourists. Many became permanent residents who dug in, created camps, and drove Indigenous people from their land. The forty-niners permanently altered the region's landscape and—with more than half of them coming from outside the United States—its demographics.

Reinvention—as well as gold—was part of the allure. It's hard to travel anywhere in Central California without encountering the name Sutter. The German-born entrepreneur Johann August Sutter fled to what was called the New World from Europe in 1834, leaving behind his wife and five children, several failed businesses, and a mountain of unpaid loans. On the way to New York he recast himself as Captain John Sutter, a well-traveled European with a military past—an aspect of his persona he enhanced by dressing in a military-style uniform when he arrived in Alta California, following detours to Oregon, Missouri, and Hawaii, in 1839.

Sutter was extremely successful at earning the trust of merchants and businessmen and consuls in Yerba Buena (now San Francisco) and Monterey, where he met the governor of Alta California, Juan Bautista Alvarado. He sold Alvarado a sparkling vision of a vastly profitable Central Valley agricultural and trading utopia, a new colony within Alta California, with himself installed as a kind of king/patriarch. His idea was to call the place New Helvetia, or New Switzerland. Worried over Russian settlements in Northern California, and arriving Americans, Alvarado deeded Sutter a forty-eight-thousand-acre land grant near the confluence of the American and Sacramento Rivers, to settle and make a rancho of his own. It would act as a buffer between the frontier and what the Mexican government saw as Alta California proper—as all colonial settlers do.

Sutter's Fort, as it became known, operated as a microcosm for America as a whole. The settlement was built by the indentured labor of hundreds of Native Americans (mainly from Miwok and Nisenan tribes) and relied on outright slavery to function. The European settlers whom Sutter coaxed to arrive were paid in land for their loyalty, but in time they would push Sutter off. Meanwhile, Sutter built and deployed a private army to defend his fiefdom, and used it to control his workers as well, many of whom he didn't pay. He may not have been a captain before arriving in America, but through a brutal type of commerce, Sutter became one. And then one of his employees, James W. Marshall, discovered gold at Sutter's Mill, in Coloma, forty-five miles northeast of Sutter's Fort.

Once gold was discovered, the word went out fast, and people began arriving from all across the globe. President Polk even mentioned the discovery in his State of the Union address in December 1848. Newspapers all began to run stories of gargantuan fortunes to be made. So did the Chinese-language newspapers in California. By 1849, letters coming from Chinese relatives in the US and Chinese-language newspapers meant word of the rush had spread to mainland China, especially southern Canton. The reasons for people coming varied—not everyone came looking for gold; they were also seeking work in agriculture, on railroads, as domestic servants, in the mines. Ever since China's defeat in the Opium War of 1839–1842, foreign merchants had fled into the East, including Canton, one of the five ports China was forced to open to outside influence in accordance with the Treaty of Nanking. All told nearly thirty thousand people arrived from China in San Francisco and the Sierra foothills, bringing with them history and culture and food and family. By the end of the 1850s, of the people living in the four counties where the majority of the mining was being done, one in five was a Chinese immigrant. The Chinese were often met by "frontier justice," as it was euphemistically called. What couldn't be done by outright force was eventually upheld by law, with legislation directly aimed at Chinese migrants to make prospecting prohibitively expensive, such as the Foreign Miners Tax of 1852. Eventually, the goal was to shut down Chinese immigration altogether. First, though, it made the state a lot of money. By 1870, when there more than sixty thousand Chinese in America, 77 percent of whom lived in California, Chinese Americans contributed $5 million to the state's bottom line, fully one-quarter of its revenues.

At last there is a novel that looks right into this history and imagines it from within. It might be a stretch to call it California's *Beloved*, but C Pam Zhang's *How Much of These Hills Is Gold* moves with the same rough magic and has a similar relationship to America's radicalized indentured labor as Toni Morrison's haunted masterpiece. Only here, the children survive and the ghost is history. We never hear the word "California" in this novel, and it's nearly one hundred pages before the word "gold" appears. The book is primarily about two children, Lucy, twelve, and Sam, who is eleven. They've lost their mother, Ma, and as the book starts, their father, Ba, expires too. Broke, hungry, and aware that their situation is not safe, the siblings saddle up a stolen horse and carry their father's body on the run. Their behavior quickly begins to map onto the skittery emigration pattern their father charted when he brought them to these hills with dreams of gold, land, a farm, good living. He didn't want an empire; he wanted a home. That was before drink and grief and the violence of resentful miners waylaid him. The book unfolds mostly in Lucy's point of view as she seeks to keep them safe in a world without parents. She is cautious, eager to find official paths, to seek approval—even from a dubious East Coast teacher writing a book about people like their family. Sam has inherited the wildness of their father; he sneaks out and prospects at a young age, and is always ready for a fight. Lucy hasn't forgone risk; she simply takes different ones.

Zhang takes a huge gamble herself here, stepping out into the well-trodden territory of the Western, but she's a writer of immense poise. Having grown up and lived in thirteen cities, she wrote the first draft of this novel in Bangkok, far away from the golden hills where the book unfolds. Clearly her mind's eye is lucid, though. She writes lean but sensual prose that immerses us in the stench and muck and wonder of traveling across a landscape that has been brutally used. The moon hangs high on cold nights. In Zhang's universe, buffalo might still be alive somewhere, and tigers roam those hills. Each day, the siblings find something new—a dying if still hardy prospector needing help one day, a dried-up salt lake where they can preserve their father on another.

One of the things Zhang is pondering here is discovery: Who gets to experience the shock of something new, and what sort of claim can they lay upon it? How quickly does it become knowledge? As Lucy and Sam travel, discovery takes on several shapes for them. On one hand, they begin to piece together the story of their father's life, assembling the portrait of a man who (like many) left debt behind—and their mother too—and who held a secret that clearly haunted him until his final moments. Meantime, the marvels of the land do not reveal themselves in neutral terms to Lucy and Sam. There are forms of violence that cannot be untethered from it and its allure, something their father had tried to teach them before he died. At one point, noticing the way the landscape is stripped and contains untold treasures, Lucy feels she is "parched and quenched all at once."

> If she believes that tigers live, then does she believe that Indians are hunted and dying? If she believes in fish the size of men, does she believe in men who string up others like linefuls of catch? Easier to avoid that history, unwritten as it is except in the soughing of dry grass, in the marks of lost trails, in the rumors from the mouths of bored men and mean girls, in the cracked patterns of buffalo bone. Easier by far to read the history that Teacher Leigh teaches, those names and dates orderly as bricks, stacked to build a civilization.

How Much of These Hills Is Gold is a tale about what happens when two children try to find out for themselves which stories they want to believe and which ones matter to them. That they are undertaking this quest as they search for a proper burial site for their father lends their journey a spiritual dimension. The deserts, forests, and landscapes they travel through and across have a stark, luminescent quality, as if the children are moving through a realm of the afterlife. The world without their father. Doing so draws the siblings close, and in sudden piercing moments they are yanked out of this near dream state into the harsh realities of the present.

Being Chinese puts both siblings at risk, and defying the ways boys are meant to be makes life harder for Sam, who would be called gender-nonconforming today. Zhang never uses pronouns when Lucy is thinking of her sibling—we only get to them in actions and qualities. Sam is vulnerable, internally tilted, and aware that the costumes boys are expected to wear are but that. Zhang writes into the field of gender and its performance with a steady rhythm to her syntax, one that makes it possible for us as readers to liberate ourselves from the prepackaged roles with which this history has often come to us. In "Sam's mind," Zhang writes, "the shadow is the true height, the body a temporary inconvenience. When I'm a cowboy, Sam says. When I'm an adventurer. More recently: When I'm a famous outlaw. When I'm grown. Young enough to think desire alone shapes the world."

Zhang creates an epic tale in a small space here; her story reaches back and back and then yokes forward the lives Ma and Ba lived before, the incredible voyage Ba underwent so they could have the privilege of living on the precarious edge of a nearly fictional enterprise, in which military captains who aren't captains found new colonies to start over on a land that wasn't theirs. "All your life you heard people say the story starts in '48. And all your life people told you this story," Zhang writes at one point. "Did you ever question why? They told it to shut you out. They told it to claim it, to make it theirs and not yours. They told it to say we came too late. Thieves they called us. They said this land could never be our land."

How Much of These Hills Is Gold is an act of imaginary reclamation. Not only because it inserts a Chinese family into the heart of the Gold Rush but because it refuses to start history at the previously agreed-on year zero. The novel is a story of a series of arrivals, a sequence of events that stretch far back into the past and involve Ba's and Ma's families, their lives in China, and what made them leave. The novel imagines these stories to be worth at least as much as gold.

What is gold anyway? Among the painful realizations Lucy and Sam experience as they search and search for a place to bury their father is that he fell prey to the madness of it. The tragedy of this rupture is made evident when Ba's voice breaks through into the narrative and you hear in his memory the delusion taking shape. We hear in moving flashbacks and stories how their father ordered and told the world to his children, in fables that shift like water. As Sam and Lucy come of age in the shadow of this inheritance, crossing paths with others who have a similar brokenness, the past as evanescent as California rain, Zhang makes it possible for us to appreciate how hard it is for them not to be infected by that longing. That desire to get lucky, make it big, buy some dignity from a world that doesn't freely give it. Do they move toward great gambles, and, if it's required, violence? Or toward finding ways to know and contain official history, so that they might write it themselves? Write it right into the record. Do they light out, or circle back and remember just how history felt to live? Taking a risk, as Colson Whitehead did in *The Underground Railroad*, to imagine history as even stranger than we allow, C Pam Zhang has proved it's possible to do both.

THE WOMAN WARRIOR

by Maxine Hong Kingston

Every family has a word for it—for what they do when they get together and talk about the past. Some have a natter; others go down memory lane. But what if that lane has to stretch across an ocean? Or that natter must twist itself into a new language? Or both? In a state made up of people born elsewhere that is as multilingual as California, these are key questions. Can family stories travel by suitcase, or in something as portable as a voice? Say you are born in a village and now live in a city two hundred times its size, like San Francisco. Do you scale old stories for the new present? And what if moments of shame are still buried there—wouldn't it be a betrayal to drag them up in this new, unforgiving California light?

Here are some of the far-reaching questions that power Maxine Hong Kingston's *The Woman Warrior: Memoirs of a Childhood Among Ghosts*. From the very first line—"'You must not tell anyone,' my mother said, 'what I am about to tell you'"—the book announces itself as a telling on, an account of an account by a daughter–betrayer of family secrets. *The Woman Warrior* shatters their power by stating these secrets baldly, then doing something miraculous: Kingston reveals them to be merely one part of a whole ecosystem of family stories. Tales of strength, romantic love, and regret, but also gossip, hearsay, and total speculation, not to mention vaudeville comedy and so much folklore. Hers was a family made by stories; it was no wonder that one held so much power.

Nominally, the backdrop for these stories—where they are told and retold—is Stockton, California, in the 1940s, where Kingston was the third of six children born to her mother and father in America. Two other children were born in China. For fifteen years her parents had been separated while Kingston's father tried to make his way into the US. The Chinese Exclusion Act—the law passed in 1882 when the Foreign Miner's Act didn't stop immigration entirely, but instead stoked and legitimized anti-Chinese discrimination and violence—was still in effect. He eventually made it to Manhattan, but alone. One night, in a gambling house in Chinatown in New York, her father won $600 off a man who couldn't pay. The man gave Kingston's father his visa papers instead, which he'd use to ultimately send for his wife. In the years Kingston's father had been away, her mother had become a doctor—a job she wouldn't be able to practice in America. In Stockton, where they resettled, she'd help Kingston's father run a laundry and a gambling house.

This arc, supplemented by things that Kingston has said in interviews, is revealed to us across the entire book in fits and starts, digressions and casual asides. It is not the book's melody, nor is it something like the score to her family's tale of immigrant arrival. Immediately, powerfully, Kingston inverts the frame of what matters. And in her family, what matters, where matter lives, is the past—the spirits who come from there, those left behind—and not disturbing the past, which is why it's so powerful that on the very first page Kingston goes after the biggest story of them all.

Long ago, in China in the 1920s, Kingston's father had a sister who got pregnant and drowned herself in a well. Within a page, this secret is suddenly out there in the open. "The real punishment was not the raid swiftly inflicted by the villagers," Kingston writes, reimagining the time, the villagers whipped into a fury, "but the family's deliberately forgetting her. Her betrayal so maddened them, they saw to it that she would suffer forever, even after death. Always hungry, always needing, she would have to beg food from other ghosts, snatch and steal it from those whose living descendants give them gifts."

Fifty years after this event, Kingston announces she will honor her aunt, the first in a series of recognitions and reimaginings, something she likens to seeing ghosts. To Kingston, ghosts are not just the undead—they are spirits, they are the unacknowledged, they are people, like her, girls or women, who are barely even seen or seen as her aunt was, as less important than boys, than men. Across the book, the the word ghost expands to include people detached from others, from where they are from. It comes to also mean most white people, some Black Americans, many of the customers who frequent the laundry her parents run. She uses the term so much it becomes emptied of its fright-night quality, and becomes something sadder, warmer, and, eventually, worthy of attention.

There is a lineage here, an alternate one, which Kingston is claiming. *The Woman Warrior* is so many books in one, but on a fundamental level, it is a series of linked portraits of moments when Kingston, her mother, and other women in her family, real and imagined, confront ghosts and either conquer them or become conquered by them. In one chapter she retells the fantastic story of a girl trained to be a woman warrior in an underworld and who comes back to vanquish a ghost army; in another chapter she imagines her mother's long journey to becoming a doctor, a key moment during which she sleeps in a room haunted by a ghost because none of her classmates will; in yet another chapter Kingston's aunt, Moon Orchid, comes to America after thirty years of being supported by her husband and confronts the man, who has taken a new wife in California, at his fancy downtown Los Angeles medical clinic, thus becoming the ghost he refused to see. This is the saddest of all tales, for his unwillingness to recognize her ultimately destroys Moon Orchid's mind.

There were clues right away, though, that Moon Orchid had not clicked in America. When she moves in with Kingston's family, she follows young Maxine and her siblings around the house, narrating all of their actions in a state of astonishment, as if struggling to pair their actions with reality. "She bent over them. 'Now she is taking a machine off the shelf. She attaches two metal spiders to it. She plugs in the cord. She cracks an egg against the rim and pours the yolk and white out of the shell into the bowl. She presses the button, and the spiders spin the eggs. What are you making?'"

The Woman Warrior is astonishing because of how Kingston listens. Tilting her ear this way and that, remembering what it felt like to hear tales told, she resurrects all the ways her family, as she calls it, "talked story." The rhythm, the syntax, the storytelling modes of every character in this book are not just part of their character; they *are* their character. Kingston's mother, the lodestar of the whole galaxy, has a huge variety of storytelling modes. She tells stories as parables; she recounts others as myths; still more unfold like Shakespearean comedies cast in a telenovela mode. This is how the confrontation with the errant husband begins. Kingston's mother endlessly goads her sister into driving to Los Angeles to confront the man, and as they drive south, she plays out, rapid-fire style, all the different ways the scene will unfold.

> I can charge through the door and say, "Where is your wife?" And he'll answer, "Why, she's right here." And I'll say, "This isn't your wife. Where is Moon Orchid? I've come to see her. I'm her first sister, and I've come to see that she is being well taken care of." Then I accuse him of murderous things; I'd have him arrested—and you pop up to his rescue. Or I can

take a look at his wife, and I say, "Moon Orchid, how young you've gotten." And he'll say, "This isn't Moon Orchid." And you come in and say, "No, I am."

Moving between these stories, how they are told or witnessed, and how Kingston feels hearing them and witnessing them, creates a powerful sense of a fracture. In the world of the story, her mother is powerful, hilarious, full of force. In reality, she is almost as silent as her sister when faced with the realization that the errant husband has become a rich American. That he never wanted to go back to China or bring Moon Orchid to America. After the confrontation, Moon Orchid's mental health goes downhill rapidly, and ultimately none of her sister's ministrations can make her well. She is institutionalized, and the young Maxine watching this concludes: "The difference between mad people and sane people . . . is that sane people have variety when they talk-story. Mad people have only one story that they talk over and over."

Kingston's gift as a child was her ability to listen and to record these stories; years later, she learns how to expose their variety of effects on her developing self. Even though she recalls how she did not speak for long stretches of time, and her IQ was measured at one point as zero, her mind was fed by the fabulous myth of the woman warrior. In telling her childhood, Kingston realizes that her spirit was tuned to ghosts too. Both actual and metaphorical. Ghosts of overlooked people, people who toil unseen, people who by force or circumstance have been exiled. Her mother in that sense is the greatest ghost of all. Kingston's sense of fairness was stoked by an awareness of the tremendous amount of work her mother undertook to become a doctor.

The discovery that there is a gap between how you see your parents or ancestors and how the world sees them is one of the most painful and disorienting experiences of youth. This all-powerful god reduced to a type or a job or a service, or worse. Maxine Hong Kingston was never presenting her own family as a model of any kind of Asian American family. But the *way* she presented them in *The Woman Warrior* and the follow-up book about the men in her family, *China Men*, opened the door for generations of writers, from Viet Thanh Nguyen to Hua Hsu, from Rachel Khong to Barack Obama, to refuse or explode or invert that gap between how people like them were presented and how people they knew lived, loved, told stories. Doing this also meant redrawing the boundaries of where America began and stopped—after all, even in her older age, when Kingston's mother was working in tomato fields, she was sending money back to relatives in Hong Kong.

> The relatives there can send it on to the remaining aunts and their children and, after a good harvest, to the children and grandchildren's two minor wives. "Every woman in the tomato row is sending money home," my mother says, "to Chinese villages and Mexican villages and Filipino villages and, now, Vietnamese villages, where they speak Chinese too. The women come to work whether sick or well. 'I can't die,' they say, 'I'm supporting fifty,' or 'I'm supporting a hundred.'"

As a storyteller, here, Kingston is doing something similar. *The Woman Warrior* is her story too, and it charts her development as a thinker, as a writer, as a girl who later becomes a woman, as a daughter—but it is a book bowed with the responsibility of many, of all the family members whose stories have been crammed into her ear. No wonder that when Kingston fell in love with writing it was Walt Whitman who spoke to her budding sensibility. "I contain multitudes," he wrote in his great poem, "Leaves of Grass." Quite literally, so did she.

"What I'll inherit someday is a green address book of names," Kingston writes in the last chapter of *The Woman Warrior*. "I'll send the relatives money, and they'll write us stories about their hunger." Kingston is referring to the terrible privation of life in post–Great Leap Forward China. But there's a metaphor here—that Kingston will inherit the whole world of responsibilities her mother carried with her, which made her so great at talking story. One of Kingston's other big influences as a writer, though, was Virginia Woolf, whose essay "A Room of One's Own" connected deeply to a young writer so plied with stories of her family, it was years before she spoke.

Obligation is entwined with liberation in Kingston's life, perhaps because it was through broken narratives about the former that the latter was clandestinely or overtly taught. "When we Chinese girls listened to the adults talk-story, we learned that we failed if we grew up to be but wives or slaves. We could be heroines, swordswomen.... Perhaps women were so dangerous that they had to have their feet bound." In the decades since she wrote that line, Kingston has continued this tale of emancipation by reremembering and by reframing, across novels, poetry, and anthologies, one long book that is the story of her life. It is an epic of love and despair, of war and peace. In it she is everyone and no one, a spirit passing through who has the power, through her extraordinarily agile voice, to say, "Look, here: There are ghosts all around us. Can't you see them?"

A PARADISE BUILT IN HELL

by Rebecca Solnit

Of the many grim moments in the first Trump presidency, one in particular represents a loss of almost unimaginable scale. And that is the degree to which the Trump administration played down the coming pandemic, all while knowing how bad it would get. "You just breathe the air, and that's how it's passed," Trump told reporter Bob Woodward privately over the phone on February 7, 2020, adding that it was much more dangerous than a regular flu. Meantime, standing before microphones, Trump was telling the nation just the opposite. Trump later explained to Woodward the rationale behind such duplicity. "I wanted to always play it down. I still like playing it down, because I don't want to create a panic."

The casual cruelty and duplicity on display in this moment are breathtaking, but the assumptions behind Trump's thinking are hardly new. In fact, if you read Rebecca Solnit's remarkable 2009 book, *A Paradise Built in Hell*, this notion that people panic in a crisis (and need to be treated like children) has been around a very long time. It can be traced back to the 1640s, as Solnit points out, when Thomas Hobbes fled England to Paris and began to work on developing a theory of strong central government. "The condition of man," he'd write in *Leviathan*, published in 1651, "is a condition of war of everyone against everyone." And without strong authority, the thinking goes, we are in chaos.

One of the great problems of this theory of humanity, Solnit writes in her immensely absorbing book, is not just how wrong it may be but how it has obscured our ability to see the utopian possibilities unleashed during times of disruption, particularly disasters. What if we are better than these notions? she wants to ask. What could we possibly build? Or better yet: What have we begun to build, only to be stymied by a desire for control?

To answer her question, *A Paradise Built in Hell* is three things at once: a historical salvage job, a work of political philosophy, and a group biography of the people who have dedicated their lives to unlocking the possibilities of people, particularly in times of crisis. It is a sprawling and very often arresting book, one particularly suited to our times in which each week brings a fresh disaster and, fast upon its heels, calls to alter or suspend civil liberties, property laws, and other forms of the civic contract to contain the chaos some strident voices claim looms behind these events.

Solnit's account is particularly powerful because you hear it first in the voices of people who were there. Drawing on diaries, newspaper reports, and eyewitness accounts, Solnit has essentially written a people's history of five major disasters of the twentieth and early twenty-first centuries, from the San Francisco earthquake of 1906 to Hurricane Katrina in New Orleans nearly a century later. Along the way she zeroes in on the lives of activists from Dorothy Day, who was just eight and a half when the temblor struck, to Felipe Chavez of Welcome Home Kitchen in New Orleans, showing how disaster was a catalyst for meaning for them.

This is a massive project, greatly aided by Solnit's qualities as a writer. As a psychogeographer, Californian, and cultural historian, Solnit has always found ways to map experience onto places, and spaces back onto people. It seems hardly an accident that her largest project prior to this book was *Wanderlust*, a wide-ranging study of the possibilities inherent in walking, and her most significant project to immediately follow it was a series of atlases (three-dimensional anthologies, really) of the cities of San Francisco, New Orleans, and New York.

A Paradise Built in Hell begins in San Francisco in April 1906. Solnit introduces us to the firefighters, short-order cooks, washerwomen, and people who—rather than panic or grab every last roll of toilet paper—turn and help one another as the blaze bears down on them, and survive. On the morning of the quake, for instance, a police officer named H. C. Schmitt was on patrol downtown. After stopping a few thieves from stealing some cigars, and helping others, he made his way home and—using two huge pots normally dedicated to boiling laundry—set up an impromptu kitchen.

This pop-up soup kitchen is just one of many organizations to emerge almost immediately after the quake. To which one could add a whole host of other services. Mail was delivered without postage; speakeasies bloomed; local firefighter brigades began putting out fires with what water they had left and, when that ran out, with blankets soaked in vinegar.

What's remarkable to read here, even now, freshly reminded of how generous some people were during the COVID-19 pandemic, is how virtually *everyone* chipped in. As Solnit writes, all but two butchers in the city began to donate every last cut of meat. Cattle, sheep, hogs, beef. "None of this meat was lost or destroyed," a slaughterhouse manager remembered. "Every bit of it was distributed to the people, and the supply lasted seven days. We started distributing at five o'clock the afternoon of the earthquake. . . . The two firms that did not open up their warehouses had all their meat rot on their hands."

As a Californian used to moving freely in a lot of open (but contested and often stolen) space, Solnit is extremely well equipped to describe the conditions that made this magnanimity possible.

Twenty-eight thousand buildings were destroyed in the San Francisco earthquake, she reminds us, and there was no place to hide. Suddenly in close proximity to one another, their horizons reduced to the present day, the citizens of the city were overwhelmingly generous to one another. "Self-interest is more often about amassing future benefit than protecting present comfort," Solnit writes; and people gave, often regardless of color or creed, because a future beyond the very moment was inconceivable.

As a political theorist and activist, Solnit is especially good at showing the way various minds are shaped by interactions with disaster. In the opening segments of the book, she traces how in response to the San Francisco earthquake both Dorothy Day and William James developed ideas that were crucial to their evolving understanding of human nature. Day, the future founder of the Catholic Worker Movement, experienced the call to help as a kind of love. James emerged from his walks around the city, talking to survivors, with a sense that the human self was far more resilient to suffering than he'd previously thought: "Suffering and loss are transformed when they are shared experiences," he concluded.

Threading these accounts with some of the destruction that followed, Solnit creates a rousing portrait of how quickly a utopian social flattening—however built from disaster—can be brought to a brutal end. Brigadier General Frederick Funston, the commanding officer at the Presidio military base in San Francisco, "perceived his job as saving the city from the people, rather than saving the people from the material city of cracked and crumbling buildings, fallen power lines, and towering flames." In essence, he was protecting the elite during their panic—indeed, of the many terms introduced here, *elite panic* is an especially helpful one in times of great disparity.

Were this book to stop here, it would already be a significant rewriting of how disaster has informed the California imaginary. But Solnit moves on to reimagine four other disasters to tease out other lessons. From California she brings us to Halifax, where on December 6, 1917, a Norwegian ship, the *Imo*, collided with a munitions ship, the *Mont Blanc*, which was loaded with three thousand tons of explosive power, setting off the most powerful explosion the world had seen prior to the dropping of an atomic bomb. She writes,

> An air blast rolled over the city, knocking down buildings, tearing through doors, windows, and walls, crushing the bodies of those who were hit head-on nearby, exploding eardrums and lungs, lifting people and hurling them into whatever was nearby or carrying them away, snapping trees and telegraph poles like twigs, reducing whole neighborhoods to splinters and rubble.

Solnit's account of this devastation is grisly, forensic, and some of the best writing about disaster alongside Stewart O'Nan's *The Circus Fire* and many works by Leslie Marmon Silko. It could have been much worse, she points out. Vincent Coleman, for one, rushed back into the telegraph office to send a warning to a train coming into town. "Guess this will be my last message," he said signing off. He died in the explosion, along with several other men and women who'd sent out crucial messages for help.

What motivated such people? And why, as opposed to those in San Francisco, were soldiers in Halifax less trigger-happy when conducting rescues? Out of the Halifax explosion, Solnit writes, the field of disaster studies grew, and from this point forward she takes readers on a guided tour of some of its early and key texts, such as Samuel Henry Prince's *Catastrophe and Social Change*, which he wrote after studying what unfolded in Halifax. In the course of his dissertation, Prince referenced a revolutionary Russian book called *Mutual Aid: A Factor of Evolution*, Peter Kropotkin's study that took issue with the notion that life was, by nature, fundamentally competitive. "If animal life itself and earlier and simpler forms of human society were not ruthlessly competitive," Solnit summarizes, "then the justification for the selfish side of contemporary human society as natural or inevitable would crumble."

Far-flung in its reach and exhaustively reported, *A Paradise Built in Hell* sometimes feels like a continuation of Kropotkin's project. In the course of writing it, Solnit steers away from simply attacking power, and instead, time and again, finds in the reporting about one disaster or another, stories of resilience, belief in civil society, and the ability of people, from Mexico City to London to the suburbs of New Orleans, to form what is essentially a government of people. This in no way plays down the suffering of those who have lived through such disasters, but instead pays tribute to their knowledge. Drawing out the fine difference between altruism (which is love channeled freely) and charity (which is love directed with a price of return regard), Solnit has created a possible framework for how we might need to live all the time. If our catastrophic era is to be judged, we will need this book more and more with each coming year.

ARRIVALS AND MIGRATIONS

DEVIL IN A BLUE DRESS

by Walter Mosley

American literature features some killer first lines, and here's why Walter Mosley belongs right up there with the best spinners of them, from Toni Morrison to F. Scott Fitzgerald: "I was surprised to see a white man walk into Joppy's bar."

That's how Mosley introduced us to Easy Rawlins in *Devil in a Blue Dress*. Mosley was thirty-eight years old, working as a computer programmer. It was his first published novel, and, carried by Easy's smooth, skeptical, brilliant voice, *Devil* launched one of the best hard-boiled mystery series of the twentieth and twenty-first centuries. So much moves beneath the surface of that one line: the easiness of its tone sliding over the unease of its content; the segregation of the times and the arrival of something new.

The book gets off to a hot start. It's 1948, and Easy (born Ezekiel) Rawlins has just returned from World War II, where he fought alongside white, Japanese, and other Americans at the Battle of Normandy. ("I ate with them and slept with them," he says of white soldiers, "and I killed enough blue-eyed young men to know that they were just as afraid to die as I was.") But prejudice never left the good ole US of A, even in so-called paradise. Casual, persistent racism is everywhere in Los Angeles; it's part of why Easy lost his job at Champion Aircraft—a problem because he has a mortgage and likes to pay his bills.

Enter this white man with an errand. A woman—named Daphne or Delia; Easy can't keep it straight—needs to be found. And Easy can look in places this white man—whose name is Mr. Aldridge—can't. Easy can also probably get this done quietly. Against his better judgment, but also because he was raised on a sharecropper's farm in Texas, Easy takes the man's money and sets out across the city to ask a few questions.

It's worth pausing here to appreciate the time frame Mosley has chosen for *Devil in a Blue Dress*. In 1948, the United States was transitioning out of a wartime economy; factory jobs like the one Easy had held were drying up, and corporations were cracking down on labor. Chester Hime's great 1945 protest novel, *If He Hollers Let Him Go*, reminds us how quickly that work went away when a Black man complained. Meanwhile, the Second Great Migration was under way, with anywhere from fifty thousand to a hundred thousand Black Americans moving from the South to Los Angeles in search of better lives, a life without Jim Crow. Many of them settled in South Central Los Angeles, in Compton and Watts.

It should be said, too, that this was not simply a choice. By 1940, 80 percent of housing in Los Angeles and Chicago, two cities where Blacks were settling, had restrictive racial covenants effectively barring Black ownership. Thus Blacks went where they could go, which was South Central. *Devil in a Blue Dress* is set in this Black city within Los Angeles, and the way that Blacks lived next to but separately from whites, who were entitled at will to cross any real or imagined border, creates some of the key context for the novel's plot. The last place Daphne was seen might have been John's, an illegal club that Easy already knows well. "Being on the bottom didn't feel so bad if you could come to John's now and then and remember how it felt back home in Texas, dreaming about California. Sitting there and drinking John's scotch you could remember the dreams you once had and, for a while, it felt like you had them for real."

At John's, Easy runs into some old friends, which leads to a night of drinking that is memorably portrayed in the 1995 film adaptation with Denzel Washington and Lisa Nicole Carson as Coretta, his friend's sultry girlfriend. With his friend passed out on the couch, Easy and Coretta go at each other, each plying the other with questions while their bodies are entangled. By the time the sun has come up, Easy departs with what he thinks is the information Aldridge has been seeking. "When I finally made it back to my house, on 116th Street, it was another beautiful California day. Big white clouds sailed eastward toward the San Bernardino mountain range. There were still traces of snow on the peaks and there was the lingering scent of burning trash." What a forensically accurate description of a Los Angeles morning.

Here is one key way that Mosley is making some updates to LA noir as a genre. Private eyes, which Easy is in the process of becoming, often live light and sleep at work or even in their cars or at hotels. Throughout *Devil in a Blue Dress*, even after it has becomes abundantly clear that he is being watched, that it is dangerous there, Easy always comes back to his house. In the film, Washington is always doing yard work. In the novel, Easy loves his mail. "Once I'd become a home owner I got mail every day—and I loved it. I even loved junk mail."

One of the letters Easy gets is from his friend Mouse, whom he had left behind along with some questionable circumstances back in Houston. As a narrator, Easy often sounds as if he is recounting events for someone like Mouse. He is new enough to Los Angeles to compare it to home, and the way people live is just different. Take looking out the window. "Looking out the window is different in Los Angeles than it is in Houston. No matter where you live in a southern city (even a wild and violent place like Fifth Ward, Houston), you see almost everybody you know by just looking out your window. Every day is a parade of relatives and old friends and lovers you once had, and maybe you'd be lovers again one day."

And then there are the cars:

> Because in LA people don't have time to stop; anywhere they have to go they go there in a car. The poorest man has a car in Los Angeles; he might not have a roof over his head but he has a car. And he knows where he's going too. In Houston and Galveston, and way down in Louisiana, life was a little more aimless. People worked a little job but they don't make any real money no matter what they did. But in Los Angeles you could make a hundred dollars a week if you pushed.

Easy is here to push, but he is done following orders. "A job in a factory is an awful lot like working on a plantation in the South," he says at one point. "The bosses see all the workers like they're children, and everyone knows how lazy children are." Thus he finds himself getting in deeper and deeper with Mr. Aldridge, who eventually has Easy at his beck and call. Not Easy's happy place, but if he can find this Daphne, who is tied up with a white mayoral candidate and a Black gangster, then he can get on to the next thing. So when the phone rings he answers it, and off he goes into the night.

This moment, where a noir novel lays bare its insider access to a place, is one of the genre's great delicious pleasures. There are so many ways that Mosley feasts on postwar LA in *Devil in a Blue Dress*, summoning the city's fractured past, its still farmland roots. Its secret nightlife. He also captures the small touches, things that may have struck new arrivals adjusting to life in a new home. The play of light through windows on an afternoon spent trying to drink away one's personal history. We follow Easy between tense interactions with whites and more genial ones with Black residents at work, in poolrooms, on his front porch. Eventually, Mouse shows up and helps him in his quest to find Daphne.

One can feel Mosley working in the slipstream of Chester Himes and Raymond Chandler here. The fury and the style of each inform his voice, but there's a lot that's new, too. Easy is indeed easy in situations that ought to cause distress, with white bullies on the beach, cops who pick him up and shake him down for information. But he's no simple errant knight: He has a vulnerability and disquiet which mean that when Mosley shows the constant adjustments Easy must make for white men's expectations of him, we feel it from the inside. The city within the city has a mirror in the self Easy must develop to stay alive in LA.

There's another mirror to these continuous appeasements, and that is in the character of Daphne. Easy eventually learns that she is passing as white, and that her secret has been used against her boyfriend, the mayoral candidate, by another mayoral candidate with his own far more sinister secrets. She eventually grows to trust Easy, as much as one can in a crime novel set in a fallen world. But Easy can't trust her affection. "Daphne was like the chameleon. . . . She changed for her man. If he was a mild white man who was afraid to complain to the waiter she'd pull his head to her bosom and pat him. If he was a poor black man who had soaked up pain and rage for a lifetime she washed his wounds with a rough rag and licked the blood till it staunched."

As in all hardboiled mysteries, what begins as a simple question— Where's the girl?—unravels a secret network of crime and dependencies. But ultimately the deepest network is the one that lurks inside its hero. Easy may not be a good man, but he is trying to be, which might mean he is good. He is also just finding his feet in *Devil in a Blue Dress*. Over the dozen-plus books that follow, he will change dramatically, become more introspective, harder even, and his losses will pile up. He might acquire financial security, but he doesn't get safety.

That's because the series spans Los Angeles from 1940 to 1960, a period of the city's history rife with growth but also terrible violence, open Klan marches, and people all over the city—from Chicano students to Black activists to Asian Americans—all taking to the streets for their rights. The Watts uprising is at the heart of Mosley's 2004 Rawlins novel, *Little Scarlet*, which takes place just in the aftermath of that period, and Easy, who has already become mightily skeptical of the LAPD, is asked by them to investigate the murder of a Black girl called Little Scarlet.

The city was in ruins that day because a routine traffic stop escalated to a terrible bloody beating of a Black motorist, twenty-one-year-old Marquette Fyre. For days the city burned in rage, a precursor to the uprising that would kick off thirty years later after the beating of Rodney King. It is surely not an accident that Easy's home in *Devil in a Blue Dress* is on 116th Street—the same street where Marquette was stopped, though perhaps not the same corner. Mosely himself was born at 116th and Central. The latter street plays a key role in *Devil in a Blue Dress* and the books that follow; it is the thoroughfare where people go out, meet up, and live.

In a good crime series, the hero traverses the city so much in figuring out whatever crime they have been roped into that the writer remaps it, makes the place their own. Mosley does this and some in his Rawlins books, but he goes much further. Writing with great sensory delight, poise, and a lashing sense of humor, he upends LA and finds pockets of Houston and Galveston there, not to mention many other elsewheres.

In other words, he restores the city to its rightful complexity, and in Easy Rawlins he gives us a Virgil we'd follow just about anywhere—to do anything, talk to anyone, or simply spend a day drinking vodka and grapefruit soda with, napping and waiting for the sun to go down. Decades after it was first published, Mosley's book is every bit as vital and glorious—and every bit as uneasy about the safety of its hero.

A PLACE AT THE NAYARIT

by Natalia Molina

Tenderly, thoughtfully, *A Place at the Nayarit* reaches into the recent past and resurrects a restaurant. To the author, Natalia Molina, historian of race and ethnic studies, this is not simply an act of research; it is also a personal errand. The Nayarit, the Mexican restaurant in Echo Park, hangout of well-known stars and too-tired-to-cook construction workers, was founded and run by her grandmother and namesake, Doña Natalia Barraza. This book chronicles Doña Natalia's life's work, a masterpiece of engagement and care: a restaurant that didn't just feed people and feed them well but also built structures of protection, joy, and financial security for a whole community.

Doña Natalia moves through the pages of *A Place at the Nayarit* like a busy patron, flashing in and out of view. Part of this movement is to do with how archives work, Molina points out. Dependent on official records, census questionnaires conducted in English, they tend to distort and erase. They often reify structures of power, and what interest would those nodes of officialdom have in a Mexican woman who came to the United States at barely twenty-one years old, not speaking English? It's astonishing how quickly, though, Molina picks up her trail, describing how her grandmother founded one restaurant, which failed, then another, called the Nayarit, located first on Sunset in Downtown during the 1940s, when postwar Los Angeles was booming and Mexican and Mexican American workers longed for food from home.

Doña Natalia's greatest gamble—moving the Nayarit to Echo Park, a racially and ethnically mixed neighborhood in Los Angeles—was her biggest success. Molina delivers an exquisitely modulated capsule history of the place, from the early days in which Spanish missionaries took land from Chumash and Gabrielino/Tongva people, to the rise of surrounding neighborhoods and their racial covenants, to the resulting densifying of Mexican, Vietnamese, Chinese, and Filipino communities, which together with a large gay population gave Echo Park a decidedly bohemian air. Within the neighborhood, people lived vividly in opposition to primary ideas of what the city was—a fantasy of whiteness that ran from pop culture to policing to the way loans were given out—while also establishing alternate centers of wealth for Echo Park's communities.

The Nayarit sat at the intersection of these contested crossroads. Over the years, it employed more than a hundred people and fed thousands more, people who were grateful for a space that reminded them of where they were from, a place open late, a safe place—Doña Natalia made savvy bargains with LAPD officers, feeding them for free so that they would keep an extra eye on the restaurant—and also a place where they could be themselves. Where they could speak Spanish and not feel as though it needed to be translated, where they could be queer and not expect that would put them in danger. Where Latinx people, some of them new to the United States, could feel as if some part of home had come with them to Los Angeles.

Doña Natalia played dozens of roles at the restaurant. She was its maître d', its icon, its social planner, its advertising guru, the entrepreneur smart enough to run ads in newspapers back home in

Mexico so that by the time people arrived, it already loomed large in their imagination. She was a financial sponsor who put up family members and friends upon their arrival in Los Angeles, lent them the expertise of her attorney so that they, too, could apply for documentation—a key element of Depression-era forced repatriations, not too far in the past. She was a paramour-maker who introduced lovers; she was a protector who played den mother to the women, keeping an eye on Marlon Brando and others who came to the restaurant with swiveling eyes. She was a fixer, a political power broker, a mentor to future restaurateurs, a pipeline of money back to Mexico, a culinary historian, and a mother of two adopted children, because, of course, why not take on more responsibility? The scale of her generosity is simply breathtaking.

Molina is a historian, so as close as she gets to Doña Natalia, she also respects her singularity, her scope, the limits of her knowability. Rather than make this book a story about only her family, Molina has made it about all the families involved in the Nayarit. She speaks to former busboys, waiters, waitresses, hostesses, customers, and food critics. This narrative large-heartedness with her family's legacy has two effects. First, it opens the book up to the knowledge and history that reside in the lives of everyone her grandmother touched; second, it demonstrates the very principles she is musing about with regard to reconciling how people actually inhabit a place with how history is told.

In early parts of the book, Molina discusses the difference between community institutions—like libraries or governments—and community anchors. The former tend to rely on top-down approaches, even if what they do can be very helpful. The latter tend to be made from the community up. By seeing the Nayarit as the latter, Molina also gives herself the excuse to remember and address the careers of early community figures—like Representative Edward Roybal, the first Mexican American councilman in the history of the United

States—thus contextualizing Doña Natalia's work in light of their efforts on behalf of their community.

There are moments in this book when you can feel Molina—a fabulous writer whose prose is supple and feels addressed to you as a reader—realizing that if this sort of history is going to be written again, she will also need to address historians and make her methods part of the story here. She has to lay the blueprint for the kind of book *A Place at the Nayarit* is so that it can be written in other neighborhoods, about other communities, other restaurants, other spaces, from bowling alleys to jazz clubs. Watching her build the framework for these future works is incredibly moving. To see someone of such immense erudition turn her novel creation, something she could raise up on a pedestal, into an invitation, an open-source work of memory, is powerful. True, there are other books set in motion by this impulse, such as Saidiya Hartman's intimate history of Black women and queer people in New York and Philadelphia during the early twentieth century, *Wayward Lives, Beautiful Experiments: Intimate Histories of Riotous Black Girls, Troublesome Women, and Queer Radicals*, but by proceeding from what she calls an "urban anchor," Molina has pointed toward a new way of bringing back the past—framing, perhaps, what has so often slipped through history's too-stingy register.

It also simply makes for pleasurable reading. When you accept that a territory is not merely what can be seen but what was lived, a fresh spirit of possibility enters. New incidents are drawn to the historian's magnet. Indeed, by pulling from interviews, stories, and the whole panoply of memory that exists within a community—orally as well as in print—Molina has resurrected the way in which spaces, not simply institutions, are where we become, where we work our lives out relationally, picking up and putting down different identities based on whom we're with and in what context. The variety of happenings at the restaurant attests to this, from a forty-five-minute boxing match that occurred between two leading prizefighters, to the promenade of musicians after midweek sets, to the idle Friday-night takeout order of a family who lived nearby and simply didn't feel like cooking.

Of course, the restaurant doesn't exist anymore; of course, it isn't forgotten. In later chapters, Molina describes the way the memory and possibilities of the Nayarit live on, even if it's not serving up delicious food at three in the morning. What an uncynical way to think about loss, while respecting what it means: to follow the lives into which care was poured, at all hours of the night, with afterlives so long they are almost comical. One interview subject with whom Molina sits remembers how Doña Natalia intervened to pay his gas bill because he needed help. The bill arrives to this day with her name on it, even though he has long since resumed paying it.

Now, at last, a few more people will know the place and the many other generous things this great woman did, made possible, most important of them being the restaurant she created and kept open for a while, making the nights more hospitable, more fun, more tasty, more worthy of their sweet music.

THE DISTANCE BETWEEN US

by Reyna Grande

One day in May 1985, nine-year-old Reyna Grande was called to her grandmother's house and told to listen for a phone call. When she arrived, she found a man waiting there.

"Nobody had to tell me who the man sitting on the couch was," she writes in her memoir *The Distance Between Us*. "I thought about the eight-by-ten-inch photo I had placed on my grandmother's altar. He had put on weight. He wore glasses now. Instead of black-and-white, he was in color, and I could see that his skin *was* the color of rain-soaked earth."

Thus ended an eight-year period of waiting. For most of her childhood in Mexico, all Grande knew of her father was what he had left behind when he went north to El Otro Lado. Grande's father was a bricklayer, and he'd gone north to pursue a dream of making enough money to build a great house. When he arrived there, he discovered he needed help, so Grande's mother soon joined him. Grande and her two siblings stay behind in Mexico and go to live with their father's mother, Abuela Evila, a bent-backed older woman who takes out her frustrations on her granddaughters.

Great books about childhood often have saints and villains—it's how some children see the world, in a way—and this book has both. Even taking into account Evila's already heavy burdens, she treats the children appallingly. She constantly favors her other grandchildren over Reyna and her siblings, to whom she assigns extra chores, as if they need to work off the cost of their boarding. They even eat last. "Abuela Evila always made sure that her favorite grandchildren ate first, and whatever was left, that's what she gave us. Sometimes there wasn't much left, and we would go to bed with our stomachs growling."

Day by day, as their parents find their way up north, Reyna and her siblings are recast in their own lives. No longer are they prized, beloved children but burdens who require maintenance. Like so many children, they wind up in a school with a louse problem, so their grandfather deals with it the old-fashioned way: by chopping their hair off. Grande's hair was the nicest thing she possessed, and suddenly there are scissors hissing near her ear. "I squirmed even more at watching my curls land on the ground and on my lap, falling one by one like the petals of a flower. Then my grandmother's chickens came clucking to see what was happening, and they picked up my curls and shook them around, and when they realized they weren't food, they stepped all over them and dragged them with their feet across the dirt."

In stories of the migratory journey from Mexico to America, we do not often see this part: the time spent waiting, the loneliness of children, the imperfect emotional support they receive from overtaxed or indifferent grandparents or aunts and uncles, the way this period of abandonment creates coping mechanisms and familial bonds that will last a lifetime. *The Distance Between Us* is a masterpiece of portraiture in people changed by their various mechanisms of survival. It shows just how much anguish such a separation can put children through, even if a kindlier relative steps in, as ultimately happened in Grande's case, when her other grandmother, a healer, took her and her siblings in.

Looping forward, and staying mostly back, Grande narrates from a child's-eye point of view. Nothing makes sense, and all around her is a world bursting with animated life. Grande remembers so well the sights and smells of her hometown of Iguala, with its ring of hills, its pouring rains, the hot summers. The scorpions trying to sneak in at night. The luxurious mangoes sold at school that she could never afford. Not to mention new clothes, a quinceañera, and many other things her next-door neighbor and cousin could.

With childhood comes an acute awareness of fairness, and Grande deploys this moral centering to observe the way distance operates on her family. The trying times draw Grande and her two siblings closer together. When her brother, Carlos, sneaks out, she and her sister, Mago, work to distract their grandmother from realizing he's nipped across town to where he knows he'll be fed. They also watch out for one another, and then for their mother, too, when she comes home heartbroken: Their father has met another woman.

Everyone in this book has a wound, and one of Grande's skills is to allow us to see it inflicted before some of her characters know it. For instance, it will be years before Grande's sister understands the cost to her psyche of not having a complete childhood. When their parents leave, she is thrust into the role of caretaker; she learns to be strong for others, a lesson that becomes a habit of self-sacrifice.

In her second memoir, *A Dream Called Home*, the ultimate consequences of this period will come home for Mago, Reyna, Carlos, and their mother in ways that are heartbreaking, seemingly arbitrary. For some in Grande's family, the memories of abandonment lead them to seek out safety; for others—like her father, her brother—it leads them into habits of self-destruction.

There is a long history of cross-border tales in North American literature. Mexicans and Central Americans have been coming to what is now California for centuries, and since it became the US following the Mexican-American War. Though the story the country has often told itself is one of exceptions and success, the best of literature acknowledges the pain, loneliness, and heartache of the multistage journey north, the search for work, the hard labor of forging a life in a new language.

One of the most significant of these tales is Daniel Venegas's satirical novel, *The Adventures of Don Chipote: or When Parrots Breast-Feed*, first serialized in the Los Angeles newspaper *El heraldo de Mexico* in 1928. The novel follows the fate of one Don Chipote, lured to the US by dreams of escaping the daily grind of ox herding in his native village. "All you have to do is make up your mind to do it, an' you'll suck the nectar from the tree of life," Don Chipote's friend Pitacio says on a return trip home. Don Chipote drinks these tales down straight for two weeks.

Then one morning he's up at dawn with his dog, Skinenbones, walking to the border and hopefully California. After a month they wind up in Juárez, where Don Chipote approaches the gringo entrance to America and is treated like an idiot. It's the first of many humiliations the journey will heap on him. A trip to jail sends him fleeing into the hands of a local coyote, who manages to get Don Chipote to El Paso, where he picks up work washing dishes, and eventually gets roped into working on the trains that go all over the Southwest. Swinging a pickax for this last job, he misses and drives the blade right into his foot.

Before there were highways and industrial farming, the railroad was where many migrants came to work. They worked laying tracks, and on the trains, which meant having a life that was portable. In the first half of Venegas's novel, not a day goes by when they aren't moving. On they move toward Los Angeles. Like many early accounts of arrival and immigration, Venegas's was a story about labor, a tale about what it took to survive and how that felt. Venegas constantly breaks the fourth wall to address the reader directly, pointing out—in case they missed it—the lessons poor Chipote is learning. Number one among these is that there is no milk and honey in America, and not nearly as much work as everyone had hoped. "The result of this multitude of braceros immigrating to Los Angeles is that they do little more than pluck the goose bare and raise the height of the tortilla basket," Venegas comments in one of these asides, "because those who have jobs to offer, upon seeing this horde, steel themselves and pay the braceros as little as they can. Because we workers never have much cash to begin with, necessity forces us to work for whatever they are willing to pay us. Thus, we are never able to get our heads above water."

This cycle plays out across *The Adventures of Don Chipote*, as Venegas's hero tries to climb the slippery pole of American life. His foot heals, and he eventually gets work as a dishwasher again. After what he spends on a suit, he still has some left over to send to his family back home. He starts to date a flapper on the side, which his wife back home is beginning to suspect. She eventually decides to sell the oxen and come for her husband, Pitacio in tow, since he speaks English. We relive Don Chipote's journey again, this time with a family—and in the ultimately somewhat comic ending, Doña Chipote brings her chastened man home.

It's hard not to think of this novel when reading Grande's memoir. What Venegas deals with in satirical comedy, Grande addresses through the eyes of a child. In the time her mother and father are away, as distance becomes both emotional and literal, the children's imaginations fill in the gaps of what is happening. Reyna and her siblings tease each other that they will be replaced. Finally one day, new clothes—gifts from El Otro Lado—arrive, and they're the wrong size. "If they don't know something as basic as the size of our shoes and clothes," Reyna wonders, "what else don't they know about us? And what don't we know about them?"

The Distance Between Us does more than address physical distance. It imagines how little children know of context, and how this causes them to come to judgments that estrange them from one parent or the other. For instance, when Grande's mother returns after a few years with a new baby but without their father, the kids subtly take his side—it is somehow their mother's fault he is not there. Grande, however, is happy her mother has returned.

Occasionally *The Distance Between Us* steps outside the child's-eye view to give us key pieces of information, and when it does the effect is powerful. One of the most important moments is when she tells us that two and a half years after her mother had come to the US with Grande's father, he told her that he had fallen in love with another woman. He then kicked her out. The woman who returned to Mexico with a baby and such a palpable sense of a long journey completed that even taxi drivers asked her about El Otro Lado was returning a broken woman.

Not much is known of Daniel Venegas, but he did for five years edit his own satirical newspaper in Los Angeles. He also wrote plays that appeared in some of the city's theaters, often poking fun at the Mexican American community. It's fair to say his novel about an entire family's journey north moves in the way a satirist's tale needs to, it finds the pressure point and pushes. But there is a world of feeling one cannot address in humor this way, especially in what it means to be left behind, to be the other family, to be a child with a life put on hold.

When it is at last Grande's time to depart for El Otro Lado, she faces another leave-taking. Her mother will stay two thousand miles behind. *The Distance Between Us* is divided nearly in half, the second part beginning in September 1985, three months after Reyna, her brother, and her sister have arrived in their new home, in their new country, and where the shock of having been initially left behind comes with them. There are real and persistent physical symptoms of trauma. To add confusion to this ache, when Grande goes to the dentist for the first time in her life, she's told to answer to "Cindy," the name of the daughter of Grande's father's girlfriend.

Grande's teenage years are a welter of sweat and confusion. Her father—the man she loved from afar, longed for—has changed, and now here she is in a new country in a new language, and she senses that if she is to make it, she must rely on herself. She becomes a hard worker, a good student, a driven young woman who sometimes might look—at a squint—like a people pleaser. The way this memoir sketches this development is so psychologically rich and full of sympathy for Grande's young self, I found myself praying that the book will be taught more and more in California, where a quarter of the people living in the state were born outside America, and nearly half of all children have one parent who is an immigrant.

Grande is especially wise about the capricious ways success dodges some family members, and the distance that puts between them. Her mother eventually starts life on her own terms, in Los Angeles, her fate entering a completely different splinter. While Reyna grows up and becomes a star student in spite of her father's harsh rules, her mother's life begins to enter a barbed spiral. A bad relationship, a series of missed opportunities, and she never fully recovers from the distance between her and her children, which opened up those many years ago when all she wanted was to take them to a new country for a better life, a better opportunity.

This is a tremendously affecting book, a chronicle of a prototypical Californian childhood, and a reckoning with memory. As Grande describes her teen years, the shadows of her family's dispersal grow. Memory becomes less a possession than a force, something that enacts itself upon Reyna when she least expects it. Certain smells—the wax in a beauty salon—send Grande zooming back to her kinder grandmother's home back in Mexico. Meanwhile, in California, her father is ever a stranger, even more so when he tells her, offhandedly, that her own mother is there too. How to hold all this in one body? Grande's memoir seems to ask—so much disparate family, so much distance? It is impossible, but on the page this complex family and the journey they undergo are drawn with exquisite care, like a map that is still being written.

AMERICA IS NOT THE HEART

by Elaine Castillo

Elaine Castillo's debut novel, *America Is Not the Heart*, spans a century in the lives of two families from the Philippines—one rich, one poor—who wind up entwined in Milpitas, California, at the turn of the millennium. If you've been sipping frustratedly from the tepid bubbler of literature, thirsty for a big drink of a tale, look no further. This is a hilarious, bawdy, bear hug of a novel. Drawing from the Philippines' colonial history, its mythology, and several of its languages, Castillo charges with breathtaking confidence into the multilingual future of her form. If this novel doesn't wind up on the curriculum of every American high school in the future, God help us.

At the center of this book is Hero de Vera, a former medical student from an upper-class family turned radical, who arrives from the Philippines at her uncle Pol's house in California scarred from torture she suffered in guerrilla fighting back home. In his old life, Pol was an orthopedic surgeon from a landed family; he could have stitched up his niece and given her a wallet thick with cash. Now he's a security guard at night, and what he can offer is a bed and an important job:

looking after his amusing, fisticuffing daughter, Roni, who has a case of eczema so terrible that one of Hero's first jobs is driving the girl to visit a faith healer.

Pol's wife, Paz, is the family rock, a nurse who works two jobs and who has taken over the bread earning in the wake of their arrival in California, where she pulls double shifts so she can send money home. She grew up working class in the Philippines and has never assumed that a life without labor was hers to demand. Hero is yet another responsibility heaped on a life already heaped with sacrifice, and Paz is not thrilled, at first, to have a privileged kid on her doorstep; she has never had the luxury of a life of ideas—why should she pay for this kid's brush with the brute realities of life?

Castillo's novel is a spiritual and historical update to one of the great classics of Asian American literature, Carlos Bulosan's *America Is in the Heart*, a fictionalized chronicle of his own journey to the West Coast of the US at the tail end of the second great wave of migration from the Philippines, in the wake of the colonization by the United States in 1898. Thousands of men came to Washington, Hawaii, and California, where, like the men Daniel Venegas described in *The Adventures of Don Chipote*, they worked in canneries, domestic service, and agriculture. Bulosan encounters brutal work conditions and racism in the canneries of Seattle and Northern California.

While in America, Allos, Bulosan's main character/stand-in, is shocked to discover a double standard. For whites there is one set of rules, one system of justice, one set of expectations; for everyone else there is another, or none. He witnesses lynchings, jubilant exploitation of workers, and rampant corruption among ownership, all of which reinforce his own perilous precarity. He moves frequently, from Oregon to Washington, down to California, where he hopes things will be better, but they are not. "I was surprised to know that after eight years in the United States I had only one old blue suit, a cheap suitcase, and three shirts."

America Is Not the Heart

At the end of this odyssey, Allos's dream of what America could be is nearly crushed—but he holds fast to an idea that America is in the heart, even if it doesn't exist in the world itself. Castillo's novel takes this idea and runs with it, setting her tale smack in the middle of the biggest wave of migration from the Philippines to America, following the Immigration and Nationality Act of 1965, which removed racial quotas. Many people from the Philippines who already had family in the US came to join them, many of them winding up employed in California hospitals.

How discrete and containable such periods sound when they are simply described as facts. *America Is Not the Heart* does the important imaginary work of envisioning all the relationships that make a new home a home for people. It's not about what jobs are available, although that is important; the experience Castillo has conjured is of what acts of care and love made it possible. Whose floors were offered, who cooked the meals, what looks across the room made people feel alive, what music? What parts of language were carried over into America, what names for things were retained so that estrangement did not totally overwhelm new arrivals, like her character Hero? And what does Hero bring to people she meets?

Early in the novel, Roni tells Hero that her skin is a sign that an *engkanto*—meaning a mystical spirit—has come in human form. Roni's grandmother said it was a *kapre*, a tree god of sorts. One of the great metaphorical questions Castillo poses throughout this book is, How do we know where love will come from, and what if we can't speak its language? Also: Where will it take us, and what will it ask of us? Take Paz, for instance. Raised so poor in the Philippines that as a child she chased crabs for food, she collides with Pol when he is the *babaero*—the ladies' man—of the local hospital where she works as a nurse. She can't stand his smug confidence, his ease, yet she falls hard for him anyway.

Years later, in America—Pol's cologne mostly worn off, his prestige too—Paz will pay for most of their living together, much

77

of her extended family's education, and some of his family's living expenses also as these relatives make their way to the United States over decades—all on her nursing salary. Or salaries. After all, she works not one but two and a half full-time jobs for years. The awesome dignity of that labor and its effort is paid exquisite loving tribute in this book in all the ways Castillo describes how Paz survives it. How she bears down on providing, what she allows herself, and what she keeps private.

In America, it becomes clear that what Paz knew back in the Philippines has come true: Hero likes girls. Slowly, gently, and then with fabulous erotic power, Castillo is rewriting the queer coming-of-age story in this novel. Instead of hustling into San Francisco for nights out, *America Is Not the Heart* lands in Milpitas and stays there. Like so many people who live in the suburbs, Hero falls in love with someone she encounters at the mall. She doesn't have to go anywhere to become herself: She simply has to meet the right woman.

It is not an accident that Castillo has put a love story at the heart of this novel. For all the important acts of witness Bulosan's novel performed, Castillo is deeply wary of performing her people's labor and suffering for an audience to whom these agonies are simply news or, worse, evidence of their humanity. After all, in the seventy-five years since Bulosan's book, a style of reading for empathy has emerged in which the act of witnessing has become a new moral consumable, one that falls especially hard on writers of color. In her book *How to Read Now*, Castillo succinctly summarizes the perils of this form of documentation.

> The unfortunate influence of this style of reading has dictated that we go to writers of color for the gooey heart-porn of the ethnographic: to learn about forgotten history, harrowing tragedy, community-destroying political upheaval,

genocide, trauma; that we expect those writers
to provide those intellectual commodities the way
their ancestors once provided spices, minerals,
precious stones, and unprecious bodies.

Putting a relationship based on affection and pleasure at the crux of her novel allows Castillo to subvert the effort to extract anything from the book. Pleasure and pain, work and relief, erotics and resistance are too bound together for any one element to be plucked out—and still the novel still operates as a romance. As a love story, *America Is Not the Heart* is at once skeptical of romance and fluent in all its stages. Castillo also knows that the most powerful of all stages of love is the feeling that all the stages can be skipped, that in becoming smitten you are simply meeting a person you've always known. Hero has this arrow shot right into her heart. At one point, she looks at Rosalyn, the woman she has fallen for, and "she saw that Rosalyn had been studying her for longer than she'd been aware, arms around her knees, the gaze alert and considering. She looked at Hero like she'd looked at her this way a million times before and would do so a million times more; like she was looking at something she was used to but not tired of, something she could trace on paper with her eyes closed." Find a person to look at you this way and hold on tightly.

It should be said that *America Is Not the Heart* extends Bulosan's project in another significant way. It takes the large frame around the word *America* and finds a more livable one at the scale of place. *America Is Not the Heart* is also Castillo's love letter to Milpitas and the East Bay in general. So many everyday aspects of life there are transmuted into this novel with fond and hilarious attention. The longer Hero stays, the more she connects to the place through her niece, Roni, and her friend Jaime, who becomes like an extended part of the family. In one scene Jaime picks her up at the train station. "Jaime was waiting outside the BART station in his brown Supra, idling illegally at the curb, an Oakland A's cap on his head, smoking a cigarette that he flicked out the driver's side window at the sight of her."

The humble, the real, the mundane, the lived-in: Castillo sings the praises of life as it is lived, narrating with such warmth and linguistic brio that it reminds you that sometimes the most fundamental escape hatch a novel can provide is back into the everyday. The language used to order soup at the grocery store, the words one offers a sister when it's her turn to grieve.

Castillo has also made a harmonious weave from the many languages her characters speak. Each one of them is simultaneously reinventing themselves and keeping a language back for the heart. Pol speaks only Ilocano to Hero, whereas he'll use English on the phone, Tagalog at home; and somehow Roni sees them all as one superlanguage. Happily, Castillo doesn't pause to translate these shifts so much as note them, showing that every character in this memorable family is translating at all times. Even when speaking to any of the others.

Long before Elaine Castillo began work on this book, she studied Greek classics at UC Berkeley. Reading *America Is Not the Heart*, you feel she has made the most of their influence. This is a grand book full of epic battles, long journeys into the unknown. Family schisms. A Dolby surround sound conception of love and its place in life. No young writer in America understands quite so well the anguish of wanting to give and receive love in language that's not taxed at the border. No debut in recent years holds you aloft with such mighty tenderness and sings its song with such beauty.

SOLITO

by Javier Zamora

When extraordinary journeys are rendered normal—or even invisible so that abstract feelings like safety or security or greatness can reframe public debate—writers have work to do. Roque Dalton knew this. The revolutionary Salvadoran poet was constantly reframing resistance in the context of love and life, and life in the terms of political upheaval. This led to a peripatetic existence, not unlike the lives of the Magonistas, who resisted the reign of Porfirio Díaz. Once, the revolutionary poet was spared death by firing squad in 1959, and he fled to Mexico, where he wrote some of his most famous poems. The best of them dealt in love, like the classic "Poema de Amor," in which the exiled poet declares (in Katherine Silver's exquisite translation) his affection for

> those farmers who grow corn in foreign jungles
> those kings of the crime page
> those who nobody ever knows where they're from
> . . . .
> the eternally undocumented,

> the do-it-alls, sell-it-alls, eat-it-alls,
> the first to draw their knives,
> the saddest sad people in the world,
> my compatriots,
> my brothers and sisters

The poem has become something of an anthem in El Salvador, and it's not hard to see why. Rolling between sarcasm and bardic social yawp, it claims everyone who was expelled from the country during the violent buildup to its twelve-year civil war, not to mention all the people labeled as thieves and whores, anyone tarnished, anyone who did what they needed to in order to survive, and loves them.

It took years for this work to gain the prominence it deserved in North America, likely because of the author's politics. During his brief lifetime, Dalton would end up shifting bases to Cuba, even going so far as—legendarily—to have plastic surgery to reenter his country so as to fight for its freedom. He was murdered in 1975, and four years later, the civil war in El Salvador began with a bloodless coup of Carlos Humberto Romero's government, followed by brutal repression of any anti-coup protesters. Over the next dozen years, the United States (under Jimmy Carter and then Ronald Reagan) poured military and financial aid into the hands of the repressive government, which murdered tens of thousands of Salvadoran citizens, largely because the rebels were being funded by the Soviet Union.

Among the policies the Salvadoran government pursued—with US backing—several stand out. One was targeted assassinations. Anyone, be they a journalist or a doctor, accused of speaking out against the government could be erased. The other was called "draining the sea," which grew out of the US strategy during Vietnam of attacking the Vietcong by destroying the metaphorical water in which they swam. This essentially meant ecocidal bombing campaigns of the jungle and any area in which the guerrillas operated, as well as massacres of civilians. The idea being that with enough lethal encouragement, a population will turn on the resistance being done in its name. This strategy has never been successful, and as A. C. Grayling has written of the Allied bombing campaigns in Germany and Japan in World War II, the opposite happens.

Still, when bombs are dropping on their heads, many people flee for safety, and thus revolutions of the future are sown. For example, in the mid-1980s, one of the people who had to leave El Salvador in fear for his life was the father of Javier Zamora. The writer was merely a toddler, and he would soon after lose his mother, too, when she crossed over. Eventually, when he reached the age of nine, they sent for him, and Zamora began a two-month journey by bus, by boat, by minicab, and by foot from La Herradura, El Salvador, across Guatemala into Mexico, and finally—after two unsuccessful crossings—to Tucson, Arizona, where he now lives today, twenty-five years after his perilous, miraculous crossing.

The reason we know of this journey, among so many others like it, happening all the time right now, even as you read this sentence, is twofold. In 2017, Zamora published his debut collection, *Unaccompanied*, a series of lyrics and odes to the family he left behind, those who crossed with him, and the landscape of the desert, which both sustained and endangered him. It is one of the most powerful debut collections in recent American history. Adopting the voice of his mother and father, imagining the history of his grandfather and aunt, the book also captures the long aftermath of his country's civil war.

And then, in 2022, Zamora published an astonishing memoir, *Solito*, which re-creates his journey north from the perspective of his nine-year-old self. While many of the family members who animate *Unaccompanied* appear and then recede as he makes his way, *Solito* trains its sights on the adopted family with whom young Zamora travels. Whereas migrant journeys are often seen as exploitative and ill-conceived, composed only of the hardships they contain—which are many—*Solito* shines as a book about love and help. Time and again, during parts of the trip where such things shouldn't happen, there is laughter, aid, protection, care, and affection. In this way, Zamora has emerged as the greatest living inheritor of Dalton's revolutionary value: love.

But Zamora is loving in different ways in his two books. Poetry adores silences, acknowledges them, gives them their music, or indeed, as Dalton did in "Poema de Amor," their so-called names. Meanwhile, prose narrates toward what is possible: It does so by imagining a story. There is no way that Zamora, in his early thirties, could have retrieved every conversation, every spongy piece of white bread, every agua fresca that was part of his trip as a nine-year-old. That's not the point. The book exists to say, Will you imagine with me how it was for me? Will you come on this journey and meet the people who saved me—the people who were not angels but simply on the trip too? And—most radically—it asks us whether we can imagine loving a stranger, him, the way these fellow travelers did.

In this fashion, Zamora carries Dalton's legacy forward in the most intimate twenty-first-century way. You can see that Zamora is up to the task in the opening pages of *Unaccompanied*. The book doesn't begin with the poet writing about himself but to his Abuelita Neli, whom we later meet in the first pages of *Solito*. It is the eve of Obama's election, but all Zamora can think of is how at sea he has become.

> I've got nothing left but dreams
> where I'm: the parakeet nest on the flor de fuego,
> the paper boats we made when streets flooded,
> or toys I buried by the foxtail ferns.
> "¿Do you know
> the ferns I mean?"

Here in this first poem is one of Zamora's key syntactical moves: to begin a sentence with Spanish punctuation and to end it with English, like a memory being swallowed by a language. How heartbreaking it is, too, that even if this poem were written around the time of Obama's first election, in 2008, that would make the poet eighteen years old, yet here he is grasping at the receding tide of childhood memories, of things he did with the aunt who took care of him after his parents had left for the United States. "Last time you called," the poem continues, "you said my old friends think that now I'm from some town between this bay and our estero." In a way, they're not wrong. The poet is suspended between the life he once had and the life he has begun to live.

Unaccompanied is the opening act of retrieval. It conjures life in El Salvador, as the poet lived it, but it also strobes these portraits and memories with scenes from his flight north. The effect reads like following two stories at once: In one, we see a traumatized adult population trying to get on with life during a civil war. A grandfather who drinks, a father who flees, a mother who decides it's time she dates; perhaps her husband is never returning. Meanwhile, there is this child racing north, unsure of where he is or whom to trust, the landscape around him as unfathomable as the political realities he travels in.

As a poet, Zamora writes with a superior metaphysical engineering of the line. When writing of repeating memories, he retreats into tercets so that what is recalled has the elegance of ceremony. In shards of what can be recalled, his lines break abruptly, as if the reality reel has become unspooled:

> Against the herd of legs,
> you sprinted back toward me,
> I jumped on your shoulders,
> and we ran from the white trucks, then their guns.

This poem describes an incident that later appears in *Solito* during Zamora's second crossing. Before they're caught, Chino, who has come to look after young Zamora as though he were the brother Chino had lost years earlier, puts Zamora on his shoulders and runs with him. It is an image that is hard to forget: a man putting a child on his shoulders, the way one does at an amusement park when the child is tired, only this time to run to safety.

It is startling to reread *Unaccompanied* after reading *Solito*, as here are many of the key incidents of the second book, told in a slightly different register. Zamora remembers keeping his departure a secret, but he does so by imagining in a poem his father's final morning in El Salvador and how he may have had the same homesickness before leaving that Zamora later did. "I miss our son," Zamora writes, in his father's voice. "I miss the faint wick / on his skin." Later, we hear of this departure in his abuelita's voice: "When you mist / into tomorrow's dawns, at the shore / of somewhere, listen to this conch. / Don't lose me."

Unaccompanied places these sentiments in the context of the heavy cost exile has rendered on Zamora's family. His grandfather, who has seen what the government does to people who speak out, drowns his thoughts in drink and tries to control the last daughter who hasn't left him. Meanwhile, Abuelita Neli hides the letters that her daughter sends home to young Zamora so that he will stop asking her to read them—a poignant detail, since it clearly is an act of double preservation. In another narrative poem, Zamora describes an aunt who was raped and murdered by soldiers, and the psychological devastation those acts wrought on an uncle he never truly met. A man who might be alive today, but who is more likely dead.

> Some say you still pace some street without the chain
>   around your foot
> That kept you home. You went crazy. Only the streets know.
>
> We're tired of looking at strangers' left feet
> To see if the big toe and the two next to that are missing.

> Uncle, your brothers gave your mother the key
> To the steel chain tied to your right foot,
>
> The good one. Around her neck, the key waits for you.

What is notable in *Unaccompanied* is how disassociated Zamora is from himself. When he narrates stories of his family, the tone is sweeping, nourished, and deep, as if what is being recalled has been experienced, whereas when he writes of his own memories, or his own journey, the camera eye retreats, and it is as if we are watching the experience from above, from outside his body.

> I could bore you with the sunset, the way water tasted
> after so many days without it,
> the trees,
> the breed of dogs, but I can't say
> there were forty people
> when we found the ranch with the thin white man,
> his dogs,
> and his shotgun.
> Until this 5 a.m. I couldn't remember
> there were only five,
> or seven people—

Patient and careful with this fragile record of the journey north, *Unaccompanied* begins the act of reassembly, not just of the past but of the instrument of past-making. It waits for details to emerge from silence, and it slowly descends back into the poet's body. This poem, "Let Me Try Again," appears near the end of the book, after Zamora has told some of the harder-to-tell stories about his family, about his trip—this one ending, however, with a happier conclusion, in which the border guard who arrests them, inexplicably, lets them go.

This act of kindness is one of the apertures through which *Solito* is tugged, not so much the generosity of guards everywhere but the capacity of people trapped in an inhumane system to do more than think of themselves. And that flinging oneself into the unknown can be—amid terror and danger—an adventure. If *Unaccompanied* imagines love as an act of retrieval in the face of an ongoing tragedy, *Solito* conceives it as acts of joy and kindness remembered when a tragedy is sometimes all that people see. They are two sides of the same act of love, inextricably linked.

Zamora is a superb prose writer, certainly one of the best of his generation. From the very beginning pages, *Solito* grabs on to words and rides them all the way to shore. Words like *trip* and *nicknames*, *La USA* and *your parents*. Young "¡Javiercito!," as he is known to Abuelita Neli, is his class valedictorian, and his parents have finally decided that now is the time to send for him to cross over. Within two pages, the memoir has acquired the tiny mythic quality of childhood, in which the world is vast but what is known is small and most of everything else has to be intuited.

The entirety of the book takes place during his crossing, from the day Zamora leaves to the day he arrives. It is an astonishing chronicle made up of expert portraiture, a surprisingly detailed geographic mapping, moments of adolescent self-consciousness, and a journey toward intimacy with chosen family along the way. As the book describes, Zamora's grandfather paid a man to watch out for his grandson. From the beginning, however, this paid guide is aloof and cruel and ultimately betrays Zamora and the others they are traveling with—although we later find out that he is the one who, upon his own arrival in Los Angeles, calls Zamora's parents after their boy has been traveling for seven weeks (and not heard from) to tell them their son will probably make it.

How in the world do children survive this trip? In Zamora's case, for the early part of his voyage north, he traveled alongside his grandfather.

One of the saddest moments in *Solito* is when he and his grandfather part. Getting inside a bus in Guatemala, Zamora recalls thinking, "He's taught me so much. About the sky. About my family. About maps. I can almost tie my shoes correctly. I can poop and flush by myself now, I'm less scared. He's been on the other side of the door every single day. Everyone else is already inside the bus except for Don Dago, who waits for us, one foot on the ground, one foot on the bottom step."

Don Dago is the first of many coyotes who guide Zamora in a group north. Everyone gets sick, and the biggest man on the boat nearly loses his mind. At each stage of the ordeal, young Zamora's group disassembles and recombines so as not to draw attention to themselves, sometimes gaining a new coyote, in other moments retaining the old one. By and large, the coyotes are kind and, in addition to delivering them to safety, often the people who bring Zamora's group sustenance, from fresh water to—on one occasion—fresh fried fish.

It's useful to remember here that this passing takes place in 1999, by no means easy, but before the world of human trafficking was taken over by cartels—and before the US border became so heavily militarized, importing the same guard towers used in occupied Palestine that are made by Elbit Systems, the same drones, the same facial-recognition software. By comparison, the world in which Zamora was traveling was practically analog. In several locations, the coyote simply points in the direction of "La USA," and only at the end of the book do Zamora and the people he travels with learn that the border is also patrolled by airplane.

The frame of *Solito* then is close-up, and it spends most of its time describing the underground railroad of helpers who aid Zamora. In one city, an older woman in an apartment cooks the group two full meals a day, as if the greatest risk of migration was hunger. In another, the men in Zamora's group go out and get drunk, so he winds up sharing a room with a woman, Patricia, and her daughter, Carla, thus binding him ever more to them. When later they find themselves in a mixed room, Chino, who when the boat was crossing kept Zamora warm by rubbing his arms, sleeps by the bedside so they are safe, and because they trust him.

What *Solito* does is refute its title. If you had to list the cast of characters who help Zamora cross the border, it would run to three or four pages. Though it's true he is traveling without family or his parents, he is brought closer and closer to Patricia and Chino by the fictions they are required to make—that they are a family. What begins as acting, as resistance, sticks, and in the final passages of this book, as they begin the stretch of their journey where they walk, the greatest tension comes from whether they will make it through together. Not alone.

Solito might be a version of what happens, but it does something striking, which *Unaccompanied* could not. It puts the poet back into his body. At one point, when they're switching coyotes, young Zamora begins to worry about who is leading them forward, and Chino reassures him with a hug. "Besides the boat, this is the first time I'm in his chest again, and he called me hermanito. I can smell his cologne. His cigarettes. But through all the smells, *his* smell: dry dirt before it rains. His hug warms me. Makes me feel protected, like it's Mali, Grandpa, or Mom here with me."

It would be another few weeks before Zamora made it into their arms, at 9 a.m. on the morning of June 10 in Tucson. There were other close calls before that. The migrants were caught, caged, let go without money back in Mexico, and caught again. The risks were incredibly high. But there were joys and pleasures in that hard time, and *Solito* retrieves those amid a group of characters who are funny, complex, and deeply alive but who today would be called illegals— by either political party in the US. Were he alive today, Roque Dalton would no doubt write a poem to them, for them—or perhaps he would simply herald this great book, written in his example and spirit, which, like bread, is for everyone.

BUILDING CITIES

CLARK AND DIVISION

by Naomi Hirahara

History is not made by incidents. It is forged in their aftermath. The way that people adapt to events, the way they break down, the way they tell stories or hold them—these are as much our understanding of the past as time itself. In an era of the celebrity-driven biopic and widespread book banning, of legislating American history out of student curricula, and of a yawning cultural memory hole, a novel like Naomi Hirahara's *Clark and Division* is a bold, necessary text. Not just for the vivid portrait it paints of nisei (second-generation Japanese Americans) freed from the Manzanar camp, remaking their lives in Chicago, but also for the remarkable way it shows how an unfolding story—even one built on fine qualities, like loyalty and hard work—can trap people.

The trap is set in Aki Ito's life by her place and times. Raised in the Glendale neighborhood of Tropico, the heroine of Hirahara's novel grows up rooted in Los Angeles, which is a landscape and a home but also a world of vanishing maps. Tropico incorporated with Glendale in 1918 just before Ito's mother arrived in America from Kagoshima— her father was one of the issei who had come to work in its strawberry fields. By the time Aki was born, Tropico was—as a separate place—disappearing. Aki's family had one another, though, and that would get them through a lot.

Hirahara's life as a crime writer and social historian has revolved around telling stories that excavate these lost cities within cities—especially Los Angeles—revealing how they remain very much alive. *Clark and Division* marks a turning point in her work, however, for it animates the way these old geographies are carried over to a new one—this time in America's heartland. And how the habits of old places don't always suit new places and their realities.

Within thirty pages of *Clark and Division*, Aki has been born, and she has grown up, been shipped off to Manzanar, and then set free. In the full swing of war, America needs to draft nisei men into the army, and by answering test questions correctly, first Aki's sister, Rose, and then her family are released to Chicago, with careful instructions not to gather in groups of more than three. "I understood the resettlement agency's strategy," Aki says. "If I were working for the government, I would send hundreds of Rose Itos out into the wide plains of the Midwest. . . . If anyone could convince a suspicious public that we Japanese were patriotic Americans, it would be my older sister."

It is there, in 1944, on the corner of Clark and Division Streets, that the novel begins in earnest, following a terrible tragedy. Shortly before the Itos arrive, Rose is killed from a fall onto the train tracks. Her death is labeled a suicide, but Aki cannot believe that her sister would take her own life. From the coroner Aki learns that her sister had also recently undergone an abortion. This information she keeps to herself, knowing her parents are already in shock.

The novel descends into the tumult of World War II–era Chicago, within a population told it is being watched. Nisei from the camps are piling into Chicago, overtaxing the job market, the housing market, and everyone's assumptions. Every day is a test of what must be known—some of this new knowledge stark and sinister, some of it a delight. In her first days, Aki meets a nisei woman just up from Arkansas and discovers that at Greek diners you eat something sweet before sitting down to the main course.

There is a lot of quiet teaching going on in *Clark and Division*, character to character in an informal network of instruction. Hirahara has also precisely re-created the many formal overlapping structures of support and mutual aid that quickly assembled in Chicago after the war: the church groups and dance halls, the underground bars and daisy chain of employment recommendations, the mafias with their tentacular reach. Rose, Aki learns, had been employed at a bra factory, making cheap undergarments, while taking precious good care of her own dresses, which remain like a set of clues to the life she led. Grief-stricken, Rose's parents can barely say her name.

As it builds its story, *Clark and Division* threads between secrets and well-known facts and memories of the past. Aki and her parents are poor, twice relocated, fearful of losing their new freedoms, and dependent on the kindness of strangers in a new place. The book's title reveals just how precarious their existence is in that time—their world not a house number, or an address, but merely an intersection. Until their incarceration, Aki was raised somewhat protected from the peril her family faces simply by being Japanese American. Her parents would have known how much California had restricted isei from accumulating land and wealth, from the Alien Land Law of 1913, which prevented immigrants from owning land or entering into leases of more than three years, to the racial covenants with "no persons of Japanese ancestry" clauses rife across Los Angeles, including in Glendale where they lived.

Aki narrates the book in a wide-eyed, somewhat posttraumatic register, desperate to believe the best of people. She doesn't have much choice, given how estranged she is from the streets of Tropico. When she meets a part-time gangster—or screwup, it's not quite clear—also from Tropico, she suspends judgment due to the tenacity of hometown ties. It takes the rest of the book for us to find out whether this is a good choice or not.

The novel's absorbing power comes from how well it suspends us in equivocal states. Just like Aki, we need to weigh what is true and what is rumor. As Aki retraces her sister's steps, encounters the friends Rose made, and rubs shoulders with the men she met—everyone from the man at the registration desk of the nisei hotel and pool sharks to icebox deliverymen and priests—yet another ghost of doubt enters the text. Was Rose Ito really like her sister? In essence, a well-behaved, hardworking young woman? Or had she gotten herself involved in something she could not control? This question rises up from Aki's upbringing and gently lays its shade on each one of her sleuth-like interrogations. Nothing takes place in this book only in Aki's head: We are always navigating her perceptions, projections, and the shared space of people who do the same.

As these questions bloom in *Clark and Division*, the scale of Rose's vulnerability becomes clear. Rose was a recently released nisei, told to be loyal, and a woman, no less—her behavior was at once publicly monitored, prodded. She would have also privately had to entrust her safety into the hands of people—men, mostly—to help her gain access to certain spots, places for a respite, a bit of privacy, a drink. In the streets around Clark and Division, in the dive bars and underground gambling dens, Aki begins to realize that there are places Rose could have become lost—or where a man could have hurt her and easily gotten away with it. When it becomes clear that other women may have had similar trouble to Rose, Aki tries to get these women to talk. Not all of them want to. Some shut the door in her face. Some scold her. Some listen, and a very few help her.

Everyone in this novel, it could be said, is suffering from a form of PTSD. Some have been freed from camps easily; some have had detours in reform zones. The varieties of coping on display in *Clark and Division* are acutely rendered, even when quickly sketched. Aki's parents bear up as many do when trying to carry the weight of the world: by working. And by drinking. Periodically through the book, Aki's father returns home very late, paralytically drunk, and it doesn't require much commentary to explain why. When Aki gets a job at a nearby library, she makes friends with a Black coworker and a Polish coworker, and wisely, Hirahara never turns these into instrumental plot points. Aki merely discovers in their care and shelter friendship outside Japanese American circles, and that softens the blow of her own circumstances. It also steels her resolve to achieve justice for her sister.

In truth, Aki desperately needs this resolve. Chicago might have a river too, but in many, many other ways, it is different from Los Angeles, a comparison Aki makes in one of the book's most touching passages. "I knew the bend of the winding streets and the pitiful concrete bed of the Los Angeles River without looking," she says. Meantime, the Chicago River courses through the city without apology. Without the familiarity of the land and with precious little help from the Chicago Police Department, Aki falls back on a part of the city map that she feels she could understand: the press. "The more sensational rags, not to mention the *hakujin* ones, would have featured an attack on a Nisei woman on their front page. Rose Ito's plight would not have been ignored."

Hirahara, who edited the *Rafu Shimpo* newspaper, is an ink-stained crime writer. She clearly loves newspapers. They appear throughout this book, from the various newspapers of the camps, which are referred to in passing, for news of Rose's death could have traveled there, to the Chicago dailies. Aki has more faith in these humble publications than in the police. They are to her inherently trustworthy. Including these quasi-public spaces gives the facts and whispers Aki collects by asking questions a kind of minor, official echo chamber. They give an already enclosed city another form of enclosure.

The truth, Aki knows, though, will never be found in them in its entirety. But a crucial part of it might be—especially if she works with a newspaper reporter to bring her sister's case to light. And thus we begin our race to a finale. What an arc this brisk, moving book traces. Aki grows up in California believing she belongs, save for discriminatory comments by a classmate's mother. The actions of the US government shatter this feeling, and then that same government demands loyalty as the condition of her family's release from an unlawful prison. The terms of their freedom are so clearly designed to break them, to break their community. *You cannot gather in groups of more than three.* One by one, Aki threads around that line and finds the grim, real truth to life in Chicago after the camp, at least for her sister. It is a new world, all over again. "Nothing could be trusted in Chicago," she writes, "not even the weather."

I HOTEL

by Karen Tei Yamashita

One of the biggest obstacles to writing about revolutionary change is the form of the novel itself. Conventional ones thrive on the blinkered certainties of a few points of view. Meanwhile, truly transformative uprisings depend on the strength of the many: on overlapping and even conflicting interests being allowed space to coexist within, say, a larger goal or commitment. Making this conception of political action work in life is difficult enough; in fiction, getting this many people in the room often winds up feeling busy and unwieldy.

Neither of these words comes to mind while inhabiting—and there's no other word for how one lives inside it—Karen Tei Yamashita's 2010 masterpiece, *I Hotel*. What is this strange, huge, remarkable book? Well, to put it baldly, it comprises ten linked novellas, each set in a year from the period of 1968 to 1977, spanning the birth of the Asian American movement in the Bay Area, from the era-defining Third World Liberation Front strikes in the fall of 1968, when students went to war with the administration to create Asian American Studies departments, to the violent eviction of tenants from the International

Hotel in Manilatown at 848 Kearny in August 1977, after which the building sat empty for years. If a better novel about San Francisco in the 1960s and 1970s exists, it's doing a great job of hiding.

That Yamashita crams all of this history into the book is an astonishment; that she manages to weave it through events of global import—Kissinger's trip to China, the assassinations of King and Kennedy, the mass migration of Filipino people to the Bay Area, Castro's trip to Moscow—is breathtaking. All of it set to a funkadelic soundtrack of James Brown and Creedence Clearwater Revival.

How does she do it? From the beginning, design is Yamashita's strength. Each novella features two events, one global, one local; three major characters; and a theme, marked at the section's beginning. The unity of design in another writer's hands might be imprisoning, but Yamashita works like a poet, allowing juxtaposition and repetition to do their mysterious but potent work unfettered. Gently, elegantly, each section calls back to the ones before it, drawing characters forward into new settings.

Yamashita also respects the integrity and boundless mystery of each life she holds. While *I Hotel* is a book thronged with lives, many of them circumscribed by restrictions, no one is meant to stand in for any one aspect of themselves or their time. There are aging Chinese immigrants who've come to America thanks to "paper families," from whom they've had to buy fictional relations, because of the Chinese Exclusion Act aimed at miners and other early arrivals. There are Indigenous men who've come from the same area that once held the Japanese incarceration camps. There are Yellow Power activists who've learned from Black Panthers how to resist arrest. And yet none of the characters' actions are predictable.

The book opens with the sudden death of a Chinese American writer's father. Already motherless, too, Paul spends his father's funeral with a family friend, Chen, who is part confidant, part translator, part connection to the China of his family's past. Through Chen,

I Hotel

Paul winds up searching out literary ancestors of his own voice. Chen, who himself is orphaned, in a way, takes a shine to the young man, but knows what lies ahead of him.

"He knew that if Paul and his generation of writers wanted a history, they would have to dig it up and invent it for themselves," Yamashita writes from Chen's point of view.

One of the primary stories of *I Hotel* is that of a large, disparate group of people, many of them not white, having similar simultaneous revelations all across the Bay: revelations about self-determination and civil protection and the necessity of representation in these quests. It was out of this energy in the late 1960s that the Indians of All Tribes movement and the United Farm Workers and Asian American student activists all wound up sharing an area and changing their time.

I Hotel doesn't romanticize an entwinement of fates: It does something far more difficult and interesting. The book records it and also refuses to fall prey to the one-man theory of social change, which is how even recently made artifacts of culture deploy stories about social change and upheaval. *I Hotel* takes you into all the kitchen-table meetings, the coffee shops where people killed time, *a lot of it*. It burrows into student committee conferences. One scene will resonate with anyone who has been to a protest in recent years—which in the summer of 2020 alone accounted for more than twenty-five million people. The entire set piece is a series of protocols for what to do when arrested.

If this sounds at all boring, it isn't. Yamashita is a restless, bold stylist, so as we fall through the years, meeting new characters, hearing echoes of previous ones in new lights, she constantly varies her narrative technique. Some scenes unfold in a screenplay format, with directions to a camera; another chapter is simply a dossier of its main character. One chapter is structured as two fables with notes on how to read them or questions to ask oneself, as if this part of the book were a test document. There's also a comic strip, monologues, and straight-up *War and Peace*–style enchantment. Other sections would function easily as a recipe book, as a protest song, as a kind of collective first-person anthem.

"We grew up here, and we lived here," goes one such section, narrated in the collective voice of people about to be evicted from the I Hotel in 1977,

> in Chinatown under colorful pagoda roofs and serenaded by flower drum songs down Grant Avenue; in Filipinotown in heroic Bataan bars and courted with sampaguita flowers along Kearny Street; in Japantown between jazz spots and cherry blossom festivals around Post and Buchanan. We lived in the centers of our city's Oriental tourist attractions, our li'l towns described as "exotic Kodak moments" in *Sunset* and other travel magazines. We were always smiling for our customers, saying that if they visited our towns, it would be the next best thing to traveling to the real countries, even if some of us had never even been there.

This book reads like a three-dimensional map of these places, one that is at once spatial and sonic. *I Hotel* channels the voices of people who grew up in them and called such spaces home with a supremely gifted ear, one that, if we look back at Yamashita's first novel, surely has enabled writers like Julie Otsuka to exist. The book also describes long-gone pharmacies, poetry houses, bars, and side-by-side arrangements—Black- and nisei-run businesses in, say, San Francisco—that are no longer so, just as Nina Revoyr has done in her Los Angeles novels, or Naomi J. Williams in her stories about Sacramento in the 1940s. Whoever feels as though history has drowned the novel hasn't come across this one.

Ribald and hilarious, furious and tender, *I Hotel* does not pick up the past with silken gloves. It shoves it back at us, raw, unredeemed, unjust, still unfolding. The goals of the people it conjures here are still, in many instances, unmet in twenty-first-century California—fair and affordable housing, proper representation, a liberation from prisons. It reminds us, spectacularly, with warning, that they, too, were spurred on by ghosts. *I Hotel* does not promise them atonement, but it does something just as powerful: It gives them a glorious structure to call home.

SOUTHLAND

by Nina Revoyr

It isn't only in the American South that the past is "not even past," as William Faulkner wrote. Anywhere marked by migration has this quality. When residents carry their histories with them, in their own bodies or in stories they tell, the place they live might be called undead. Los Angeles is such a space, and in the twentieth century, it was shaped by several ruptures, the ghosts of which speak loudly: the Northridge earthquake, the 1992 uprising, the Watts Rebellion of 1965, and, during World War II, the incarceration of Japanese Americans.

Molding a tale from the past is nothing new; it's a genre—the historical novel. But in *Southland*, Nina Revoyr accomplishes something fresh. She has written a crime novel in which mapping these ruptures—essentially sketching the landscape of trauma, as it's experienced collectively—forms the core of her narrative drive. The book begins in 1994, just after Northridge, and Jackie Ishida is dealing with a convulsion at home. Her grandfather Frank Sakai has died, leaving behind two daughters, a suspiciously well-organized AOL account, and, at the back of his closet, a stone-colored box with $38,000 in it labeled "STORE." Accompanying this pile of money is an unofficial will with a name Jackie has never heard: Curtis Martindale.

Jackie feels guilty over having been an inattentive granddaughter, so she decides to find this Curtis Martindale for her aunt Lois and restore the inheritance to him. The money, she quickly infers, comes from the sale of Frank's store, a corner deli in Crenshaw he left behind after the Watts uprising. He moved his family to Gardena, just a dozen miles away but a universe apart in terms of class differences. Jackie's parents became doctors; she's now in her third year of law school and on her way to a corporate job that will probably catapult her all the way to the Westside. Why Frank kept the money—and why he wanted to give it to Curtis—is a mystery.

Much of this is long-ago history to Jackie. To her, Frank was a kindly but somewhat antiquated figure, a reminder of a Japanese-ness that never quite embarrassed her but from which, as an adult, she keeps a distance. She's dated enough white women that one night at the Palms, the historic lesbian bar in West Hollywood, a Japanese American friend says to her: "What's the deal with you, anyway? You're like a reverse missionary. Rescuing the lost white children."

Following Jackie across Los Angeles in search of answers to questions about her grandfather is like following a cartographer across an inland sea. Names like the Palms bob to a choppy surface alongside tales anyone who has lived in Los Angeles long enough will have heard from elders. The year it snowed on New Year's Day; the way South Los Angeles used to flood so badly, milk was delivered by boat. The building of the freeway to Pasadena and the miracle of disparate villages essentially being connected.

Once her quest begins, though, Jackie stays close to and starts island-hopping through South LA's various communities, stopping to talk and listen—sometimes eat—and ask questions anywhere people get together. In return she's buffeted by gossip, old romance, nostalgia, and sorrow. *Southland*, at its heart, is a gorgeous hymn to the way Los

Angeles is an archipelago of such spaces: community centers, church barbecues, farmers markets, the corner stores where owners once put out milk crates for people to sit and enjoy a beer at the end of a long day.

Novels struggle to respect the way a community is made. There's so much static but deeply felt time that goes into knitting one together. Conversation in a community isn't just exchange; it's partly recitation. Who is related to whom, and who dated whom, and who left and why. Some stories get told all the time, others hardly ever. Telling all this, capturing its syncopated rhythms, takes time. It requires an ear and, frankly, manners: knowing there's a time to listen and one to ask questions. *Southland* demonstrates these actions and values in motion. Everyone in this book is related to everyone else in small ways, sometimes big. Everyone has secrets. Every place was once someplace else—once inhabited by a slightly different mix of people from elsewhere.

Jackie has a fellow traveler in this metaphysical search. James Lanier's family also comes from Crenshaw, and now he manages an after-school program at the neighborhood's Marcus Garvey Community Center. Upon arriving there to ask questions, Jackie feels like "an overseas visitor," noting that hers is the only non-Black face. Lanier, as he's known, isn't sure what to make of her at first. He's an activist used to a small degree of cultural tourism from outsiders. But when he discovers why Jackie has come, their mutual interests collide. Curtis was Lanier's cousin; he died during the Watts uprising, his body found in a freezer in Jackie's grandfather's store alongside those of three other Black teenagers; a particularly brutal white cop was suspected. Thirty years later, Lanier wants justice.

Southland reveals what an epic desire this is in a city like Los Angeles. Getting to the bottom of what happened to Curtis and the three other victims means unpeeling what layers of police loyalty, redlining, and lethal racism have done to family after family, not to mention a neighborhood like Crenshaw. Passing through farmers markets and private spaces such as people's living rooms, where the departed are still missed, *Southland* creates a kaleidoscopic portrait of how people come together and fall apart as a result of trauma. As the novel tacks forward in 1994, each alternating chapter dives into the past, bringing up buried stories from Jackie's family's history, as well as Lanier's.

Both of these pasts float on a sea of loss. Some of the most sharply rendered passages in the book describe life in Manzanar, where over eleven thousand Japanese Americans were forcibly sent in 1942—an experience first captured in Jeanne Wakatsuki Houston and James D. Houston's memoir, *Farewell to Manzanar*, but painfully sketched over time in *Southland*, from the terrifying buildup to the slow, shamed fallout in the months and years afterward, as people tried to pick up their lives again. We also see the camp experience several times—first in Frank's life, then in the life of a friend and fellow World War II veteran.

While very different, Jackie and Lanier share some aspects of their backgrounds. Both Lanier's father and Jackie's grandfather survived particularly brutal tours of duty overseas, Frank in the famous 442nd Regimental Combat Team—the division made up largely of incarcerated Japanese Americans, the most decorated division in US history—and Lanier's father in Korea. Both of their families made homes in Crenshaw and then watched as different types of violence claimed those homes. Both have sets of grandparents or great-grandparents who got jobs as domestic workers.

Like Walter Mosley's *Devil in a Blue Dress*, *Southland* is a story about economic crime, one born partly of the loss of manufacturing jobs at places like Goodyear and partly of racism that made jobs like that so precarious for Black or Japanese American workers, who could lose them at any time. Both Revoyr's and Mosley's books also remind us how segregated leisure was in this era, cycling through similar beach scenes in Santa Monica, where whites-only policies are enforced. In *Southland*, however, the scene is viewed through young Frank's eyes, and it's a moment when he needs to decide to which side he belongs. Oscillating between the past and present, *Southland* shows how parts of Black and Japanese American experiences in Los Angeles have mirrored each other.

This structure is doubly ingenious and daring, for within each chapter Revoyr also does something only Toni Morrison and Louise Erdrich and a few other novelists have managed so successfully—which is to deploy multiple points of view in the same chapter, *sometimes on the same page*. This prismatic approach to narration turns Jackie from a search lamp (which produces its own blind spots) into an orienting point around which we see multiple angles.

For instance, when Lanier goes into a precinct to talk to a Black police officer who might know something about the cop many in the neighborhood believe was behind the murders, we see the interaction from at least three perspectives: Lanier's, that of the officer he's questioning—for whom taking the uniform was a differentiating step, proof he wasn't just another knucklehead—and later Jackie's, when she listens to Lanier unload not just the details of his exchange but also, for reasons he cannot at first comprehend, the particulars of the murders his estranged father committed when stationed in Korea.

This can be the way of trauma: Even if you feel stranded on an island, suffering alone, very often one form of it is connected in ways, at first mysterious, to another's—and once the thread joining them has been pulled, there might be no stopping the whole linkage from emerging from beneath the sea. *Southland* is such a warm and deeply skilled act of narrative recovery. The novel hauls up the past's wreckage from the deep, and it shows the effects that confronting that past has on the lives of characters so complex that they are as endless as the city they call home.

THERE THERE

by Tommy Orange

Perhaps in the future what we will say about film is that it rescued the novel, not that it destroyed the form. Well into the twenty-first century, novels of great quality continue to be written, books of wide variety and spoken musics, many of them informed by the techniques of filmmaking. The novel reinterpreted as rolling documentary (Svetlana Alexievich's *Last Witnesses*), the novel as fractured archive (Valeria Luiselli's *Faces in the Crowd*), the novel as endless jump cut (Olga Tokarczuk's *Flights*), the novel as mood piece disguised as cultural history (Rachel Kushner's *The Flamethrowers*).

Film has long since tempered the intensities of modernity's idea of consciousness. Now, in the twenty-first century, the symbiosis between forms is at its most powerful in the gestures and methods that create areas of space, sound, and portraiture. And here is where Tommy Orange's genius achieves its full complexity. *There There*, Orange's 2018 debut novel, is a series of linked stories set in Oakland about a group of Cheyenne and Arapaho men and women who are preparing for a powwow at the Coliseum. Even though their tribal affiliation links back to Oklahoma, where they gather and consider home is the East Bay. The powwow is an event of symbolic importance, in which people can see one another and be seen for what they believe they are—Native. But of course even the characters in this book, many of whom struggle mightily, privately, with what it means to be Native, know that external performance is only one aspect of identity. How else, this novel seems to ask its participants and readers, can we see one another?

There There is Orange's magnificent answer. The novel is structured like a series of tightening loops. We meet each character in a longish chapter, then we see them again in shortened moments. As we get closer to the book's denouement, an act of violence we know is coming from the early appearance of a gun made with a 3-D printer, the chapters get shorter, more associative. The depth and range of the early portraits of each of the book's twelve main characters are deployed, put in motion, and scrambled.

Drawing a character rapidly is intensely risky in fiction because it tends to channel broad characterizations. Orange circumvents these risks with his amazing ear. From the very beginning—with its bravura prelude chapter, a rapid driving tour of Native history in America and the reasons modern life is so rarely seen—the book is sonically rich. Poetic. Recalling the test pattern that once closed down every station broadcast in America, it makes the connection between static and sound and the distortions through which much of America sees Native life right before them:

> If you left the TV on, you'd hear a tone at 440 hertz—the tone used to tune instruments—and you'd see that Indian, surrounded by circles that looked like sights through riflescopes. There was what looked like a bull's eye in the middle of the screen, with numbers like coordinates. The Indian's head was just above the bull's eye, like all

you'd need to do was nod up in agreement to set the sights on the target. This was just a test.

There There sets out to deprogram this coinage with a dozen portraits of people connected to the powwow. They range from a groundskeeper at the Coliseum to the newly sober grandmother of one of the young dancers. One of them is a budding filmmaker with a grant to record Native people talking about their lives. Each chapter and portrait sets up the next, through lineage and contact, so the overall feel is of disparate connectedness.

The most lonely of the figures is at the center of the wheel, the provocatively named Tony Loneman, who was diagnosed with fetal alcohol syndrome as a child—the result of the drinking his mother did when he was in utero. Doctors and counselors say it hasn't affected his intelligence, which is proof in other ways that it has—and Tony knows this. He's aware when he is being handled, managed, treated as though he is a walking syndrome.

Tony also sees people seeing him, a potent moment of disintermediation and an apt place for this cycle of tales to begin. "The Drome first came to me in the mirror when I was six," Tony begins. "Why's your face look like that?" a classmate asks him. Back home, Tony turns on the TV, and for a split second, he sees himself as a stranger: "I saw my face in the dark reflection there. It was the first time I saw it. My own face, the way everyone else saw it."

This moment of confused reflection occurs and recurs throughout *There There* as various characters pause before mirrors, shiny surfaces, and even their iPhones, puzzled by what they see—a modern interpretation of the dilemma that haunts the hero of James Welch's 1974 classic, *Winter in the Blood*, about a dissolute young Native man, spiraling in conversations and suicidal bouts of drinking, wondering if he'll survive: "The distance I felt came not from country or people; it came from within me. I was as distant from myself as a hawk from the moon."

Orange's book awakens from a similar inner chill, but its power comes from its astonishing enmeshment—the way it has found a narrative rhythm and sound to portray people deeply grooved into one another's lives. Even when they are absent. Many of the people in this book have missing fathers, who've stamped their lives onto their children's faces and then reemerged in the modern-day arcade of copied images—Facebook. One of the characters, Edwin Black, sneaks onto his mother's account on the hunch that she's been talking to his birth father. "You look like me," Edwin types to his father, Harvey, now thirty years sober and living in Arizona. After seeing a selfie of his son, the man types back. "Well shit."

That little utterance is so typical of Orange's huge register of speech. Brief, aural, absolutely hearable. Everything from slang to song to poetry emerges here and creates a rich weave of speech across generations. Many of the younger characters talk and rap and interrogate one another to a direct degree about their traditions, displaying a self-consciousness that is schooled in curation and sometimes even comforting. Orvil Red Feather, who will dance at the powwow, thinks about why he keeps gazing into a mirror, dressed up like an Indian. And yet it's "important that he dress like an Indian, dance like an Indian, even if it is an act, even if he feels like a fraud the whole time."

Orange is patient with his characters' self-doubts. He acknowledges that in many of our lives, that's where we live—in the space between faith in ourselves and self-hatred, between belief in traditions and embarrassment over their old-fashionedness. In *There There* Orange shows his characters clocking one another's doubts and acknowledging them. "Like what's a pow-wow," Lony asks his peers at one point, which invites a round of rippling derision, before one of them says, quite simply, "They're just old ways, Lony. We gotta carry it on. . . . If we don't they might disappear."

This tension between remembrance and forgetting forms one of the many infinite loops of *There There*. For Gertrude Stein, whose quote about Oakland after she left and returned—"There was no there there," she wrote of it, in *Everybody's Autobiography*—gives the book its title, forgetting is a force that can be absorbed. Stein moved to Oakland in 1874 and left in 1891 after her parents died and she went back East to college. She didn't return for forty years, when as an unexpected celebrity she was on one of her cross-country trips, promoting *The Autobiography of Alice B. Toklas*. She tried to find her childhood home and discovered it had been torn down, which is why there was no there there—a neat syntactical joke, but also, as it so often was with her work, a kernel of philosophical disquiet. Erasure is the ultimate proof of time passing.

There There succeeds so brilliantly because it folds the huge scale of epistemological concerns of being Native in a world after genocide into intimate, endless family issues. Should Edwin's mother forget or forgive the horrific way she came to carry a child? Is the way his uncle drank a disease, a way to forget, or a slow-motion way to commit suicide? And before he goes, what should he tell his nephew and kids? Finally, what do the stories that the many people in this book tell themselves about one another carry forward—and what gets left out?

Moving from one conversation to the next—if this book were a film, it would proceed from one chat to another in a series of jump cuts—*There There* creates a sound of wonder, of mourning, of future-seeking. Of people talking themselves toward a deeper sense of place. It orients this discursive music the way Stein slid though spoken registers in her own poetry, finding the unlikely hinges between images and sounds, between expressions and feelings. Orange is different, though, because by layering his linguistic treatment of being Native in the city across Oakland like a string of pathways, looping past Fruitvale Station several times, pausing at crosswalks, he asserts a fundamental connection between language and place, between belonging and city life. By the book's end you can almost retrace its peregrinations by memory.

What is this Oakland? It is a place more realistic than the orderly neighborhoods of the ensemble-cast novels of America's past: the Winesburg, Ohio, of Sherwood Anderson; the Brewster Place of Gloria Naylor, the Main Street of Sinclair Lewis. Although *There There* belongs among these books, it does something new. It creates a soundscape for a place and makes the place come to life through the way it manipulates that acoustical depth. Read the book even casually and patterns emerge—echoes, melodies made from questions.

The great sound engineer and sometime Bolinas resident Walter Murch once wrote that "most of us are searching—consciously or unconsciously—for a degree of internal balance and harmony between ourselves and the outside world, and if we happen to become aware—like Stravinsky—of a volcano within us, we will compensate by urging restraint." What Murch is addressing is an equilibrium between our inner and outer voice. But what if neither has ever been heard? What then? In *There There*, for reasons this book makes forcefully clear, Orange's characters are no longer going to listen to that voice of restraint. Thank God their author didn't, and now we have this astonishing, noisy, tremendous book.

THE SWIMMERS

by Julie Otsuka

One of the saddest stories in American literature is also one of the most magical: John Cheever's "The Swimmer." The tale begins on a lark. Getting drunk at a summer party, Neddy Merrill decides he'll swim home that afternoon, crisscrossing backyard pools all the way. At first, the journey is full of light amusements. He is greeted triumphantly at each house. There are pauses for gin and tonics, for kisses and handshakes. He is the Forrest Gump of suburban explorers!

Quickly, though, the trip takes on a more somber hue. One house is missing most of its inhabitants; at another, a tree has dropped its leaves; at a third, the neighbor's pool is drained dry. By the time he reaches this point, Neddy is good and drunk and has swum himself into a lugubrious solitude. The prank, begun in the blustery spirit of youth, has become a parable of aging and alcoholism. He returns to his own house later than he imagined he would, to find it empty, the doors locked.

What a small miracle this story is—a triumph of Cheever's sumptuous style, which lures us, one aperitif after another, into the spirit of the swinging '60s and boozy suburban parties.

Another writer in American literature possesses this same luscious elegance—writing like a poet and possessed by destruction too. Her name is Julie Otsuka, and in her third novel, she has written a tale to rival Cheever's own, one in which swimming becomes a metaphor for the final isolation we face, whether we drink or not.

The book is called *The Swimmers,* and as with all of Otsuka's work, part of its resonance comes from the collective first-person voice she has made into her trademark. Used in her first two books to address the collective experience of Japanese American immigrants to California, here it speaks like a wry, observant chorus, from the lanes of a community pool. "Most days, at the pool, we are able to leave our troubles on land behind," it announces early on, and what a simple, perfect sentence this is—for what else is swimming but learning to float.

After offering the reader a tour of who comes to the pool—"we" includes a famous actor, successful doctors, onetime athletes, and retirees—the book bevels down to the rules everyone has agreed on in order to function together. There will be no tailgating, no excessive splashing, no diving into the sacred space without a shower first. Everyone must wear a cap.

Tone here, as in Cheever, does so much exquisite work. It is warm, brisk, and somewhat prim. Each one of Otsuka's sentences has been polished to its finest point, so the contours of the society bloom vividly into view like flowers against a crystal-blue backdrop. There are slow-lane, medium-lane, and fast-lane people. Once a year, in mid-August, the pool is drained, causing relief and consternation in turn as the daily swimmers miss their patterned existence.

The overall effect of this introduction strongly recalls Chekhov's great stories, wherein a society unfolds in all its grandeur and absurdity against the backdrop of an institution. In *The Swimmers,* ritual and routine combine to bring a waltz-like pace to the prose—an order that seems eternal, until something happens. The swimmers begin to leave.

> From time to time one of us will disappear for a
> week or two and aboveground inquiries are made.
> Emails are sent. Voice messages left. . . . Usually it
> is nothing serious.

It is in this context that we meet the soloist of this collective, the center of the book, and ultimately the point around whom it orbits. Just as gently as the book creates its world, it reminds us that the world, and the participants, are not forever.

> You forget to change the battery in the smoke detec-
> tor. You fail—just this once—to look both ways
> before crossing the street. You wake up one day and
> you can't even remember your own name. (It's *Alice*.)

Alice is the only one whose presence is sustained through the length of this short but intensely imagined book. Otsuka's prose is so enchanting, it curls so neatly around our inner eye, that it's easy to miss Alice's presence at first, just as it's easy to forget it when a crack develops in the bottom of the pool. The fissure is a tiny thing, a small hairline fracture that someone notices passing over it. But it grows—or does it, some wonder?—and experts arrive. Seismologists. Strange and ominous, this sign ripples through the community.

The shape of *The Swimmers* is one of the most marvelous aspects of the book. It begins like a portrait of a community, then it seems to head toward a magically real fable, and just as you adjust to this abstract shape, it plunges headlong into the medical reality out of which it proceeds. Alice has dementia and has forgotten so much around her—and yet not all of it.

> She remembers her name. She remembers the
> name of the president. She remembers the name

> of the president's dog. . . . She does not remember how she got the bruises on her arms or going for a walk with you earlier this morning. . . . She does not remember to comb her hair.

The Swimmers ultimately settles into its final form: a short prose song to the miracle of memory, and the awful spectacle of its erasure in a parent. Like the novelist Rabih Alameddine, Otsuka began her creative life as an artist, first with sculpture, then with painting, and she sketches Alice in a series of naturalistic details. Alice is a combination of what she remembers and forgets. A love affair, a marriage, a stillbirth; a trip, a shade of orange; a daughter's name, an address, her own name. Every detail Otsuka introduces is painted as if in watercolor, as if its very substance could at any time be washed away. By that chapter's end, it nearly has been.

How far we are now from Cheever, and yet so close. The tragedy of Cheever's swimmer was his self-imposed isolation. The destruction of Alice's world, by contrast, is not her fault. It is simply the bad luck of a gene splice. Still, like Neddy, Alice doesn't entirely realize how alone she is until it is too late. As a story, "The Swimmer" gives us only one point of view; as a novel, *The Swimmers* brings us, in how Otsuka introduces "you," an anguished daughter who has been caring for her mother—those who are affected.

It will happen to us all, this slow or sudden excision. In her first novels, Otsuka used her collective first-person voice to bear belated witness to the collective experience of Japanese Americans coming to the United States as picture brides (*The Buddha in the Attic*) and the shame and rupture presented by time spent in an incarceration camp (*When the Emperor Was Divine*). Jeweled and specific, drawn from a mountain of research, yet light as air, those books feel like steps of the eternal rescue California literature must perform on its amnesiac history.

But who rescues those physically losing their memory? It is family and carers. It sometimes is those who shared an office or those who shared a pool. *The Swimmers* is Otsuka's most intimate book yet, for it reminds us that even if art can create a public remembrance, those who lived it, the individual lives, every single one of them, will be poured into a much bigger body in the end. Here she uses a pool as the metaphor, but in truth, even the ocean isn't big enough to describe the enigma that awaits and the numbers who have gone there before.

IV

OF LANDSCAPE AND LOVE

UNDER THE FEET OF JESUS

by Helena María Viramontes

One of the most powerful things César Chavez is credited with saying wasn't uttered by him alone but written alongside playwright Luis Valdez and civil rights activist Dolores Huerta. It's a phrase that comes from "El Plan de Delano," the manifesto they wrote to be read on the eve of the United Farm Workers *peregrinación* from Delano some three hundred miles up to Sacramento. The goal of the march was to get California grape growers to recognize their union. "Our sweat and our blood have fallen on this land to make other men rich," Chavez and Valdez and Huerta wrote. "This Pilgrimage is a witness to the suffering we have seen for generations."

How anguished and loving is that possessive pronoun—*our*. It honors work, it says, implicitly: *our* bodies, *our* spirits, *our* faith. It also claims those who have perished while doing such work. But it isn't exclusionary. In March 1966, to raise money for the peregrinación, for things as humble as "shoes for the marchers, sleeping bags, raincoats, cars, medicines and food," Chavez wrote a letter to friends and added, "This will be a pilgrimage by members of all races and religions. . . . Although this is primarily a march of farmworkers, it is important that all we who have a concern for social justice and human dignity demonstrate their unity with us."

It is impossible to use the word *our* expansively without touching questions of faith, of who and what we are—so it's not a surprise that so many of the great leaders of protest movements, from King to Chavez to Mary Brave Bird (Crow Dog), deal in questions of faith. But how about novelists? Surely the best of them deal sensitively in what our spirits contend with—but can novels born out of anguished ground deal in questions of the spirit, and if so, how can they do so? How can they possibly let us all in?

Helena María Viramontes's *Under the Feet of Jesus* is one answer. First published in 1995, it follows the fate of a family of grape pickers in search of work in California's Central Valley. The book reads less like a novel than a long lyrical poem, one that moves in sequences of escalating clarity into a predicament any precarious worker fears: What happens when you get sick? Who will tend to you?

Drawing in both form and value from the Gospels, which proceed in episodic fashion and tell the story of Christ, *Under the Feet of Jesus* imagines, What if Christ was not a parable-spinning prophet? What if he was a fifteen-year-old boy who got sick working in a farm field, or what if he was a thirteen-year-old girl, moved to take care of the boy? What would we know of them? What would the story of how they survive tell us?

Viramontes is best viewed as a cosmic miniaturist who can in a tiny space cut to the core of life, but also show you the vaulting sky. Prior to this novel, she had written just one book of tales, *The Moths and Other Stories*—eight short stories about people caught within roles, be they fathers or mothers or young girls struggling with what is expected of them. In the title story, a young girl whose grandmother is ill struggles to come to grips with a universe that might snatch such a beloved person from the face of the earth.

As good as Viramontes is with a single character, the nimbleness of her attention lends her a godlike ability to dip in and out of lives, giving her tales the feeling of intimate murals. "The Cariboo Café," for instance, begins with this exquisitely balanced opening line: "They arrived in the secrecy of night, as displaced people often do, stopping over for a week, a month, eventually staying a lifetime."

It's easy to see the beginnings of *Under the Feet of Jesus* in this story—a family unit disassembles and reassembles in a café, a refuge from *la migra*. In the novel, a family that has broken down under the pressures of migration reassemble in a barn on the edge of a field. Five people huddle together for safety, hoping to get by. Viramontes introduces us to them quickly with swift, painterly brushstrokes. Estrella is dreamy, and we know this because the first time she sees the barn she and her family arrive to stay in, she notices it "through a clearing of trees and the cratered roof reminded her of the full moon."

There is Petra, Estrella's single mother, who keeps her children's birth certificates under the feet of a statue of Jesus that she moves from one temporary housing arrangement to another. She is responsible, careful, a provider, someone who can enter a room and smell "the fragrance of toasted corn tortillas, of garlic and chile bubbling over," and it's hard to blame her, since most places she stays stink of Raid and the Quaker Oats boxes left behind.

Like the story of Jesus Christ, Viramontes's novel is a tale about poverty, not so much the structures that create it but the way people survive it. Estrella's father has long since left the family, and in his place is Perfecto, a quiet, dependable man in his seventies who watches over Estrella, who teaches her language by instructing her in how to use the tools in his tool kit, and who does odd jobs so that, from time to time, the family can go to the store and buy Spam. He has also probably, in a moment of late-night comfort, gotten Petra pregnant. The barn might become a manger, or it might just be a barn.

Two cousins travel in the wake of this makeshift family, picking peaches and grapes until one of them, Alejo, who has been mooning after Estrella from afar, gets sick from pesticide spray. Alejo had not guessed "the biplane was so close until its gray shadow crossed over him like a crucifix, and he ducked into the leaves," Viramontes writes. It then banks steeply over the trees and releases a shower of white pesticide. "The lingering smell was a scent of ocean salt and beached kelp until he inhaled again and could detect under the innocence the heavy chemical choke of poison."

One of the key issues for César Chavez and Dolores Huerta and the UFW was the working conditions of farm laborers all over America, and in particular, their constant exposure to poisonous chemicals. In one of his 1988 speeches, Chavez said that these poisons could undo all the hard work of their struggle:

> What good does it do to achieve the blessings of collective bargaining and make economic progress for people when their health is destroyed in the process?
>
> If we ignored pesticide poisoning—if we looked on as farm workers and their children are stricken—then all the other injustices our people face would be compounded by an even more deadly tyranny.

Across the novel, Estrella gradually becomes aware of the injustice of the condition she and her loved ones inhabit. Viramontes so entwines this awakening with those of young girlhood that it's hard to separate them. To grow up, for Estrella, is to find her voice; to recognize that an injustice happening is to step into a world in which she must confront its consequences. Taking care of Alejo when pesticides make him sick pulls both strands together.

It does not take much work to put this issue of working conditions at the center of *Under the Feet of Jesus*. The key task for Viramontes is making the reader feel it, and here is one of the ways *Under the Feet of*

Jesus remains a living text decades after its original publication. Viramontes is an especially fine writer of the senses. The colors that saturate this book are vibrant and rich, and they operate in mysterious ways, just as colors do in the real world. The sounds of voices at work, and joyfully expressed, give it an enthralling music. The book also knows tremendously well how important it can be to touch and be touched when working to exhaustion. "Sleeping in a room full of children was different than sleeping in a room full of men," Alejo muses, after he becomes sick and is adopted by Petra and her family. "The smells and noises and dreams were different."

Viramontes was born in 1954 in East Los Angeles in a house with eight siblings. Her father was a construction worker, her mother a homemaker and farmworker. She has spoken in interviews about the influence this upbringing has had on her writing—not just in the quality of listening such an environment instilled but in her sense of what a story is, what sacrifice means. "I always used to think of my mother and my sisters doing so much, giving up so much for us," she said in a 2020 interview.

> My parents met in Buttonwillow picking cotton. My mother used to shell walnuts. She and her sisters would spend hours, shelling walnuts, to the point where their hands would be dyed brown. My mother couldn't wash it off and when she had to go to school, she was embarrassed and kept her hands in her pockets. These are experiences that I honor in the writing.

Steeped in this sense of sacrifice, so careful in portraying the way kindness leavens hardship, *Under the Feet of Jesus* tells a tale of how people help each other. It shows that we are *defined* by what we do to help other people. In this fashion, the novel becomes a pilgrimage of sorts, as Petra, Estrella, and their family try, desperately, with very little money at all, to get Alejo the medical treatment he needs. Doing so awakens in each of them a deeper form of caritas: one that slips among them and binds them together. Moving among this band of workers, of travelers, *Under the Feet of Jesus* also powerfully evokes the spirit of Chavez's movement for dignity, justice, and fairness for all workers. It conjures love, adventure, and wonder and asks, Who among us would deny anyone such joys?

THE CONSEQUENCES

by Manuel Muñoz

The word *consequence* does not appear in the King James Bible. Oh, there are punishments reaped and fates which are sowed—but consequences, that very behavioral term, are not to be found. Perhaps *consequence*, coming to us from the late Middle English, from Old French, as in "to follow closely," is not a word for the New World. A world tipped toward the present and away from the past, even if all the effects born from the past are evident to be seen.

We are currently living in the consequence of a world of no consequence, a world in which no matter how much misinformation has been thrown at the clear links between burning carbon and our climate crisis, conditions continue to heat up, burn, and create new pandemics. The extremely rich mostly get to skip these consequences, or dodge their terrible cost—their homes are rebuilt. The rest of us, the vast majority of humans on the planet, live in the wedge of light and darkness their actions create.

Manuel Muñoz has written a masterpiece about people navigating these lights and shadows. *The Consequences* is a slim book, containing just ten short stories, but it is large with feeling and scope, and desperately close in its intimacies. Parts of it are so hushed, so moon-lit with longing, that they feel spoken into a confession booth. Other stories open up and reveal, in a few stark scenarios, the whole rotten structure of an agricultural system built on precarious laborers: working all week, to be rounded up by *la migra* the day before they are paid.

That neither of these frameworks competes with the other has to do with the steadiness of Muñoz's gaze, the patience and humility of his ear. *The Consequences* does not charge toward injustice, hurrying out in front of its characters to herd a reader toward a reaction. Instead, the stories build in close focus, in the language of a neighborhood, a place, a friend group. A bakery frequented by retired men. Not for nothing was one of Muñoz's two previous collections, *The Faith Healer of Olive Avenue*, modeled on Sherwood Anderson's great linked portrait *Winesburg, Ohio*. Here is another one of Anderson's modern successors, moving softly through the world.

This universe of the Central Valley is home to Muñoz. He grew up there, in Dinuba, California, the child of farmworkers who harvested grapes, among other crops. He spent some summers and winters in the fields from about second grade up until sixth grade. In this, he joins Sherley Anne Williams, the poet and author of the historical slave novel *Dessa Rose*, as one of the great geniuses to emerge from these fields with a feeling for their silences, the pulse of the heat, the betrayals that happen so easily. This landscape appears to have made his imagination.

As a writer, Muñoz has an extremely rare ability to situate people within the landscape. *The Consequences* swivels between the abstract geography of the Valley, in which the most potent presences are living elements—the fields, the orchards, the fog hovering over the earth and spilling into town, the huge blue sky—and specific corridors of work, transit, escape. Quite a few people in this book are moving, have recently arrived, or are planning to leave where they are—heading north, south, back to Texas, or in some cases, back to Mexico—even those with papers.

The Consequences

In one of the collection's most autobiographical pieces, "Fieldwork," a narrator visits with his ailing father, recently laid up in the hospital with a stroke. In between visits from nurses, the man and his mother jog his father's memory with conversation. "You picked crops, right, Dad?" he asks. When his father answers hesitantly, the narrator switches to Spanish, "Naranjas, right, Dad?" which provokes a flood of memories.

> When he heard the Spanish, he nodded and continued recalling in his own language. Cotton and tomatoes, too. And almonds, my father added, and figs and nectarines, there was so much work. Apricots, plums, corn, pistachios, the lemon groves over on the eastern slope of the Valley into the Sierras. Walnuts and cauliflower. Cherries and pears. He kept remembering things. Strawberries hiding in the dirt. Pecans. Persimmons. Avocado trees in the prettiest green rows you've ever seen. Olives and wheat. Hay bundled up for the horses and the cows. Apples, because the Americans liked their pies.

This is one of the most poetic paragraphs about farmwork published in an American novel in recent years. Look at the way the bounty tumbles forth in its jeweled specificity. There is awe, gratitude, and sweat here. Light with his touch, Muñoz allows the old man's voice and sensitivity to come through—"because the Americans liked their pies," "the prettiest green rows." What is most loving here, but not belabored, is that his son has recorded this life's labor, has made it as valuable as what it picked, and has held it forth as of great value.

A new meaning to consequence arises here. A consequence needn't *only* be the unwanted result of a recent action. What if a fruit is a consequence of labor, of care? What if a child is a consequence of love? And what if listening is a consequence of that love growing up? Accordioning between the generations, Muñoz's collection reestablishes connections, small and large, and in so doing reveals the world to be much more knit together than it is often given credit for being.

This is not to say that the stories in *The Consequences* merely preserve this deep network of meaning. Rather, they construct drama out of showing us how this web of connection lives and operates among friends and family. And how connections can be threatened. In "Anyone Can Do It," Delfina, a woman new to the Valley and who awaits her husband's return home—he has either been deported or picked up in a raid, or maybe run off—puts her trust in a stranger. Lis, the woman who lives next door to Delfina, is also alone, and she wants to work. All she needs is to borrow a car.

What follows from the moment Muñoz's heroine decides to trust Lis is a stomach-turning slide toward betrayal. As the story escalates to its perfect ending, we keep waiting for a reprieve, which comes in the form of the grace shown by its heroine—broke, given $20 by a foreman who recognizes the bind she's in, she buys three colas, a loaf of bread, and a package of bologna. She gives the foreman one of the colas in thanks.

Forgiveness and grace and shame pace these stories in powerful, unpredictable ways. A closeted father of a teenage boy who is on his way to becoming a player presses upon his son some advice that kindness might be the ultimate style. In another story, a man edging out of youth catches a lucky break from the plague years when he tests negative. When his ex-lover goes back home to his small Texas town to die, he follows just in time to lurk outside the funeral.

Muñoz's ability to slide, just like that, from one point of view to a God's-eye glimpse of a place in a single story has powerful social effects. It enables his stories to construct dramatic juxtapositions in a short amount of time—precarity living right next to power. Whiteness and its entitlement. In "Susto," the body of an older man is found, his head buried in the earth. The foreman involved in overseeing the fields where the body turns up begins haunting a local bakery, frequented by men like him—white, older. A waitress, young and poor enough to be allowed by her parents to work on a Sunday, takes pity on him and tells him the man was not unknown, as the police determined, but a neighbor to many Mexican people in town, Don Facundo. He simply worked with cattle farmers.

"Susto" is the darkest story in the book, a piece of gothic fiction that feeds on the shadows, on violence, and on the sense of guilt that has stalked its narrator. Most of the rest of the stories in the book surface more easily into life, even when the realities of their characters press down heavily on them. In "The Reason Is Because," a teenage mother leaves her baby with her mother so she can walk to town and go to the fair. "Later on," Muñoz writes, "when she returned to the apartment, she would endure her mother. But right now, the walk in the fading afternoon light reminded Nela that it was Friday and she could see the weekend anticipation on the faces passing by as cars drove over to the carnival."

Nela's escape has consequences, but they are not presented here as punishments, or as anything that she has sown for herself. They are simply part of living. In "The Happiest Girl in the Whole USA," a woman boards a bus to Los Angeles to try to find her partner, recently picked up in a migrant raid, who will likely have been released and who will have crossed back over the border. As the bus heads south, more and more women get on, until eventually one sits down next to her. She is young, overdressed, and clearly doesn't know what awaits her in LA. Just like that, the older woman has to decide whether to help her.

Helping, caring, loving, they all have consequences. Doing so can put a whole life—a new lifestyle—at risk. In "Presumido," a man named Juan and his partner have a good life, better than Juan could ever have expected growing up. They own a home with enough bedrooms that Juan's father, when he comes to visit, moves from room to room in a state of bewilderment. At one of the parties they attend, Juan makes eye contact with the woman catering the food, cleaning the kitchen. "Her look of hard dissatisfaction dissolved when she had locked eyes with him and Juan had seized up at the way she had looked back, as if she might have been somebody he recognized, or who recognized him."

In that moment, Juan faces a decision—to cross the room and acknowledge her, to close the distance between them, or to separate. Muñoz's great gift is to show him trying to do both at once. Here is one of the unintended consequences of getting what the narrator wanted: to be cast onto the other side of a scrim by virtue of his unease and, maybe, his guilt. That we experience this spiral in a story, which also shows us the great comfort Juan takes in his lover, the mechanics of the fights he has with him, the brusque way the man tries to control his drinking, makes the story's ending all the more devastating.

Everyone in this book wants and needs more, but even when they get it, it's not enough—in part because it's so expensive to be poor. Whether it's the young woman on the bus, using all her money to meet her partner in LA, or Juan, a long way from "the poverty scalped yellow grass and dirt driveways" of his childhood homes, the risk of humiliation remains ever present. As Juan thinks about why he didn't want to host a party at their home: "He had not wanted to be under scrutiny . . . the one on guard, the one who had to put on a good face for the rest of the group."

In this world, where a young boy can be called "as thin as his empty wallet," the edge is right there at all times. Muñoz's greatest talent might be his ability to show just how sharp that edge is, how persistent, but how it is not total. It is not the only thing of consequence in the lives of his characters. There is the long arm of the law, of punishment, of course, but there is also love, mourning, friendship, aspiration, and comfort. There are sausages cooked well, a bathrobe, and a child listening closely. There is living. Would that we lived in a world where using such a capacious optic when dealing with the poor, the documented and not, seemed less radical.

LAW AND ORDER

BAD MEXICANS

by Kelly Lytle Hernández

When revolutionaries spring to mind, one's next thought is not, typically, of stamps. Or literary journals or poetry, for that matter. Yet one of the great heroes of Kelly Lytle Hernández's riveting history of the Magonistas, the rebels who ignited the 1910 revolution in Mexico from within the United States, is not the gun but the plain old post office. Before hashtags and Twitter threads, it was by letter that a revolution's ideas traveled, and the Magonistas sent letters in droves. They had to. Due to the cozy relationship between the regime of Porfirio Díaz and US capitalists, Mexico was able to delegate its harassment of the Magonistas to local US law enforcement, who chased Ricardo Flores Magón and his cohorts across the borderlands in Texas, Arizona, and California for nearly a decade. Incredibly, out of the missives the Magonistas sent on the fly, newspapers were made, printed, and smuggled back into Mexico, from Coahuila to Monterrey.

In time, their letter codes were cracked, and many of the Magonistas were jailed, sent back to Mexico on trumped-up charges, or killed. *Bad Mexicans: Race, Empire, and Revolution in the Borderlands* tells the remarkable, disturbing story of how, in tracking the Magonistas, the United States and Mexico pioneered the full register of techniques now deployed by the US along its southern border and on frontiers around the world: deportation, extraordinary rendition, black sites, and high-tech surveillance. Back at the turn of the twentieth century, this meant simply opening—illegally—the revolutionaries' mail and directing security contractors (think Pinkerton agents, but worse) to keep watch over the Magonistas wherever they went, from Los Angeles to St. Louis, for twenty-four hours a day. Out of this heritage grow companies like Blackwater.

This is an astoundingly well-told book, and because of the volume of letters at its core, Hernández can provide us—more than a century later—with an almost front-row seat to the revolution. Back and forth, north and south, as we follow Flores Magón, his brothers, his compatriots, and their US sympathizers—from Ida Tarbell and Mother Jones to Jack London—their insurrection moves from a fringe movement to a cause célèbre. Researching this evolution must have required a staggering amount of archival work, but *Bad Mexicans* wears Hernández's efforts lightly. It is not a data dump or a book about revolutionary strategy but a deeply immersive account of how a group collectively seeks liberation, told in the voices of its central protagonists.

Chief among the book's voices, though, is that of the group's antagonist, Porfirio Díaz himself. He was a poor child, brought up by a single mother, who clawed his way into the military when a coup seemingly happened every month. Following decades of chaos, Díaz maneuvered to secure the presidency of a debt-ridden and exhausted country. His promises to the nation were stability and growth, and on these he delivered. He quickly bought back Mexico's debt on capital markets, cracked down on bandits, and hard-wired Mexico into the global economy. Within decades, Laredo and El Paso were connected to Mexico City by rail, and this in an era before passports, before extensive paperwork needed to be filed to cross into the United States.

Along the way, however, Díaz essentially gave the rights to Mexico's resources—its mines, its railroads, its oil, its land—to a very small group of US capitalists. He needed their wealth for the country to grow. The results were mind-blowing. By 1910, 80 percent of Mexican railroad stocks were controlled by Americans. Oil was even more concentrated. Edward Doheny might have been known as a Los Angeles oil tycoon, but most of his wealth came from Mexican soil. For many of the great robber barons at the turn of the century, Mexico was their treasure chest. Meanwhile, these rights to resources were being taken from Mexican citizens, especially the Indigenous, who had been disenfranchised from their own land and often even wound up working on haciendas where they had once lived.

To enforce this vast transfer of wealth, Díaz used the power of the word and the fist. The latter is expected, but the former less so from a man who'd grown up as he had. In one revealing passage, Hernández describes the president's day in his prime. He often rose at 6 a.m. and, after a bath, dedicated several hours to dictating letters. Following a break, he read some newspapers and then went back to more letter writing. Astoundingly, he responded to every letter ever sent to him and in the course of his presidency sent some one million in return. "In homes across Mexico," Hernández writes, "a drawer held a letter from the president."

Increasingly, what these homes didn't hold was criticism of him. Although he claimed the presidency promising never to run for reelection, Díaz reversed this position and didn't look back. To ensure his victories, he resorted to tighter and tighter restrictions on free speech. By 1882, as Mexico's economy had risen, he'd convinced Congress to pass a law that defined criticism of the government as libel. And this was dangerous. Not only had he quickly built a system of patronage, in which all governors owed their fortunes to him, but he had also created a set of shock troops, the *rurales*, who roamed the country and often shot Díaz's victims in the back, "a technique permitted under the *ley fuga*, the law of flight," Hernández writes, which other historians have called Mexico's version of the lynch law.

The Magonistas—led by the brothers Jesús, Enrique, and, most enduringly, Ricardo Flores Magón—had the temerity to publicly state what was happening. The brothers were, in essence, born to the impossible odds of their task. Their parents had met carrying munitions for the troops during the siege of Puebla, when a small group of Mexican soldiers held off Napoleon's advancing army. Ricardo and Jesús studied law, but Ricardo read the most widely, taking in Peter Kropotkin, whose theories of mutual aid have been crucial to revolutionary movements around the world (and formed the central idea of Rebecca Solnit's *A Paradise Built in Hell*, which challenges the notion that in crisis, social order breaks down and people fight one another rather than help).

Ricardo Flores Magón also read Emma Goldman, but he didn't need to look to the United States to find female socialists or revolutionaries. *Bad Mexicans* is full of portraits of women who took part in incendiary change, such as Juana Belén Gutiérrez de Mendoza, "an autodidact from the mountains of Durango," as Hernández describes her. "She was the daughter of a landless rural blacksmith and, like many among the rural poor during the nineteenth century, she never knew her birthdate." She lived with her husband, who was a miner, and her three children, one of whom would die during infancy. Over the course of *Bad Mexicans*, she launches her own feminist anarchist literary journal, leaves the north, travels to Mexico City, and participates in many of the most crucial turning points along the road to revolution.

There were more, some girlfriends and wives, some gun smugglers, and sundry others. Hernández records Ricardo Flores Magón's attitude toward the role of women as mixed, even as he depended on them for sustenance and often safety. They were also involved in crucial ways with the circulation of his newspaper, *Regeneración*, which began in 1900 and called out the need for reform in Mexico. These calls landed the Flores

Magón brothers in jail, which only bolstered their credibility and their determination to speak out. By 1905, the continued threat of imprisonment meant they had to move the newspaper to the United States, and thus began their life on and off the run. For as soon as the Díaz regime could, it called on its US counterpart to shut down the organ that was disseminating revolutionary fervor into the population.

It would not be easy—Ricardo Flores Magón's followers were strong and determined. New presses were often made available to them. Railway workers could carry the newspapers far and wide quickly and have them distributed within hours in major cities across the United States. A range of people were involved in the Magonistas' cause: They were landed; they were poor. They were college educated; they were day laborers.

As *Bad Mexicans* chronicles the growth of this movement, it draws a few key aspects of Mexican migrant labor at the turn of the century into focus. Mexican labor had of course built much of the United States, yet in 1900, many Mexican Americans suffered under "Juan Crow," a system of stigmatization and discrimination that assumed many shapes, from limits on where they could eat and drink and sit and travel in public to threats to their very life and safety. Hernández makes clear that they knew their rights and how unfair this treatment was, often in cases that revolved around violence.

Several lynchings of Mexican men ignite riots and protests across this book, but just as many court cases underscore the growing clarity among Mexican laborers of their rights within the United States. One of the most memorable in the book involves Gregorio Cortez, a farmer who, after a violent encounter with Texas lawmen over a crime he hadn't committed, went on the run and eluded up to two hundred horseback riders for ten days before finally being captured. A posse formed and stormed the jail where he was being kept, but a local Mexican newspaper, *La Crónica*, run by Jovita Idar and her family, kept his story as front-page news and with the pressure of the media saved his life. Later, with the power of a good lawyer, he also gained his freedom.

Hernández makes plain that in taking their revolution on the run, the Magonistas were not just doing what was necessary but tapping into old myths becoming new again in the United States about bandits who thumbed their noses at power. In many cities, Spanish-language newspapers that circulated there ensured that whenever Magonistas were arrested, held a rally, or were led from a jail, a crowd of well-wishers came out to greet them and cheer them on in their fight against what was essentially a Goliath: the full weight of the US government.

They occasionally wound up with money on their side. Camilo Arriaga, who was part of the *Regeneración* newspaper from its earliest days, brought a crumbling family fortune with him. Later, Práxedis Guerrero, who was born on a hacienda, joined their cause and helped to keep the paper alive, as the political platform that it spread became increasingly focused on the removal of Díaz. In Los Angeles, the paper was restarted with the help of well-to-do socialists. Ultimately, these connections came in handy when a member of the cadre in Los Angeles, Anselmo Figueroa, was able to call on someone he'd met at a local socialist meeting—Job Harriman, one of the most famous prosecutors and socialists in the United States—to defend Flores Magón and three Magonistas, once they'd finally been caught and arrested.

Bad Mexicans shows how often this diversity of input cut both ways. While Flores Magón's girlfriend was able to smuggle missives out of jail by offering to wash his underwear, their communications, in time, were shut down, and new and more extreme tactics, including violent raids, had to be relied on to keep revolution alive, none of which were highly successful but which, in their accumulation, created a drumbeat of worry among US capitalists and politicians. Guerrero proved that he was far more than a well-to-do poet, covering these violent raids in dispatches for *Regeneración* and eventually taking part in them himself. Unlike Ricardo Flores Magón, he would die of a bullet for the cause. Flores Magón would live to see Díaz turned out of office before succumbing to long-standing sickness—probably exacerbated by neglect—in prison in Leavenworth, Kansas.

So much of what makes the United States terrifying is on display in its nineteenth-century forms in this book: the greed of US capitalists and the speed with which the US government will break its stated principles to defend their wealth; the way the US Border Patrol has created terminologies of illegality to punish laborers who keep both countries running and in so doing also shut down legitimate criticisms of the way labor is being treated; the way prisons have evolved to backstop this approach; the deep cost this grind has on the lives of citizens.

And yet there is also something tremendously hopeful about watching a few thousand men and women using not much more than words to call into account one of the most powerful regimes of the nineteenth century. Díaz might have escaped to France with some of his wealth, but he had to do so under armed guard and tremendous duress, and he died four years later. The rights he worked so hard to deny people are enjoyed now by a few more today, thanks to the men and women in these pages, whom Hernández has written about with intensity, as if lives depended on them, which is right, because they do.

THE DARK HOURS

by Michael Connelly

Without the myth of a knight-errant, hardboiled crime fiction wouldn't exist in America. In the 1920s, cities across the country were wild places, some nearly run by criminal gangs. Sometimes those gangs were the police. It took someone beyond the law to mythologize justice in these environs. Thus, in the pages of pulps, Raymond Chandler gave birth to Philip Marlowe, an amoral detective driven by mysterious reasons—as well as money—to solve crimes. He didn't ride horses or wield a sword, as in the Arthurian legends. He drove an old gray Plymouth and smoked Camel cigarettes.

The image of a lone man, lurking in shadows, unpicking a crime one interview at a time, was dynamite for early cinema, which was long on dialogue, short on setting, and treated the women as dames. This new genre also reinforced some growing American legends in a world spinning out of order. They were double-edged tales the country told itself, though. What happens, after all, when a knight-errant answers, truly, to no one? When he's almost always a man? What you have then is not an agent of justice but a desperado. Occasionally, a vengeance killer. A punisher. Indeed, in the 1970s, San Francisco, the city of Chandler's

149

fellow crime writer Dashiell Hammett, became, briefly, the city of Dirty Harry. America became the nation of the war in Vietnam.

And so, while hardboiled crime writing began with the knight-errant myth, it would need to leave the unreconstructed myth behind or else run the risk of edging toward a spirit of punishment in post–civil rights America. Nearly unchecked power presents a powerful lure, the temptation to excuse oneself as righteous. Especially in a nation where the most powerful man in the country could also, astonishingly, present himself as an outsider. It was a few years after Nixon gave his law-and-order speech to the nation—one echoed by the president in 2020—that a young engineering student at the University of Florida went to see a Robert Altman film and caught the crime bug. It's hard not to wonder whether some of the charged atmosphere of that decade—its growing distrust of officialdom, the simultaneous real need for order—had struck him too. This sense that maybe a new knight-errant was required. The student, famously, was Michael Connelly, and it would take him another decade and a half to write his own novel, but once he began, he'd revolutionize crime writing.

Connelly's fictional universe is so narrow it is vast. His books unfold almost exclusively in Los Angeles, as seen primarily through the eyes of a detective, his lawyer half brother, and, more recently, a second, up-and-coming detective. Captured through these characters' peripheral vision, through their night watches, and through their daily interviews, decades of fictional Los Angeles life have flourished in the pages of Connelly's books, often with the actual complexity of interactions in LA. It is a city, yes, of bank robbers, serial killers, and drug gangs, but also an expansive metropolis of pain, of racial uprisings, of class yearnings, of people wanting to get unstuck from their station in life, sometimes succeeding, sometimes tragically failing.

The Los Angeles that emerges in Connelly's pages is so many-sided that it has taken dozens of novels to make a scratch at it—a sprawling, heaving everything-o-polis. It's a city, like all cities, stretched beyond its means, and perforated, still, by criminal syndicates, from China, from Central America, and, of course, transnational gangs that got their start right in LA. Murders there can emerge out of taxi medallion disputes, in the cold-case files that date back to the Los Angeles uprising of 1992, during the performance of a mariachi band.

Our guide, our Virgil, into this landscape of light and dark has most of the time been the appropriately named Harry "Hieronymous" Bosch, a tunnel rat in Vietnam turned LAPD detective, exquisitely played by a hangdog-eyed Titus Welliver in the eponymous TV miniseries. A loner, not good with love, living on a perch overlooking the city in a bought-with-movie-money house, percolated with his jazz and his strong coffee, Bosch is, in many ways, our century's Marlowe: Wearied by the murders and violence he has seen, he is equally determined to do right by the powerless. But he is different from Marlowe in one way.

The police procedural, the genre Connelly has so brilliantly made his own—teaching tens of millions of readers not just what codes are called over police radio but what forms are filled out when officers return—does not proceed from detail. Detail is its Trojan horse for a greater realization: that we are all connected in city life. Every slip of paper, every rule that is described in a police procedural connects more people to more people, meaning that its detective protagonist is often totally enmeshed in a huge web of city dwellers. Unlike Marlowe, the detective is not alone, solving a crime, but often has a large swath of Angelenos (or New Yorkers, or Romans) working alongside him—coroners, beat cops, social workers, restaurateurs, victims' relatives, chauffeurs, people without housing.

This mapping serves more than a titillating or humiliating function in city life. Yes, a pornographer might have ties to the highest and mightiest, and a dead equestrian might have links to a murdered pawnshop owner, as they have in previous Connelly novels. But if fiction is to tell us not just where we live but how and why, has there ever been a more finely designed capillary system for the network of human connection and knowledge than the reverse engineering of a crime?

Plying and perfecting this genre over a vast body of work, Connelly has brought the knight-errant back into the fold, revealing that a person who seeks justice in a flawed, even corrupt system is perhaps as interesting as, or even more so, than the fantasy of someone seeking it alone, from the outside. He has begun, in the past decade, to put a woman in this leading role. And he has also demonstrated that sometimes an institution—like the police—will fight a crime just as it perpetrates it. A city—like Los Angeles—will create the conditions for a crime just as its people fight to undo them, or help the quest for justice for those who have suffered.

This type of moral complexity feels essential if the police procedural is going to make any kind of sense in a country riven by the murder of George Floyd and thousands of other unarmed (mostly Black and brown) civilians at the hands of police. *The Dark Hours* is Connelly's first novel to address life in the post-Floyd-murder, post-COVID era of America, and it begins, quite realistically, with two officers hunkered down under an overpass, sitting in their cruiser on New Year's Eve, hoping to avoid the rain of lead that falls when guns are fired in the air after block parties.

The two detectives in the car are Renée Ballard and her partner, Lisa Moore, of the Hollywood Division Sexual Assault Unit. The two are working together to catch a pair of serial rapists who've struck twice already, but within several pages, Ballard and Moore have managed to shut their windows up against a homeless man asking for help (he has no mask) and beat back the crude jokes of two fellow male officers. So much for social change. Everyone feels exhausted and somewhat beleaguered, and Moore is more interested in getting home to her boyfriend than solving a case. Everything about the night has begun wrong, and it gets worse when a man enjoying a New Year's display is shot in the back of the head, echoing the murder from Connelly's 2014 novel, *The Burning Room*.

Ballard first emerged in Connelly's world in the 2017 novel *The Late Show*, whose title is a nod to the overnight shift she works in Robbery-Homicide. By this time in Connelly's series, Bosch has crossed one too many lines in the bureaucratic sand and been pushed into an early retirement. Tired, fueled by ghosts, he can be hard company, a crime-fiction cousin to Beckett's Molloy. By contrast, Ballard, who is part Hawaiian, young, and full of energy, is a burst of narrative fresh air. In *The Late Show*, she solves two cases in one night with a vigor that hadn't been felt in a Bosch book in a long time.

The Dark Hours has a similar double-helix structure. It's clear very quickly that the auto bodywork shop owner who is shot and killed on New Year's Eve was murdered and that the gun that was used to do it was connected to an old crime. Ballard begs her lieutenant for permission to proceed with the case, even though it's not her territory and Moore has abandoned shift work to flee to Santa Barbara with her boyfriend. Almost simultaneously, the Midnight Men, as Moore and Ballard were calling their serial rapists, strike again, and Ballard is also chasing down leads to learn how this pair found yet another traumatized victim, this one well outside their geographic pattern.

The heart of *The Dark Hours* is not, as its title says, the night per se, but the time of not knowing, when it's unclear where either case is going and when Ballard's wit, intuition, and gumshoe work lead her into charged, often tense interactions with civilians, many of whom, understandably, distrust the police, and are not keen to help them. Connelly began as a journalist, and he has always excelled at scripting these interactions, at resisting the fantasy of law enforcement being treated like the cavalry. *The Dark Hours* does not go as far as it could to draw plot points from within Black Lives Matter and the record-breaking protests against police mistreatment of vulnerable people. But it does something nearly as important: By pushing Ballard, who can read to some as white, and Bosch, among others, into civilians who are uneasy around them, this book captures the volatility of trust between a police force and the population of a city who, even if they want to defund it, still might need its help to solve murders.

Information is the drumbeat of crime fiction, and Connelly knows how to create complex rhythms with it. Watching Connelly balance Ballard's two cases against each other, pouring the momentum from one into the other and back again, is like watching a master stickman doing two separate tasks with each of their two hands. It's beyond dexterous. In the best passages, wherein plot twists create parallel portraits of minor characters—such as a manipulative ex-husband and a CI who crawls out of a life of crime by informing—the novel achieves a symphonic depth. What does it mean to scheme? This is a question that emerges in the language itself. When Ballard catches a break, she checks in with Bosch, who has begun to lob in help from the side. They decide to go "skeeing" past a person of interest's house:

> [The word] meant doing a drive-by . . . taking a measure of him. Its origin was debated: One camp thought it derived from the word schematic, meaning getting the physical parameters of a suspect's place of business or residence. Others said it was short for scheming—taking the first step in a plan to hit a house of criminal activity. Either way, Ballard did not have to translate for Bosch.
> "I'll go with you," he said.
> "You sure?" Ballard asked.
> "I'm sure," Bosch said. "I'll grab a mask."

Bosch and Ballard first met in Connelly's 2018 novel, *Dark Sacred Night*. In *The Dark Hours*, their rapport is based on mutual respect, sacrifice, and Bosch's willingness to be told, on occasion, that there are charming anachronisms, like having an old printer, and not-so-charming, even stupid ones, like not getting vaccinated. One of the novel's best intradetective moments occurs when Ballard refuses to be brushed off and simply drives Bosch over to a site where he can get his first shot.

As the novel progresses, the vulnerability the two detectives show each other leads to an even greater bond. It also means that the wide array of characters begins to narrow and we must start making, as ever, guesses about who was in on the scheme to defraud a hardworking auto body shop owner out of his business. Who was helping the serial rapists case the houses or find the victims, who, at first, seem not to have been attacked according to a pattern.

In most of the Bosch novels, he has worked with another detective, and, in the past decade, he has often worked with other female detectives, rather than had them purely as love interests. In *The Closers*, he worked with Kiz Rider, who convinced the chief of police to allow Bosch back to work. In *The Burning Room*, he paired up with a rookie, Lucia Soto, as he faced the reality of his own retirement. Since Connelly has been writing, a whole new generation of younger writers—from Ivy Pochoda to Steph Cha—has reinvented the field, and Connelly pays them tribute by having their books appear as crucial sustenance to one of the assault victims.

With *The Dark Hours*, however, he has gone the furthest yet in reinterpreting the knight-errant tale. What if the city isn't sure it needs a knight-errant anymore? What does that mean for a crime novel's sense of justice? And more aptly here, what if that knight comes with a supporting cast of men? This is a Renée Ballard novel first, even though Bosch is colisted. Its action is seen through her eyes, her gambles, her fears, and her unexpected leaps of logic—and the many, many relationships across the department and across the city that she manages. Bosch mostly helps and is along for the ride. It's a train he helped get started, but it will be Ballard's role, and probably that of the writers Connelly name-checks, to keep it going, so that the world of Los Angeles doesn't retreat into fantasy and the definition of justice keeps expanding to live up to Bosch's own motto: "Everybody counts or nobody counts."

YOUR HOUSE WILL PAY

by Steph Cha

Vengeance is a field, not an act, and as such, it requires a story to tell it right. It's all too obvious that life is not equally valued in America, but how do you measure grief? What about sleepless nights? The years it takes to return to work after, say, being released from prison? Thirty years ago, when the Los Angeles uprising began and burned for days, a line was often neatly drawn between the vicious beating of Rodney King and the spectacle of fury of those five days. Burning buildings. Looters. As if some people "looting" weren't, as Héctor Tobar pointed out in a remembrance of that day in the *New York Times*, carrying milk and diapers, and some of those store owners weren't themselves victims of discrimination as recent Americans.

The multiplicity of that moment hasn't ended. Its instabilities—not just racial, but those of class and religion—are one of the defining features of Los Angeles. In her fourth novel, *Your House Will Pay*, Steph Cha has written a Great American Novel of two families fatally entwined in these dynamics and their melodies of violence and retribution, vengeance and forgiveness. Straddling 1991 and 2019, spanning the city from Northridge to Silver Lake and South Central, the book has geographic and temporal sprawl yet is compact. Drawn from real-life events, it depicts a terrible act of violence and how it reverberates over time, disrupting two families—the Parks and the Matthewses—trying to start over. Ultimately, each must decide if that is possible.

Labor is the forge of this project, of beginning again, for both families. Cha's portrait of how each stokes the fires of improvement—of sustainability—is a deep update to the binaries of bootstraps and failure. In the Park family, the cornerstone of their life upon arriving in America from Korea was first a liquor store, then the pharmacy business Grace's father, Paul, runs in the San Fernando Valley. Unlike her sister, Miriam, Grace has followed her father into the business, but doesn't share his pride in it.

> She was grateful, and she had a lot of affection for the place, but she saw it for what it was: a two-hundred-square-foot glass box adjoining a Korean food court and supermarket in an ugly deep Valley strip mall. The walls were glass, see-through where they weren't covered with vitamins and ointments and printout ads for shampoos and Powerball tickets, but none of them faced the outside world. They got no sun, only the artificial light of the Hanin Market, a complex they shared with a Korean bank, a Korean bakery, a Korean cosmetics shop, even a fully Koreanized branch of the U.S. Post Office.

Your House Will Pay is a complex paean to the unglamorous but dependable pleasures of this world, of the shelter it provides, the food, and the different layers of kinship—many born from sacrifice. Not everyone can bear to witness this sacrifice. Miriam has decamped for

Silver Lake and a white boyfriend, so Grace receives some of her best emotional support from her father's business partner, an uncle in name only. He is the first elder to tell Grace the full truth about a long-ago secret—one that explains their family's move to the Valley and out of convenience stores into the pharmacy.

Meanwhile, over in Palmdale, the Matthews family reassembles after a series of terrible losses. Cousins Ray and Shawn have grown up together in the fallout of Shawn's mother's death and the murder of Shawn's sister just before the Los Angeles uprising. Both men would wind up flirting with gang life and go to prison. Shawn for a few years, after which he is scared straight into a moving business, and Ray for a decade. As the book opens, Ray has just been released and warily greets his family, his wife, his two teenage kids, unsure whether his place in the family has been usurped by Shawn.

The families at the heart of *Your House Will Pay* are among the most indelibly drawn in recent American literature, in part because Cha shows them being families. It is not incidental to the plot what they eat and where, who fills in for whom when babysitting is needed, and which elders wear compression socks on their legs from years of standing at work. How much such a business matters to a family that has started over in a whole new country, in a whole new language. On a fundamental level, to read *Your House Will Pay* feels, for one of the first times, to be truly brought into a contemporary American household.

Cha also gives each family space to be many things to one another. Ray and Shawn, for example, are at once rivals and friends, depending on the circumstances. When a local murder brings a wrenching loss zooming back, they celebrate, grimly, that a retribution has been delivered, if several decades later. But in the morning, Shawn is annoyed that his cousin is nowhere to be found. Still, Shawn knows he might be picking up the parenting slack and steels himself to get ready for it. Then the police show up.

Powerfully and with great subtlety, *Your House Will Pay* demonstrates how these two families, united by a tragedy, can have fundamentally different experiences with the police. When a detective visits the Parks, Grace's sister is frank and abrupt and talks to the detective as if he were in the service industry. When the officer visits Shawn in his own home, years of experience in dealing with cops, from a very young age, mean he makes no sudden moves, for fear of being shot, and answers only questions that are directly asked.

Out of this vigilance, dearly learned, Shawn and his mother and their family have wound up far more open to extrajudicial justice. In so much crime fiction, the TV media circus that feasts on public crimes is poorly drawn. *Your House Will Pay* brings a bevy of newer news sources into the plot and gives each their blind spots, their complexities. For example, thirty years on from her niece's murder, Ray's mother maintains close ties with a white reporter who wrote a book about the event, a relationship that strikes Shawn as exploitative.

In *Your House Will Pay*, telling the truth isn't so simple as uncovering what happened. Grace, Shawn, Ray, and everyone in this book must factor in how something happened and who did the telling. Who watched and why? Who made money off it? As Cha's tale of the long-ago murder is drawn together with a present-tense one, these questions become crucial. They cut to the core of who is to be trusted and who is not, a flexion that tears at the fabric of each of these families.

Three decades after the LA uprising, it was common for the media to speak of Rodney King as a symbol of forgiveness. It's a hopeful idea, but the question remains: For whom? Who is being forgiven? Into these abstractions, *Your House Will Pay* arrives like a wrecking ball, demolishing the notion that a symbol can mean the same thing to people living under different pressures, and also that fates in a city like Los Angeles are separate. Ultimately, for the Matthewses and the Parks, forgiveness is as intimate as vengeance. It is like a stain. A taste that does not go away. Something that can only be tasted on the tongue.

VI

HOW WE SOUND

THE SELLOUT

by Paul Beatty

In these times, with unaccountability's balloon about to burst—or simply fire up its thrusters and take its little wicker basket elsewhere—no writer deserves closer study than Paul Beatty.

Linguistically daring, hilarious, and driven by a torrential prose style, his work is among the finest in America these past fifty years. As a semiotician of bullshit—one who can unpack what it hides—he's in a league of his own. Who else has heard the bunk the nation talks to itself quite like him? Explored what it's saying when people utter terms like "postracial society," like "debt," like "first responders"?

"Listening to America these days," muttered the hero of Beatty's third novel, *Slumberland*, a DJ living in Berlin, "is like listening to the fallen King Lear using his royal gibberish to turn field mice and shadows into real enemies."

Since his early days as a poet, performing at the Nuyorican Poets Café and elsewhere, Beatty has taken a hard look at the cover that the language of collective identity offers an individual. Unlike George Saunders, who renders a world out of this toxic syntax, Beatty has shown us the day-to-day plight of Black characters swimming through it, dodging false rewards and even more false friends.

As a novelist, he has surveyed a cultural landscape in which the past enacts itself through a culturally significant array of tribalisms. From the empty worship of negritude that rippled through drum-and-bass circuits in the late 1990s to the latest iteration of social science's quest to put a label and a type on all, what often passes for culture in Beatty's novels is ripe for satire. And Beatty emerges from a generation of American midcentury novelists—from Kurt Vonnegut and Chester Himes to Ishmael Reed—who loved to remind us that the individual cannot be typecast. In their vein, Beatty gave us a string of memorable antiheroes—a basketball player, a DJ, an aspiring filmmaker turned local politician—who were vividly equivocal about the racial bargains their rise to fame often entailed.

The Sellout, Beatty's 2016 Man Booker Prize–winning novel, is the zenith of this driving exploration. It's an energetic, outrageous, and searching book, a novel so capacious you can only marvel at how he fits it all in. Easily one of the best LA novels ever written, *The Sellout* makes you want to follow city bus routes across town, go to a Dodgers game and grow verklempt, sniff the occasional Westside stank that creeps inland, feel the real pleasure of surfing in Malibu and the fury of living in a city where some think that's all people do. It recalls the LA uprising of 1992 and the matter-of-fact brutality of the LAPD, and luxuriates in the sprawl and heave of the place; pimp walks and drive-in-donut salons; the sadness of ex–child actors, zombie-strutting about; and the constant bustle of people trying to hustle up some kind of ladder.

The plot of the novel is absurd, and yet, given LA's history, not at all. Our hero, nicknamed Bonbon, last name Me, has grown up in Dickens, a close approximation of the part of Compton zoned for agricultural use (which is why Black cowboys exist in South LA). Bonbon's father, a community college sociologist, takes his forty-acres-and-a-mule life there literally, raising a shambolic group of livestock, all the while determined to better his son through a series of comical (were they not all of them real) experiments in aversion therapy to counteract harmful ideas of Blackness.

Among the most potent of these "teachable moments" are Bonbon's father's existential errands that he undertakes as a volunteer talking Black people in distress out of tight spots before police tackle or shoot them. Most of them are high or somewhat mentally disturbed. Beatty uses another name for these encounters, which I can't use here. There's a deep sadness beneath the humor in these scenes. For they are as common as traffic jams in LA—and most cities, for that matter—and there's usually no one like Bonbon's father there, and camera-phone footage of the decade has told anyone who didn't know what often happens next.

In *The Sellout*, it's not one of these destitute souls but Bonbon's own father who pays the ultimate price, shot three times in the back by an undercover officer for an offhand comment Bonbon's father makes upon approaching a conflagration he'd planned to untangle. With a $2 million wrongful-death settlement, Bonbon sets out to make good on his father's plot of land, first growing square watermelons. "Think of the best watermelon you've ever had. Now add a hint of anise and brown sugar." An actor and neighborhood friend named Hominy, who had played minstrel roles in the 1930s, '40s, and '50s, reveals to Bonbon a taste for humiliation, and soon he's coming by, acting out the part of a slave. "He hiked up his pants and slipped into Metro-Goldwyn-Mayer plantationese," Bonbon notes.

Although this setup begs for a father-son book, *The Sellout* is not that. And while its excesses have earned it the satire label, that, too, lets us off easy. Beatty's observations are too explosive and complex to fit into satire's narrow chimney. "It dawned on me," Bonbon says, for example, in one scene upon discovering that Hominy and Rodney King share the same birthday, "that if places like Sedona, Arizona, have energy vortexes, mystical holy lands where visitors experience rejuvenation and spiritual awakenings, Los Angeles must have racism vortexes. Spots where visitors experience deep feelings of melancholy and ethnic worthlessness."

Bonbon's observation and Beatty's genius at expansion collide in this moment, giving birth to a quest. The city of Dickens, it turns out, often called a ghetto, and the kind of place where white people roll up their windows, has been bureaucratically wiped off the map. It literally no longer exists. Bonbon decides to bring it back, and to do so forces him to go in search of an answer as to why it was erased, why it's worth preserving. While keeping his book circumscribed to Dickens, Beatty still lets his hero roam, which allows Beatty's prose to get up and gallop in long, unfurling, dazzling paragraphs. In such a passage, Bonbon hops the bus to El Segundo because his high school flame now drives it, leading to the best public transport dance party in the history of literature.

There are so many other moments like this in *The Sellout*, where spaces reveal themselves to be the containers of unlikely—but because of that, earned—*community*. It's a word Beatty uses uneasily, while acknowledging that without it we are nothing. It is friendship, family, a network for memory. So much of what made Dickens great to Bonbon has been burlesqued by culture to the point of nonsense, so much so that by himself Bonbon cannot figure out exactly what he is supposed to bring back from the dead.

How to live in a disappearing place that is being replaced by a simpler representation of what it never was? If that's not a kind of erasure, what is? Beatty's novel, at its highest pitch, is an elegy to being of a place that matters, wherever that means to the person, but especially Black LA, which has a deep, rich history that has been underestimated and reduced to a few caricatures. And because this is a Beatty novel, the book also pays tribute to—and pokes fun at—the ways that instinct draws people together.

The Sellout

Before he died, for instance, Bonbon's father had created a group called the Dum Dum Donut Intellectuals, a gathering of men concerned about their home. They meet regularly over crullers and bear claws to discuss race and philosophical issues and ways to save the old ways of doing things. At the first meeting described in *The Sellout*, one of the most feared local gangsters, King Cuz, arrives near the meeting's end, and Beatty makes great comic hay out of a gangster come to talk spreadsheets of crime rates with old heads. But what's not funny is why he's there: King Cuz is part of the group because Bonbon's father had talked King Cuz's mother off the train tracks one day, rescuing her from sure death. Bonbon's father didn't do it to do a good deed, but because it was simply not a way to go. Not for somebody who surely was loved. Sometimes it seems his son makes a similar decision about his neighborhood.

GORDO

by Jaime Cortez

There are five basic senses, and the difference between good writing and that which fades—especially writing about a place like California, so throbbed by its elements—lies in how well these senses are evoked. What is life, after all, besides what we sense and what we make of that information in the place we might call home? Is the air outside dry or humid? Does the light fall soft or sharply? Do the acoustics make you feel wary or safe? What do the people sound like? Do the skies turn copper-colored or purplish at sundown, or does the sun sink like a stone? Does the stink of cattle farms seethe? Is it cold at night? Can you smell what is cooking when you walk down the street?

Jaime Cortez has figured out a way to pack more life into his fiction than just about any writer at work today because he asks such questions of the world he creates. And the answers are fabulous, hilarious, shocking. Revelatory. Just look at his first short story collection. Set in a migrant workers' camp in Watsonville in the 1970s, *Gordo* draws on all these tactile, tangible details and brings its fictive world triumphantly to life. To say this book updates Steinbeck country for the twenty-first century underestimates the force of life that surges forth here in eleven deceptively simple stories. This is a book full of laughter and song, full of meals and funerals, jokes that are corny and nicknames that are ingenious. It is also a book of primordial stories about love and belonging, sex and death, the clasp of family and the need to grow up.

Fittingly, the sense the book evokes most vividly is touch, much neglected, but not in the pages of *Gordo*. People are hugged and kicked, tackled, nuzzled, licked, leaned on, and held throughout these tales in the ways children, siblings, parents, elders, and lovers are in life but, strangely, aren't often in fiction. How many people learned whom not to hit growing up and who could be hit and made up with? The cast of *Gordo* knows this, and they also know how to recognize when someone needs an easy touch. One of the finest of the stories takes place at a hairstylist salon, where a young hairdresser tends to make people feel better about themselves in small, tangible ways. One snip at a time.

Perhaps because they are embodied, because Cortez's tales attend to such tiny acts of decency, they spark immediately, like stone striking flint. They burn hot and fast in some instances, cool and spooky in others, with the atmosphere of moonlit fables. Their soundscapes linger like harmonies because Cortez knows how to put in just enough detail. There are the sounds of bottles clinking, of kids kicking balls in the dirt, of dogs barking. The echo of voices at a distance, the way adults sound when kids are somewhere playing in the summer and know there are some things they can get away with if they keep it down—until they can't.

To read this book is to feel part of a neighborhood, a place, one Cortez invites you into and allows you to watch as it asserts its boundaries through the eyes of a young, probably queer, slightly husky kid named Gordo. Using Gordo's nimble sense of humor as his barometer, Cortez draws all the weather systems of the camp together in a series of swift, comedic stories about Gordo's time there, moving forward chronologically. In the latter part of the book, we leave Gordo somewhat behind and meet some of the people who grew up around him.

We never see the camp from the outside. In fact, people come to the camp and mostly quickly leave: a man selling doughnuts; *la migra*, who occasionally chase down people without documents. In the middle of the book, Cortez describes a young visiting farmworker who comes to the camp and hides out with Gordo's family, forcing people to take sides with an outsider who becomes one of them.

Every tale has a kind of moral dilemma. Virtually all of the stories approach this complex territory through humor. In "El Gordo," Cortez muses on the irony of being taught to be masculine; Gordo's father gives him frankly Castro-fabulous wrestling gear and tells him a story about his boxing hero, while also asking him to be macho; in "The Jesus Donut," we meet the kids of the camp before experiencing a slapstick tableau of them turning the purchase of a doughnut into a mock Catholic Mass; in "The Nasty Book Wars," an explosive satire of coming of age kicks off when kids go to war over nudie magazines, the acts depicted in which they have yet to divine.

Humor is Cortez's sixth sense; it's how he folds and braids a world into a world so that nothing is ever as simple as it seems. In "The Nasty Book Wars," for instance, the children who are coming of age are juxtaposed with the adults of the camp, who are living in states of precariousness the kids can only vaguely sense. Primi, one of the adults, throws off such shadows with the excesses of his personality and style. Cortez's description of him is full of humor, pathos and the tiniest edge of shame.

> Primi loved a party. He splurged and rented maroon Bostonian lace-up shoes and a matching tuxedo with ruffles that cascaded down the equator of his beer belly, making him look like a downwardly mobile rain forest rooster puffing up his plumes for one last mating dance. When he stepped into the San Juan Bautista VFW hall with a living,

breathing, live, and unknown female escort, everyone whistled and catcalled. He took it all in like the pope, bowing slightly to the left, the right, and the center of the hall.

Whoever said style is a struggle was borrowing something from the spectacle of a man like Primi. Or an artist like Cookie, one of Gordo's classmates, who in a story about her has to decide whether she is going to deface public buildings where she lives or draw on paper like a fancy artist. A deep question about how to make art about where you're from lurks in parable form in that tale. Within the world of their world, Cortez's stories never ask their characters to perform or dance for their dignity. They receive it as a right, and therefore we feel when that dignity is threatened, but we also can sense why certain habits and rituals and even silences create meaning. In the latter half of the book, in a story about a gay hairdresser, Cortez shows us a version of the man Gordo might become—a man who never has to leave where he's from to practice his art.

This is a hugely important book, a once-in-a-decade book about how a home is made and the ways a neighborhood reiterates its hold on residents in jokes, in punches, in simple meals. The rough nip of a dog's bite. That the sweat and labor of working happens off-screen, so to speak, speaks volumes: What else do we work for? To make a home, to provide, to have money for food and drink, and so we can pass the hours lightly. For years, the Midwest has had its *House on Mango Street*. It wouldn't surprise me if years from now, *Gordo* has reached millions of readers with its call to Cortez's Watsonville, a place, thanks to these pages, that will forever remain on America's literary map.

THE GANGSTER OF LOVE

by Jessica Hagedorn

Deep into Jessica Hagedorn's boisterous 1996 novel, *The Gangster of Love*, our heroine Rocky Rivera has moved to New York to make a go of the rock-and-roll life. It's the mid-1970s, the waning years of CBGB, and she may have missed her moment. Rocky's band, which gives the book its title, gigs a lot, but doesn't earn much. One night, Rocky jumps in a taxi to go back down to the Lower East Side. It's late, the cabby giving her the eye in his rearview mirror. Rocky knows it's wise to be deferential. She doesn't need the hassle; she ought to call him *Sir*. A fizz of rage bubbles, though, and she thinks, "My father, I want to tell this cabdriver named Eduardo Zuniga, was so respected that he had no name in the Philippines. Everyone just called him 'Sir.' I also want to say: Eduardo Zuniga is a poet's name. But I don't."

So much unfurls in interactions like this in *The Gangster of Love*, an epic of love and shame. The novel moves like a power ballad about how these two emotions live side by side in the heart. Pumping in tandem, creating a tension in the blood. Come closer; escape. Recognize kin; put them down. As a poet and musician, Rocky externalizes this torque in her poems, in her songs, and in the bohemian life she lives with fantastic abandon. She takes whatever lovers she wishes; she sets up a life on her own terms. Her family, however, doesn't get this second life, and Hagedorn shows the pain their estrangement costs them—and Rocky.

The Gangster of Love is a small book but feels much bigger, due to its structure. The novel swirls from the mid-1970s to the mid-1980s in a moody montage of brilliant set pieces and moving character portraits of Rocky's family. We met them first at ground zero when Rocky; her mother, Milagros; and brother, Voltaire, land flat on their backs in San Francisco after her father abandoned them in Manila. It's 1970, Jimi Hendrix is dead, San Francisco is broke, and arrival is hard. Milagros, though a force, is in the waning years of her beauty; Rocky's brother has the beginnings of a mental illness; and she is brilliant but prideful, decadent, and in need of relief from her chaotic house.

Like so many sensitive kids who feel smothered at home, Rocky escapes by going out. Is there a better book on San Francisco nightlife in the 1970s? In many ways, *The Gangster of Love* feels like an update to Jack Kerouac's *Subterraneans*, without the spin of exoticism. Instead of Mardou Fox, Hagedorn gives us Kieko Van Heller, an artist and muse who is Dutch or Hawaiian or Cuban, depending on which day you ask. Men fall hard for Keiko, women too, and in her own way, Rocky is smitten. Keiko's genius for self-invention is the doorway through which she will walk into a bigger life, and Rocky will follow her, in her own way.

At a certain age, one's friends are far bigger influences than where you go to school or what you study there. Elvis Chang believes he will be Rocky's other major teacher. Sexy, silent, and sometimes a good musician, he seduces Rocky and quickly gives her the clap. These were the last days of venereal diseases that could be treated with penicillin. Already, Rocky hears whispers of something much worse happening to gay men. She refuses to be proprietary about Elvis, though, who tries to make her jealous and fails. Instead, Rocky falls deeper and deeper

The Gangster of Love

under the spell of Keiko. When Keiko and her partner skedaddle to New York, Rocky abruptly decides to go too.

Shuttling from San Francisco to New York in the 1970s, *The Gangster of Love* could be the kind of book that works due to its borrowed scenery. To having been there and escaped alive. This isn't the case. All the energy in it pours from the 500-watt amplifier of Hagedorn's prose. Her syntax is gritty, musical, rhythmic, and aural. You don't read this book so much as ride it like a wave. It jolts you with its prose power, its gum-stuck, cokeheaded surges of hilarity. Half the book is dialogue, and it's brilliant. Arguments. Monologues. And then in the latter half, the novel itself becomes a play as Rocky the musician turns into Rocky the playwright, casting her own mother to play herself in a theatre piece about their lives.

One can hardly blame Rocky for making use of what fate gave her. From the moment Milagros walks into this book, she threatens to make it hers. Dramatic, seductive, a skilled manipulator, but also loyal and loving, she is the center of gravity that Rocky must reach escape speed to flee. When Rocky moves to New York City, as Hagedorn did herself in the 1970s, you know the distance from her mother is going to be hard, but that it is also necessary—or else she would be swallowed whole back home. Still, for all the nights New York acts exactly as Rocky had hoped, she misses her mother, in her way.

Hagedorn was a playwright first, then a poet, and you can see how she deploys her skills in each form within this novel. Although Milagros looms large, she doesn't dominate the stage. We also get closer glimpses of Rocky's dreamy, troubled brother and her father's brother, Marlon, who lives in Los Angeles next door to an aging Filipina movie star, tending with courtly care to the needs of her ego and her army of tiny dogs.

He is just one of many characters Hagedorn passes the narrative to briefly, so we hear from him directly. It feels on the page as if he is stepping forward into a spotlight for a monologue. When Marlon falls ill, for example, Hagedorn gives us an extraordinary passage about him trying to imagine how to spend the rest of his days. Later, when Rocky gets pregnant a second time, her mother comes to New York City to help with the baby, and we see Rocky's life from her mother's eyes. What might have come across to Rocky as a mask of judgment is in fact concern, and care.

These emotional depths also open up the rest of the cast. One of the book's most wrenching scenes involves a family dinner Elvis grudgingly allows Rocky to attend when his family comes to New York. His parents own a Chinese restaurant in Oakland, and they have brought Elvis's high-achieving student brother to taste the sights of New York, a tax write-off given their business. Rocky and Elvis are broken up, yet she's harassing him under the table, groping his thigh, saying the right words to his parents but torturing their son, who begins to act out. The way the meal devolves into tears is real and unforgettable.

These are just the main characters, too. The Gangster of Love teems with a secondary cast, from the band's creepy, vulgar drummer, Sly, to Dr. Sandy, the acupuncturist who gives Rocky a job so she can pursue her dreams. Introduced by Marlon, Rocky manages to make this work stick where waitressing and other menial jobs bore her. In part because Dr. Sandy actually cares for her, she's not there to take anything. Or have it taken from her. Rocky says at one point,

> On one of my visits back to San Francisco, my mother asks me why I try so hard to be a man. "Look at your Grandpa Baby. So-called inventor of the yo-yo. And what did that get him?" She blames it all on coming to America. Grandpa Baby was a renowned wood-carver back in his hometown in the Philippines, but he gave it all up to come to California. First he broke his back picking asparagus in the fields, then he worked as a bell hop in some hotel in Santa Monica, where he ended up

whittling a yo-yo and starting his own company. The rest, as they say in my cynical family, is the same old shit history. Grandpa Baby sold his rights to the yo-yo for a lousy thirty thousand dollars.

Part of Rocky's search in *The Gangster of Love* is an attempt to make her way in the world without being made a sucker. How to be called Sir, even if it means playacting across gender roles. How refreshing it is to read an almost thirty-year-old book that is actually ahead of its time. In the most enlarging way, *The Gangster of Love* is a novel about queer love and about the world Rocky builds to make the getting of it and the holding on to it possible.

At one point, the band on the rocks, Elvis and Sly at their worst, Rocky and Keiko go to bed together. Here is my body, Rocky says, joking, stripping off her clothes. She's alarmed at how she doesn't feel anything as Keiko begins to touch her. In the end they wind up spooning and holding each other and that's that.

Milagros gets it slightly wrong, then, when she tells her daughter she's acting like a man: Rocky is acting how Milagros thinks men act, running away for things, for fortune. But rather than stake her claim on a toy, Rocky has put her bet on art, and love. She is going to take it all, rather than have it taken from her, which makes her an unruly character to follow. Sometimes amoral. The way she proceeds drives her further and further away from her family and the past, until suddenly it snaps back.

The Gangster of Love isn't just the name of Rocky's band; it's a title that can apply to several people. First and foremost Rocky, as she barrels into this relationship or that determined to make it out without getting hurt. Her mother also has a claim to that title, for she is a gangster who needs all love to flow up toward her. Ultimately, it might also apply to Rocky's baby, Venus, who when she is born reorders the laws of the universe as to who matters and why.

It is a minor miracle that Hagedorn manages to make such a deeply cool book about rock and roll and bohemian life and also such a warm and real book about family—about actual and chosen family. Throughout his life, Jack Kerouac went home to his mother's to write about the chosen family he sometimes drove to distraction. Here the mothers haven't been edited from the book. They are everywhere, and in many ways the song Hagedorn sings so beautifully is theirs.

LESS

by Andrew Sean Greer

Charm in literature is as misunderstood as breezes in wetlands. Those of us in the hot zone know that a breeze is more than just air moving. It's the small magic that separates you from lethargy, from the heaviness and dread of living. And so it goes with fiction. Without charm, there can be no dream, no intimacy, no pleasure. It shouldn't be an insult, then, to use the word in a description: as in, full of charm *but not substance*. To charm someone, after all, is to reach them, to seduce them, as if by magic.

From the beginning of his publishing life nearly twenty-five years ago, Andrew Sean Greer has been an immensely charming storyteller. He writes like someone who enjoys it, and his books have always tilted hopefully toward love. One by one, his novels fling characters into the emotion's gravity field and then care for them in their falling. The mood mist made by this cosmic attitude about the heart affects everything, especially Greer's sense of time. "Youth is a tender terror," Greer writes in an early story, his narrator impatient to shrug it off: to get to where the hurting stops.

But of course, the hurt living causes never does burn off. It simply changes, something the hero of Greer's sixth book, *Less*, knows all too

179

well. A middling writer about to turn fifty, Arthur Less has decided to take a trip around the world. He hopes to avoid the wedding of his ex-lover and perhaps drink some champagne. He doesn't want to give up on love. He just doesn't need his nose rubbed in it. Plus, he hopes to run away from another rejection: that of his latest novel.

What could have been a Merchant Ivory production on the page is instead a gentle riot. Told by an offstage narrator, whose identity is not revealed until the book's conclusion, *Less* begins and we are immediately enveloped by a velvety-voiced chum. Someone insinuating but not mean. "From where I sit, the story of Arthur Less is not so bad," the voice utters, slyly. "Look at him," and thus we meet Arthur.

The story-within-a-story mode, so well polished by Balzac and Chekhov, was literature's first camera lens. Here is the frame, it said, and, drawing closer, here's a person within it. When practiced well, as Greer does here, you gradually forget the frame, and the person being portrayed overtakes you, becomes you—or you him. Of course there are few fates less sad than that of a white middle-aged man—even if he's gay, as a woman in the book points out to Arthur himself, no less. But bit by bit, slight by slight, we meet Arthur and come to inhabit his body, with all its aches and pangs.

What draws us in is Arthur's at-first-not-obvious vulnerability. In Greer's handling—a sequel has come out and is great fun, too—Arthur is a fool, one of so many men siren-sung to the West Coast knowing practically nothing. So terrified by sex (he arrives in San Francisco in the midst of the worst years of the AIDS pandemic), he winds up bad at it, falling for the revered—and married—poet of the Russian River School, Robert Brownburn; becoming his lover, and then companion for many years; and thus serving as a handmaiden to his genius.

"What was it like to live with genius," Arthur is asked at an event once his trip has begun—and he thinks back. "Like living alone. Like living alone with a tiger. Everything had to be sacrificed for the work.

. . . For at the beginning, one never knew what he was writing about. Was it you?"

Brownburn teaches Arthur many minor lessons and one major one: that he is not a genius. Or so Arthur thinks. Eclipsed and nurtured and made self-conscious by this almost decades-long love affair, which he palate-cleanses with a nine-year romance with a younger man, Arthur has washed up in middle age prematurely young, having never really experienced the flower of his own youth. But he is not ready to be old. Unlike a previous generation of gay men, many of whom didn't expect to live to be middle-aged, Arthur also clearly hasn't had a model for how to be fifty.

Ironically, perceptively, *Less* sets out to correct this missing piece of training, as if part of the long tradition (which began with the Victorians) of novels as primers for behavior. From the get-go, *Less* eschews some of the sobriquets that have been lobbed at Arthur himself as a writer, "a bad gay," as another gay novelist tells him, for making his characters sad, morose, and doomed to suffer. True, the novel begins in tragic mode, but it quickly becomes a happy picaresque.

What an enviable journey! From San Francisco to Mexico to Turin to Berlin and onward to Kyoto, Arthur barnstorms from one conference and prize ceremony and teaching gig to the next, quaffing local drinks, meeting the local writers, falling gratefully into one hotel room after the other, all deftly described by Greer. During the period that Greer wrote and published *Less*, he was working at the retreat of the beloved salonnière Beatrice Monti della Corte Rezzori, the Baronessa, as she is known, and he describes the peculiarly twenty-first-century manner of literary hosting with exquisite accuracy.

There's also a sharp satire here of our modern literary world, which in the past couple of decades has domesticated novelists into accoutrements of luxury, dragging them blinking and confused like posh Pnins into the light of one international festival after another. Encumbered by an unadmitted monolingualism, Arthur is as comically tongue-tied into bumbling ineptitudes as Nabokov's character was in American academe. "I am fear of the old, I am fear of the lonely," Arthur blurts out in German at one point.

Gradually, the existential dilemma hiding behind Arthur's itinerary begins to loom in the foreground. How do you live in a new age bracket with the skills of the previous one? Arthur isn't so vain that he simply wants to hang onto youth: He wants to clasp on to a hard-won sense of how to be. "Strange to be almost fifty, no?" a handsome man on the cusp of midlife tells Arthur while the writer is on a layover in Paris. "I feel like I just understood how to be young."

"Yes!" Arthur replies. "It's like the last day in a foreign country. You finally figure out where to get coffee, and drinks, and a good steak. And then you have to leave. And you won't ever be back."

This exchange is so typical of *Less*, in which Arthur's endless journey proceeds at a madcap pace, its darts of mortal seriousness disguised as punch lines. Around the world we go, buffeted by champagne, maladroit translations, and a proliferation of travel sickness. "This isn't a birthday," Arthur yells at one companion when another traveler in his group is felled by stomach upset in Morocco. "It's an Agatha Christie novel!"

Arthur protests, but this, in fact, is precisely what he signed up for when his ex-lover's wedding invitation arrived in the mail. Not a gay *Eat, Pray, Love* but something to mix up the routine of life before he settles into the routine of getting old and, like Brownburn, who remains mostly offstage, dying. Saying yes to a backlog of what he imagined were throwaway invitations draws Arthur out into the world, where, outside the hothouse of American literary reputations, he realizes what he already is, what he has been for some time now. A decent man, a fool, a lover, a traveler, a writer of books people actually read. A happy ending in a literary novel? How in the world did we forget we needed such crucial breezes?

COLORED TELEVISION

by Danzy Senna

Every other country's caste system always seems more absurd than one's own. At home, where we are steeped in a culture that transmutes its codes, the directives of caste can feel so ubiquitous that they can be mistaken for logic. *Elsewhere*, it's simply absurd. There are so many colors in Brazil's population, for instance, that the Portuguese Language Museum once dedicated an entire room to the dozens of descriptives Brazilian novelist Jorge Amado uses in his novels to identify the skin tones of his various characters, from "green" and "blue" to "cinnamon." And of course, social apartheid exists there today, very much of it based on ideas about color.

All these skin colors and more exist within America, too, and because whiteness seems to swirl in perpetual peril, the minute someone in America identifies as biracial, especially Black and white, an entire mythology boots up. One of this mythology's central strains is the well-worn trope of the "tragic mulatto," a piece of cultural coding that surfaces and emerges in literature about characters who are Black and white, from Harriet Beecher Stowe's *Uncle Tom's Cabin* to Philip Roth's *The Human Stain*, characters who seek acceptance in the white world only to be thwarted and brought down by the discovery of—or character of—their Blackness.

How many directions this briefly sketched trajectory skips. For what if a fictive biracial woman were to turn to her Black ancestors? What if Blackness were, in fact, a source of strength? More important, what if, rather than seek acceptance from a white establishment, she turned to a burgeoning Black institutional culture—even if it is tied to white funding—for approval? Danzy Senna has spent her career as a writer sapping the unsleeping bombs of racial tropes, and in her explosive, hilarious new book, *Colored Television*, she allows for these land mines as she rewrites racial comedy, and says a few things about class, too.

Jane, the book's heroine, is a struggling novelist and professor, mother of two, daughter of a mixed New England marriage who grew up in boho poverty. Her precarious childhood seeded a deep longing within her for stability, and her formative years in front of the television have made her particularly swoony to the images of Black opulence filling up the big screen and the little one on her Instagram feed. It hasn't helped that, living in Los Angeles with her Black artist husband, Lenny, who makes no money selling his abstract paintings, everyday things—a house, a car, air, light, shade—cost far more than a novelist makes, even one with tenure, which Jane doesn't have at the moment.

What Jane does have is a sabbatical and rich friends. How wise this book is about the fickle vibes of wealthy friends. Their extravagant gestures can sweep enormous change into a family like Lenny and Jane's, lifting them up to a higher shore, and just as easily and abruptly retract these gifts, yanking them back out to financial sea. The entirety of *Colored Television* takes place during one such tidal window, as the couple and their two kids, Ruby and Finn, move to the Hollywood Hills into the architecturally significant home of Jane's vastly successful writing school friend Brett, also biracial, who has made a small fortune writing and showrunning zombie series.

Lenny and Jane, who are from different social classes, respond in contrasting ways to their new, borrowed life. Lenny, the child of Black professionals, who has a secret love of tennis and an ability to code-switch into country club manners, sets up his studio and keeps painting. The house doesn't turn his head one bit. Jane claims Brett's outdoor writing lab and begins to spiral. Her overdue and out-of-control novel, a kind of unified field theory of what she calls the mulattoes, spanning the Melungeons of Appalachia to well-known TV figures, suddenly seems like the Frankenstein's monster it is. Even as she works, she is drowning in self-doubt.

Writing is not the only perilous part of this "new" life. Stepping into social life should have come with a hazard sign—not for their kids but for Jane. In simple activities, like taking their kids to playdates, Jane confronts a barrage of social signifiers, all of which Senna skewers better than any novelist working on the West Coast. The strollers that look like Volvos; the brittleness of white middle-aged women in their adopted neighborhood. "Women who had not made enough money to send their kids to private school but who made just enough to live in this neighborhood with the blue ribbon public school."

Everything costs more. Rather than confront this, Jane evades it, pretending the house is hers, that the life she has essentially slipped on like one of the muumuus in Brett's wife's closet isn't on loan but nearly part of her skin. *Colored Television* paces the escalation of these lies brilliantly: how one fib makes another bald-faced one more possible. When Jane's agent and an editor turn down her novel, it becomes easy to let Lenny think otherwise. This is, as they might say in television, the inciting incident. Her willingness to forestall acceptance of her failure produces an even balder lie or betrayal.

Betrayal is probably the better word, because one night, chatting with Brett, lying about the state of her novel, Jane learns that he might finally write about growing up biracial. Jane, annoyed, since he'd always avoided the subject before, decides she's going to also borrow this idea and pitches it to Brett's TV agent, whose business card lies on his desk. In contrast to the decade Jane had spent waiting on her novel, she wakes to an email in the morning and a request for a meeting. Just like that, her fortune begins to turn, and all it took was betraying her art and her friend and lying to her husband about it.

In her debut novel, *Caucasia*, published when she was just twenty-seven, Senna narrated this constant push and pull from a child's-eye perspective. It was not that her protagonist had to choose to be white or Black, to turn her back on one or the other, but rather that she was constantly observing a set of instructions—as if she only needed to know what to do. "In those years, I felt myself to be incomplete," Senna wrote in *Caucasia*—"a gray blur, a body in motion, forever galloping toward completion—half a girl, half-caste, half-mast, and half-baked, not quite ready for consumption."

In her subsequent novels and one memoir, Senna has explored the ways that biracial Americans are often expected to narrate that evolution, often to undo the supposed lie of Black and white races intertwining. As if to say, How could people of different shades be together? How could love and impression be so . . . inseparable? "When there is a gap—between your face and your race, between the baby and the mother," she wrote in the novel *New People*, "between your body and yourself—you are expected, everywhere you go, to explain the gap."

At what point borrowing equals theft is one of the key moral questions that *Colored Television* revolves around, deepening the meaning of what is stolen, as in not offered. Talking to television producers in her meetings, Jane senses them fracking for emotional material. In meeting after meeting, she is so desperate that she begins to serve up morsels of her life for the sake of securing a deal with a major entertainment network.

This burlesque earns her a meeting with with a famous Black producer, Hampton Ford, who is fresh off the success of a show and has just inked a seven-figure development deal to provide more *content*. With his high-tech sneakers, expensive T-shirts, constant projected patter, and externalized thinking processes, Hampton is one of the best portraits of what a Hollywood producer is like up close, especially when their own reputations—however huge—hinge on the next deal.

Making Hampton's task all the more stressful, for him and for Jane, is that it goes without saying that what he wants her to make is *Biracialism for Dummies*. The money man he needs to sell the show to is white, and many of the viewers he will have to win over are white too. How Hampton talks to Jane has nothing to do with how the characters will be allowed to talk on the show.

To measure up to Hampton's task, to provide a money man with a new idea, Jane becomes a veritable hurricane of ideas for episodes of a sitcom about a mixed-race family. As these pilot ideas grow more and more outlandish, it's clear that what Jane will ultimately have to harvest is not her life, her dreams, scrambled-up versions of her fears and desires, but her sweat and blood. Her ten-years-in-the-making novel. It will need to get fed into the idea whirlpool too.

Watching Jane harvest all of the most meaningful aspects of her life for the ravenous "content" industry of Hollywood makes delicious and brutal reading. The Hollywood writer story as soft zombie story. Bitten by the bug of aspirational culture, Jane can't stop chasing what—even when she has it, if borrowed—is unattainable. It's not acceptance that Jane wants. It's the stuff. Looking into Brett's glass-walled home, observing Lenny watching TV, her kids quietly playing, Jane should be wowed by the image. Instead, she fears loss. Skittering along the surfaces of scenes is a barely contained terror that she'll never have what she wants.

Colored Television is a powerful portrait of what money does to a marriage when it works its way into the foundations like so much groundwater. At times, Jane understandably resents Lenny's easy assumption that everything will be OK. His background made that feeling possible.

Meanwhile, he watches her changing and starts raising the possibility that they move to Japan, what Jane calls "the witness protection program lifestyle that Lenny craved for them." He wants to uproot the kids not just from Los Angeles but from America at large, and it's hard to blame him. Were Jane not so astutely drawn as a character, it would be easy to pin their unraveling marriage on her for refusing.

For anyone who has ever felt the undertow of impostor syndrome, *Colored Television* may provide cold comfort. The reasons Jane can't leave LA, can't stop giving ideas to Hampton until she's given him everything, have to do with her desire to achieve something that is hers. She has spent a decade pumping her best ideas into teaching students. Nearly every pathway to her writing studio has been interrupted by something to do for the kids; Lenny takes care of them too, but not in an equal manner, which has lit a burning fuse of resentment. It's not that she wants it all, but Jane wants pleasure, she wants luxury, she wants relief.

Colored Television takes its title from the corny old Black TV shows Lenny and Jane used to watch when they were first together, when the future was unscarred by disappointment. Like the "belly-rubbing" R&B Jane likes to listen to, they're a guilty pleasure, overwrought, outlandish, but real in that they acknowledge the ridiculousness of simply expressing oneself through a mask.

The saddest part of *Colored Television* is that the times Jane starts to feel most like she's doing that is when she's speaking to her husband. Intricately, the novel avoids in its plotting a question of who is at fault. Instead, as the stakes of Jane's lies grow—the ones she tells to Lenny about her book, what she's working on—we are drawn simultaneously into the inner narrative of Jane's life, as seen in the images that bewitch her.

These can be humble tableaux, like the ones prompted by visiting an open house in Jane's favorite neighborhood in the city. Jane and Lenny have been subletting or house-sitting nomads for nearly a decade. Isn't it time for them, Jane wonders, to find a permanent home for their kids? Other images are highly specific. Almost comical. Later, during a camping trip to Joshua Tree to recapture the zest in their marriage, Jane looks up into the open desert sky and "felt like a white girl in a Mountain Dew commercial."

These images storyboard Jane's inner life in *Colored Television*. They are part advertising, part filmic set pieces, and all come with a form of subtle instruction. "The thing about being a woman," Jane concludes at one point, "a mother, a wife, was that if you wanted to be any more than those things you had to hire another wife. . . . Rich women got to pay somebody else to be them—a stunt double to make it look like they were doing everything well when, in fact, they were doing only the fun parts."

The ways that envy, longing, and fury feed off one another in *Colored Television* is so sophisticated, so raw, and so like a current that the novel makes an overwhelming case that only fiction gets us inside the experience of experience. Television may entertain. It may do so elegantly or with crude, broad humor. But only the novel immerses like this, makes us feel submerged in the forces moving around Jane, tugging her this way and that. In the end, Jane has to make a decision—whether she'll heed this latest call to represent her life, or live it. She might be new at the game, but the TV writer in Jane knows what ending to give readers.

VII
THE STATE
OF POETRY

ON CITY LIGHTS AT FERLINGHETTI'S 100TH

We didn't drive in over the bridge. That was one surprise. I remember thinking we'd see the Transamerica Pyramid piercing the fog or the bay sparkling in the distance. Instead, when I first visited San Francisco in the 1980s, we arrived by tunnel. The BART train from Berkeley spat us out into the noisy, echoing canyon of Market Street downtown. This was 1984, the city in near collapse, AIDS a full-blown crisis—the Reagan administration mocking its sufferers. As my family trudged up Kearny, we were stopped every few paces. Men so derelict they barely wore clothes asked us for money, food, *anything*. You'll encounter destitution like this in the city today; tech wealth merely rivers around the derelict. But it was worse then. To my child's eye, it seemed apocalyptic. How could a city pretend it wasn't so?

By midday we stumbled into a bookstore. Perched on the corner of Columbus and Broadway, City Lights emerged from the murk like an oasis. Stepping into the shop, I recall thinking it had a very different idea of what we needed to drink. Books about revolution, the theft of the North American continent, and community action sprawled over several levels. Poetry had an entire floor. I may have been ten, but my parents were radicals; I could recognize the tribal hallmarks of left-wing thought. Everywhere you looked, there were the city's problems, written about in books. In Broadside poems. In slogans sketched right onto the shop walls. The store was promising an escape by showing you how to escape *back* into social engagement. I'd never been anywhere like it.

In 2019, I went back because not only was the store still open—it was thriving. So was its eternally hip hundred-year-old cofounder, the poet, publisher, and community activist Lawrence Ferlinghetti. With America trapped in the fever dream of its most mendacious government in a century, lurching toward one of the worst decades in, well, decades, Ferlinghetti's call to revolutionary action was and is more relevant than ever. Also, with hashtag resistance becoming a kind of social media meme, it's worth remembering that no one in American letters has ever pushed back against power through words as a poet, bookseller, and publisher, over such a long time, quite like Ferlinghetti. Reading his 1958 million-selling volume of poems, *A Coney Island of the Mind*, generations woke up to the nightmare of the military-industrial complex in America. In City Lights, the first all-paperback bookstore in the country, readers found fellow travelers at cheap prices. From City Lights Books, publisher of everything from Allen Ginsberg's "Howl" to Rebecca Solnit's first book to a then recent title on drone strikes, an engagement with the moral values of empire kicked off and never stopped.

It's an aging history, to some degree, judging by Ferlinghetti's 100th birthday celebration, or maybe I just came for the early part of the shindig. For the longest time, City Lights was a young person's holy site. That Sunday afternoon, though, the store was crammed with people in their fifties, sixties, seventies, and older. Many men wore hats—bowlers, watch caps, fedoras, berets, even cowboy hats. The young were, at least early in the day, outnumbered. Following a rousing opening address from Elaine Katzenberger, the store's director, the day began with a reading of a Ferlinghetti poem by eighty-six-year-old Michael McClure, one of the five poets who'd been on the bill for the famous Six Gallery reading that Kenneth Rexroth emceed in 1955, which scholars often pinpoint as the start of the Beat Movement. The other four were Ginsberg, Gary Snyder, Philip Lamantia, and Philip Whalen. Ferlinghetti published Ginsberg and Lamantia in the store's Pocket Poet series. Jack Hirschman, eighty-five-year-old former San Francisco poet laureate, followed, reading Ferlinghetti's great poem "The Sea," in "which he gives death a kick in the ass at age ninety," Hirschman's voice the gravely sound of the Ancient Mariner.

Over the next six hours, North Beach—the still-scuzzy neighborhood of strip clubs and Italian eateries that City Lights barnacled itself onto—hosted a daylong celebration. I wandered into Cafe Zoetrope down the street from the store and listened to one of America's most exciting young poets, sam sax, reading Ferlinghetti's great poem "Dog," which follows an animal across the city, "looking / like a living questionmark / into the great gramaphone / of puzzling existence / with its wondrous hollow horn." A group of actors performed one of Ferlinghetti's interventionist plays from the 1960s in Jack Kerouac Alley. Former US poet laureate and longtime Berkeley resident Robert Hass talked about the way that having Ferlinghetti in the Bay Area was like having a benevolent sun forever shining, making seeing clearly possible. Ishmael Reed showed up, and Paul Beatty too, although he was just watching. As the chill burned off, more young people appeared and the store became what it always is—a many-ventricled heart, pumping out light and ideas.

Ferlinghetti wasn't around. The all-male choir the Conspiracy of Beards sang him "Happy Birthday" shortly after dawn, serenading him in his North Beach apartment from the street. He came to the window, natty as ever, wearing a red scarf, and waved. For a person at the center of things, he was, as always, a little off to the side, eschewing the light—preferring instead to reflect it. You see this in the work. *Ferlinghetti's Greatest Poems*, published by New Directions in 2017, covers an astonishing sixty years of production, and no matter where you dip into the book, there's a cascading movement across and through the day's darkest events—Vietnam, the ecocidal creep of climate change—back into lightness. Like Walt Whitman, Ferlinghetti writes a long, prosy poetic line, but its "I" is softer, stranger, and less verbose. His lineation steps across the pages with sudden, perfectly timed enjambments that allow for swerves toward desire, wonder, and mourning.

The magic of Ferlinghetti's writing exists entirely in those transitions. They allow for his politics never to become the hinge on which the door of a poem swings, but rather something larger and more eternally humane, even hopeful. In "Two Scavengers in a Truck, Two Beautiful People in a Mercedes," the poem smashes together two opposite social classes at a red light and, briefly, finds a chink of optimism in that sudden juxtaposition: "all four close together / as if anything at all were possible / between them / across that small gulf / in the high seas / of this democracy." In America, one hundred years after the revolutions of modernism, Ferlinghetti is a hard poet to place. Unlike T. S. Eliot, whose "The Waste Land" he revered, Ferlinghetti was deeply allergic to the idea of art for art's sake. Simultaneously, unlike the confessionalists, like Sylvia Plath and Robert Lowell, whose lives unfolded alongside his own, he was skeptical of the self and ego and mythologizing.

The key to how Ferlinghetti found a line between these poles was his time in France. It was to France he went on the GI bill for a graduate degree at the Sorbonne, and where he read in great depth the surrealists, like André Breton and Antonin Artaud, both of whom he'd later publish. He also read Jacques Prévert, whose *Paroles* was published in 1948 and which Ferlinghetti translated for the first time into English (publishing it in the Pocket Poet series). Prévert's playful realism, his rhythmic repetition of lines, such as in "Barbara" ("in the rain" appears three times in the short poem), and his bent conception of the real are all also hallmarks of Ferlinghetti's own work. Asked once by Dwight Garner of the *New York Times* about the Beats,

Ferlinghetti named their only committed surrealist, William S. Burroughs, as the best writer of that generation.

Ferlinghetti's affinity to Burroughs wasn't just artistic, though—it was generational. The two of them were born a decade *before* Ginsberg, Kerouac, and Snyder. Born Lawrence Ferling in Yonkers, New York, in 1919, he'd been sent off to France as infant. His father had died, and his mother had been committed to an insane asylum. (He later restored his original family name.) Ferlinghetti didn't learn English until he returned to America at age five with his aunt. She raised him in a suburb of New York City, where she worked on an estate as a governess. She later abandoned him, and he stayed with other family members until the stock market crash of 1929, when he was taken in by yet another family, which sent him to boarding school after he was caught stealing.

Though technically an orphan twice over, he somehow wound up with degrees from the University of North Carolina, Columbia University, and the Sorbonne, when the cultural capital of the world was shifting from France to the US. His patriotism had carried him there: In World War II, he captained a submarine on D-Day, but when he saw with his own eyes in Nagasaki what the atomic bomb had done, he instantly became a pacifist. He stayed away long enough that he had begun, like so many expats, to identify with elsewhere. "When I arrived in San Francisco, I was still wearing my French beret," Ferlinghetti once told me, laughing, in an interview. "The Beats hadn't arrived yet. I was seven years older than Ginsberg and Kerouac, all of them except Burroughs. And I became associated with the Beats by later publishing them."

He wound up a bookseller almost by accident. A friend, Peter Martin, had been publishing a literary journal called *City Lights*, after the Charlie Chaplin film, and needed revenue to keep the magazine afloat. Martin suggested opening a bookstore, an idea Ferlinghetti loved because he had just returned from Paris where books were sold from stalls along the Seine as if they were loaves of bread. It turned out to be a savvy business decision. City Lights opened at the height of the paperback book revolution, in a city crawling with avid readers.

"We were filling a big need," Ferlinghetti once told the *New York Times Book Review*: "City Lights became about the only place around where you could go in, sit down and read books without being pestered to buy something. That's one of the things it was supposed to be. Also, I had this idea that a bookstore should be a center of intellectual activity, and I knew it was a natural for a publishing company, too."

While some of the Beats drank their talent away, Ferlinghetti worked diligently on his own poems. His second collection was *A Coney Island of the Mind* (1958). Its jazzy, scabrous rhythms resonated with a generation of antiestablishment readers, especially these bardic lines of resistance:

> I am waiting for my number to be called
> and I am waiting
> for the living end
> and I am waiting
> for dad to come home
> his pockets full
> of irradiated silver dollars
> and I am waiting
> for the atomic tests to end

This message eventually reached more than a million readers, making *A Coney Island of the Mind* one of the best-selling poetry volumes of the twentieth century. The book trails Ferlinghetti like a friendly ghost. It also bought him the space to continue experimenting. In the 1960s alone he published his first novel (*Her*), an environmental manifesto, a broadside about Vietnam, a book of a dozen plays, and his own Whitmanesque third collection, *Starting Out from San Francisco*, which landed in advance of the hippy movement with a kind of warning that with liberation-lite comes responsibility. "As I approach the state of pure euphoria / I find I need a large size typewriter case / to carry my underwear in and scars on my conscience."

One of Ferlinghetti's talents was his ability to be a public and private poet at once. In the 1960s and 1970s, his poems appeared in the *San Francisco Examiner*, sometimes on the front page, as they did when Harvey Milk was assassinated. For decades you could find him in Caffe Trieste, writing, as Francis Ford Coppola later did. He traveled widely, as 2015's *Writing Across the Landscape: Travel Journals 1960–2010* made clear, with its dispatches from Spain, Latin America, Haiti, Cuba—where he witnessed Castro's revolution—and Tibet. But Ferlinghetti always came back to North Beach. His lovely poem from the 1970s, "Recipe for Happiness Khabarovsk or Anyplace," is a kind of melding of the cosmopolitan world and the one you'll find today at Caffe Trieste.

> One grand boulevard with trees
> with one grand cafe in the sun
> with strong black coffee in very small cups.
>
> One not necessarily very beautiful
> man or woman who loves you.
>
> One fine day.

And so it was March twenty-fourth, the day of Ferlinghetti's 100th birthday, an uncharacteristically bright un–San Francisco blue. There was even a pause—or so it seemed—in the never-ending welter of the president's hysterical attention ploys. As the sun dipped below the horizon, and the aging beatniks drove back to Marin or wherever they live now, I left some friends at a bar and walked up past City

Lights, expecting to find a wreck, or at least the telltale signs of dissipation. Instead, the rolling bookcases had been pushed back into place, the interior lights illuminated, people browsed. Here was the thirty-and-under crowd, lingering to do what a bookstore is for: explore. Moving about in the light Ferlinghetti had brought to the Bay and kept lit, so others could see the wreck we'd made of the world—and also, hopefully, the way to repair it.

POSTCOLONIAL LOVE POEM

by Natalie Diaz

The great poets are always expanding the language of love. Like Mahmoud Darwish when he wrote of home with words clipped by the blade of desire, or Lucille Clifton when she sang the body electric of women not seen, women the world had tried to stop. In the 1980s, before she conjured *A House on Mango Street*, Sandra Cisneros made every heartsick person staring at the moon feel less alone, especially when they were alone. And in the 1990s, after Communism collapsed, Wisława Szymborska revealed that within restraint too old to unlearn, steam yet rose, or as she put it: "Our teacups know full well / why the tea is getting cold."

It's unlikely another book will enlarge the language of love in our time like Natalie Diaz's *Postcolonial Love Poem*. Here is a linguistic house of worship big enough for anyone who deserves or needs tenderness, especially those who have been told they are not worthy of it. Diaz's word-music is joyous, erotic, sometimes even spiritual. What else is devotion, after all, but endless love? She writes of thirst, because "the ache of thirst . . . translates to all bodies along the same paths." We are not, Diaz's poems assure, our parching; we are our thirst.

That thirst takes many forms in *Postcolonial Love Poem*, from the dryness of a country unseen by rain, to the feel of growing up in want in a nation that had tried to erase her as a Native person, to wanting to be touched. Needing to be touched. The varieties of meaning of Diaz's theme do not deplete it, but rather form within the book a root structure, one that each poem travels down, sometimes overlapping and entangling with other poems. Aboveground, this book is a mere 105 pages. Beneath, though, the volume is vast, full of unexpected aquifers and sudden caves of space.

The widest root in the book grows from the title poem, in which Diaz—raised in Needles, where it gets to 120 degrees in the summer, commonly—powerfully claims "parched" as a legacy and performs the first of several forceful inversions, showing how even an inherited language—a colonial language—can ignite a thirst, a desire to be seen, for contact, awakening possibilities for postcolonial life right before it. "I learned Drink in a country of drought," she writes, continuing:

> There are wildflowers in my desert
> which take up to twenty years to bloom.
> The seeds sleep like geodes beneath hot feldspar sand
> until a flash flood bolts the arroyo, lifting them
> in its copper current, opens them with memory—
> they remember what their god whispered
> into their ribs: *Wake up and ache for your life.*

Postcolonial Love Poem speaks to that ache, sings to it in lyrics that invite the body's response. If you long for a homeland, or for a family, or for a lover, the language you use to say how overlaps and intertwines—the ache for one can feel like the other. In a lyric essay at the heart of the book, Diaz ponders whether this instinct to claim a homeland is preverbal—whether we are always translating back toward that original urge: a dilemma constantly on the mind of anyone using

English as a colonial language, which is most of us, but especially those forced into some form of exile by colonial states.

Patiently, bravely, Diaz refuses to untangle these braidings, choosing instead to dwell in their complexities. In some instances, that means Diaz repeats words until they are hollow, strange even; in other moments, she rescues them from meaninglessness, or from (solely) their meaning in English. Why are tears not called *alacranes*, the Spanish word for "scorpions"? Why not recall that *manhattan* is a Lenape word? Or that "sometimes race means run"?

In her 2012 debut, *When My Brother Was an Aztec*, Diaz demonstrated a near-mastery of lineation and enjambment, which enabled her to create and tell stories with the shapeliness of narrative, all while moving poetically across space and time, using a dazzling associative logic that opened up powerful fields of desire, longing, and regret. In one of the book's later poems, she demonstrates how a dissociated language can also lead right back to the heart of the matter, as when writing about love and war.

> What is a wall if not a thing to be pressed against?
> What is a bedroom if not an epicenter
> of pillage? And what can I do with a hundred houses
> but abandon them as spent shells of desire?

Postcolonial Love Poem never turns its head from the way the language of war, of empire, creeps into our most personal spaces. The book produces this disquiet and refuses to defuse it, as in one poem set in Manhattan:

> Somewhere far from New York City,
> an American drone finds then loves
> a body—the radiant nectar it seeks
> through great darkness—makes

>   a candle-hour of it, and burns
>   gently along it, like American touch,
>   an unbearable heat.

The instability of Diaz's imagery, its double-sidedness, is part of the postcolonial condition. In some poems, the lexicon of a beloved leads to hives and bee smoking, honey and sweetness. In another poem, that very nectar is the juice of war. This simultaneity produces immense torque in *Postcolonial Love Poem*, a feeling like danger, like risk.

Forms of address matter intensely here, as they often do in love poems. At the core of *Postcolonial Love Poem* is a series of poems to a beloved, whose hips, whose body, rise and recede in a way that is visceral and cinematic, yet equally private. Diaz's language is refracted by other forms of landscape and longing, and even routine:

>   I will enter the door of your throat,
>   hang my last lariat in the hallway,
>   build my altar of best books on your bedside table,
>   turn the lamp on and off, on and off, on and off.

A love poem is popularly thought to be a lyric—addressed to an offstage you. Diaz recalls all the other forms that can house love too. Sometimes a portrait poem can be a love poem—simply by virtue of the close attention it pays to another person, to their habits and qualities, to their way of being. On other occasions, so can something as killer as a half-joking list, for the way it does something similar, yoking together a group of people by paying attention to a world they created, one linked by a way of seeing, by inside jokes. Take "Top Ten Reasons Why Indians Are Good at Basketball," which includes, "Indians are not afraid to try sky hooks in real games, even though no Indian has ever made a sky hook, no Indian from a federally recognized tribe, anyway."

Postcolonial Love Poem is a sublime book. It is also, occasionally, hilarious. It finds in its wordplay moments of absurdity, a humor so grim it tips through darkness into a new shade of light, a breakthrough in a time of war, of suffering, in which so many of us ache for something other than violence. What else holds us like laughter? Like the memory of love? To read Diaz's poems is to surface out of memory into living, complete with the wound of existence, the thirst of it, the ache, the sweetness.

ON ADA LIMÓN

What is it poets are for these days? Increasingly, in a world where brevity matters, verse-makers are anywhere words are under pressure—which is everywhere. At school, in church, in the town square. It's not an accident that June Jordan's and Mahmoud Darwish's lines decorate protest marches. Their poems were, after all, a record of revolutionary consciousness. Not all poetry is public, though. As we saw with Natalie Diaz, even poetry addressed to us, toward us, the reader, depends on privacy. It depends on partial viewership, on interiority, on hour upon hour of time spent alone, out of which comes, perhaps, just one poem. In a world of hacking and constant drilling for social capital, the poet who can offer us the feeling of lived experience backlit by intimacy without giving (or demanding) everything—without selling us on his or her or their self—is offering something so precious that the word *luxury* comes to mind, were that word not so degraded by its attachment to goods alone.

One of the most dependable providers of this feeling is Ada Limón, whose sixth collection, *The Hurting Kind*, was published in 2022. Like Sharon Olds and Pablo Neruda, the poets she most resembles, and clearly learned from, Limón writes as a hyperporous lover of the world. She loves the Sonoma she comes from. She is a lover of men, of animals—the dogs in her life must sleep like angels—and of experience. For the heart-squeamish, there might be too much figurative saxophone in her work; that's no matter. She has learned how to speak in many languages of love. Love is not simply, in Limón's poems, an overwhelming form of desire; it is also an issue of belonging, of loyalty, of familiarity and friendship. The sheer intensity of her work has made it imperative that she parse these values from longing, from nostalgia, from memory, from grief and guilt.

Keeping up this intensity across six books has been a thing to behold, like watching a fire juggler who has never stopped, not for twenty-five years. It is, in fact, quite a radical posture, too, in a culture that treats time as a mineral and behavior as always optimizable, for a poet to again and again throw herself into the breach. "What I have / done," she writes in the 2015 National Book Award finalist *Bright Dead Things*, "is risked everything for that hour, / that hour in the black night, where one / flashing light looks like love."

One has to think of singers to come even close to this absolute fealty to love, to actionable passion. In this sense, Ada Limón is not the poet you give your friend with a subscription to the *Economist*; she is, however, the poet you give to a friend who had Dolly Parton or Tina Turner on their answering machine. Limón's poems are not manuals for love any more than are Turner's or Parton's songs, let alone Jordan's or Darwish's love poems—which are among their best. But Limón's are records of a heart's revolution. Touch even an old one, like the incredible "Miles Per Hour," which appears in her 2006 debut, *Lucky Wreck*, and you can feel its heat still, hear its pounding.

> that throbbing in the middle of my eyes
> when we knew it was over, all of it and yet
> we were still in the car, still going to meet
> the family and when we pulled over on
> Old Sonoma Road under the tree to make

love once more before the parental hand
shake made love more difficult . . .

What happens to aging troubadours, though? Anyone over thirty knows that passion requires risk and, well, an increasing amount of stretching. But can this receptivity to longing be sustained—without becoming a reflex? Or a form of decadence that shades toward lubricity? How does passion live in a heart tended by the slow-stoked fires of domesticity? In practicality—or even in regard to energy—these are not easy musings. In terms of art, these questions have plagued poets of love since the beginning of time.

If in life there are arsonists of love, addicts of love, and mathematicians of love, Limón has proved that you can temporarily be all of the above and more if you permit yourself to also question the fundamental place of a human in the world. From the beginning of her work, as she has tracked her heart's orientation, she has slipped in and out of the skin of various animals, imagined herself from one element to another, perched herself on the branches of the trees surrounding her, and tuned her animal ear to *all* life about her, like some "creek-thing" who grew up with "gobo-leaf prints on my bare limbs."

As a result of this constant tuning, Limón's work ripples with an animal's vigilance. Her poems pull you in close to their "conch-dark night" to better ponder the moral eddies of a nation when "this country's gone standstill and criminal." She beckons readers to hear with her "the massive ocean inside me" and to peer up at the "clowned-out clouds," to see the "flashlight-white eyes" of cats in the brush, to sniff "the burnt-meat smell / of midweek cookouts" and follow with her a groundhog "slippery and waddle thieving my tomatoes."

This richness gives a hint to the bestiary that lives within Limón's work, which has a species depth so broad it deserves its own Attenborough special. Her poems are full of bats, dolphins, dogs, horses, koi, cranes, and snakes, both benign and not. There are possums and fireflies, peacocks and hawks, deer, mice, crows, and eagles, the aforementioned groundhog, and still more birds—of every possible variety under the sun—from cormorants to "cardinals brash and bold / as sin in a leafless tree."

The bestiary is at once metaphorical and cosmological, qualities of force that entreat us to understand love not simply as attraction, as regard, but as a compulsion in nature that desires to connect: Think of it as where E. M. Forster (whose fictional motto was "Only connect") crosses over with Louise Erdrich. ("Some people meet the way the sky meets the earth," she wrote in her book *Tales of Burning Love*.) Creating this magnetic field, rather than just belting saxophone riffs from its sway, is where Limón the love poet pierces the lip of something vast, and eternal.

In this way, Limón's deepening appreciation for—her receptivity to—nature gives way to a meditation on how longing transforms us; it's also the ultimate way to sidestep the risk of staking a poetic life on love. This is not to say that passion recedes or that the poems grow chilly. As Limón's books progress, we watch her, in one thread, growing up and older, leaving home, falling in love, losing family and friends, then, in time, parts of her body, and learning to love in a different way. She finds her beloved and then moves to Lexington, Kentucky, for a job he's taken. They try for a child. Simply marking this trail across her work would be flatly autobiographical. Instead, parts left for us, as readers, feel like honesty, and a charting of how love asks different things of us romantically as we age.

Beneath the surface of these islands of autobiography, an alluvial power spreads, deepens, forms caverns and pools. Its greatest source is the energy unlocked by Limón's third book, *Sharks in the Rivers* from 2010, in which she roams across the rivers of her life, from the Russian in California to the Skagit up in Washington state, contemplating "what impossible longing" brings the oak and the manzanita to water. She studies a bird outside her window, whom she names Stanley, and wonders why she is not more like him, "as if wings themselves could be willed." Strange, wonderful, pleasurably hard to pin down, the book is an attempt to claim this spirit, to say from the beginning that we are creatures: "You are part weather, part flower-leaf waving," she writes, angling into an oracular mode that has stayed with her ever since. "So / much of America," she riffs, "belongs to the trees."

"Body of Rivers," one of Limón's finest poems to date, emerges in this project, carving a study of will and longing into the language of the riverine.

> The river comes to the body bold,
> dreaming of black hues and a gestured
> cluster of colored fish. This is the way
> the world runs through us, its instruments of moon-
> water and hangnails of hope.

With time, Limón has found a way to merge her slightly loquacious, headlong style with the galloping confidence of these fable-like poems in which the elements are given agency and personality equal to those of humans, and humans are seen caught up in our built environment, our cathedrals of shame and technology. In her strongest work, this scrambling of signals leads to moments of almost unbearable emotional clarity, especially when Limón is writing on what Jack Gilbert called the "great fires" of life: love and regret, longing and grief. In other words, questions of survival.

In *Bright Dead Things*, her fourth book, for the first time Limón is able to compress these styles together, in a series of poems mourning the death of her stepmother.

> Her job,
> her work, was to let the machine
> of survival break down,

>   make the factory fail,
>   to know that this war was winless,
>   to know that she would singlehandedly
>   destroy us all.

It's interesting to read Limón against a poet like Louise Glück in *Ararat*, also a book of mourning, the poems lengthening, loosening, but containing a flood and fury. Limón, by contrast, has more honky-tonk and spoken vernacular in her lines. "Sometimes, you have to look around at the life you've made and sort of nod at it, like someone moving their head up and down to a tune they like." In the wake of death, Limón watches desire bloom with fascination, writing of her own new love and her father's (as a widower) at the same time with this immortal phrase: "Still the bone / remembers, still it wants (so much, it wants) / the flesh back, the real thing."

In *The Carrying*, her fifth volume and the winner of the National Book Critics Circle Award for Poetry in 2018, shadows grow in her work where light once lurked. Fear brittles her lines, drying up their usual alluvial flow. Even long, devotional gardening poems, set in broad text-block shapes akin to that used by Robert Hass in *Meditation at Lagunitas*, cannot quite plunge their roots deep enough into ritual—what we now call self-care—to find hope there. A feeling is arising from within, spreading acid in the soil where Limón typically raked out poems of magic and nurturing, or wild gratitude. It's a fear that the world might be crueler than she had given it credit for being.

It's the rare poet who will follow such a grim thought, wherever it takes them. Limón, poet of moonlit bad decisions, has to learn, in *The Carrying*, all over again that there is a point at which hope ends and something else—not reality, but a fact of existence—takes over. Most painfully, in *The Carrying*, she learns this while trying and not managing to bear a child. The directness with which she writes of this journey, of its aftermath, of her rejuvenation, and the hardening of her attitude toward those who carelessly tell her she ought to have, should have, procreated, mark the book as a milestone in enlarging the sphere of the imaginary to meet the actual. Not having a child is not a failure; it is simply a fact.

What if we looked to the earth this way? "I am always superimposing / a face on flowers," Limón writes in *The Hurting Kind*, which arrived in a penumbra very different from that of her early work. Having already established the breezeway between human and animal in her older poems, the poems in *The Hurting Kind* benefit from Limón's easy fluency with the connection points between the two—and with the spirit level that runs beneath it all. "My beloved and I are lying in bed," she writes in "Forsythia," "talking about how we carry so many people with us wherever we go. . . . We are both expecting to hear an owl as the night deepens. All afternoon, from the porch, we watched an Eastern towhee furiously build her nest in the untamed forsythia with its yellow spilling out into the horizon."

All the animals of previous books are here, and more. The cats that, in *The Carrying*, she describes taking in after her husband's ex died; a fox; horses in foaling season, when they stand in twos all over the grass. As in other books, she relates the shock of finding dead animals on the road, or in the backyard. In one poem, she buries a fledgling dry-eyed, nursing this thought: "Seems like a good place for a close-eyed / thing."

If in previous work Limón aged desire by expanding its definition, out of the human and into longing and the animal world, *The Hurting Kind* reinterprets the elegy as part of a new evolution. In nature death is commonplace, and in observation we often breathe heavily on the wrong instrument: It's not our watching that gives breath to meaning but the turning of seasons, where lungs so huge they cannot be seen move the wind.

Cycling from spring into summer, and fall into winter, these new poems attempt to pace a natural world harassed by human handprints. The poet even feels tempted to turn away.

> I see it
> is not one tree but two, and they are
>
> kissing. They are kissing so tenderly
> it feels rude to watch, one hand
>
> on the other's shoulder, another
> in the other's branches, like hair.

    One of the greatest challenges of our time is to see the living world as having value beyond us. To acknowledge the damage done. What if, Limón appears to be asking in this wise book, the best we have made, the finest instrument we know, is our language of love? Are we really going to stand on ceremony and say, No, it's anthropomorphic thinking to apply it to these magnificent creatures all around us? Perhaps love is endless when you think of it that way: There is no aging out. No endpoint. No time in which you cannot sprawl across the car seat with heat. Who really wants to turn to a cypress and make it ask—had it the language—the question this fierce poet has asked herself, over and again, the first question of this book: "Why am I not allowed / delight?"

ON GARY SNYDER

In 1977, a few years after he'd won the Pulitzer Prize for his collection of poems *Turtle Island*, Gary Snyder passed through New York City. The colossal World Trade Center had been inaugurated. The city was mired in a deep depression, one that would culminate later that summer in the July blackout. It must have felt like a far cry from California. While on that trip, Snyder conducted an interview with Peter Barry Chowka, who was editing the *East West Journal*. They did it sitting in Allen Ginsberg's apartment, riding the heavily graffitied subway, and walking around the Village. Perhaps it was the movement or the rare combination of East-West kinship and curiosity, but Snyder gave one of his finest interviews. It began with a lucid description of how he'd fallen into a life in communion with nature. Nurturing a sense of wildness, within and without.

> When I was young, I had an immediate, intuitive, deep sympathy with the natural world, which was not taught me by anyone. In that sense, nature is my "guru" and life is my sadhana. That sense of the authenticity, completeness and reality of the natural world itself made me aware even as a child

of the contradictions that I could see going on around me in the state of Washington, in the way of exploitation, logging, development, pollution. I lived on the edge of logging country, and the trees were rolling by on the tops of trucks, just as they are still. My father was born and raised on the Kitsap County farm that my grandfather had homesteaded; he was a smart man, a very handy man, but he only knew about fifteen different trees and after that he was lost. I wanted more precision; I wanted to look deeper into the underbrush.

Snyder has been looking deeper for over eighty years now, on foot, by prop plane and aboard a dogsled, in cities but mostly not, with Indigenous elders and trackers, friends, fellow poets. He has done his probing perched on peaks, driving across deserts, and at home for the past fifty-plus years on the western slope of the northern Sierra Nevada near the Yuba River watershed. The record of this search, of the ceremonies Snyder has participated in and the animals and landscapes with which he has become acquainted, trails behind him in more than twenty numinous books. They are less the work of an explorer—who quarries for exceptional events—than a kind of practice, a form of mind that is also part of the gift of economy. Works of poetry and prose, translations, conversations with fellow travelers, and journals kept at sea, among so much else—this wide-ranging body of work reads like an offering in exchange for the hospitality the world itself has shown him.

Snyder's sensitivity to geography and our connections to land have made him one of the most vital poets in North American history. He is the fork in the road after modernism, where William Carlos Williams's key dictum, "No idea but in things," becomes a question: Well, what is a thing? Can that include me? Can that include language? Can that include everything in the world if the world also is expanded to nature? Drawing on decades of study of Zen Buddhism, a great deal of time spent out of doors, and close reading of Chinese and Japanese poetry, among other literatures, Snyder found ways to ask these questions. He used various languages for them, from the vernacular to the formal. Even though his poetic forms range from terse short lines to folding epics, like the book *Mountains and Rivers Without End*, he has a singular voice through it all: genial, trickster-y, keen-eyed, and humble. His work is as image rich as the Tang dynasty poets he read so closely and as musical as a work song.

To appreciate how steady this voice has been—how clear yet varied—it's worth looking at two of his most notable books, *Riprap and Cold Mountain Poems*, Snyder's very first collection, published (in two parts) in the late 1950s, and *The Practice of the Wild*, a stirring book of essays that dates to 1990. What the poems accomplish in language and sound, the essays open up in ideas and concepts with prose. This is not to say that poetry has no ideas but that neither the poetry of *Riprap*, Snyder's own work, nor the *Cold Mountain* poems of Han-shan, which he translates and includes, are that kind. At least not here. Composed of poems written on mountain peaks, at sea, and later in Japan, where Snyder traveled to study Zen Buddhism, the collection is a compelling interaction with the elemental world: the earth and its stones, water and ice, and the mind itself.

And it all began with a job in California. In the summer of 1955, after two years of studying Japanese and classical Chinese at Berkeley, Snyder packed himself off to Yosemite National Park to work as a trail-crew laborer. Surrounded by evidence of the ice age, exposed to the trance-inducing textures of bedrock, he found himself writing a very old kind of poem, which was a new one for him. A poem that he has said "surprised" him. "There are poets who claim that their poems are made to show the world through the prism of language. Their project is worthy. There is also the work of seeing the world *without* any prism of language, and to bring that seeing *into* language."

This description is a quintessential example of Snyder's trickster-y poetics, wherein the pathways of craft always lead back to questions of dharma—of the world and all that is. Snyder's greatness is the rigor with which he commits to this exploration. *Riprap* is certainly one of the most transcendent books ever written with such restricted syllabics. Composed under the influence of Chinese poetry, the short line Snyder adopted contains mostly monosyllabic words. Riprap, the book tells us, is "a cobble of stone laid on steep, / slick rock to make a trail for horses / in the mountains." And so we begin, in terse, lean, yet musical language, on a journey upward into the clouds.

The first poem, "Mid-August at Sourdough Mountain Lookout," begins with the poet on a peak, staring down a valley through "a smoke haze": "Pitch glows on the fir-cones / Across rocks and meadows / Swarms of new flies." Thanks to the assonance of all those *s*'s, you can actually hear the valley buzzing with insects. And thanks to the spareness of the line, it's also easy to remember—or imagine—what it feels like to look into a panoramic view. There are just two five-line stanzas in the poem—two commas and three periods. The word *I* doesn't appear until the second stanza, as if the view has obliterated or dwarfed the self. When it returns, it is nearly in the past tense: "I cannot remember things I once read / A few friends, but they are in cities." These lines were written years before W. S. Merwin would remove all the commas and periods from his own poems, yet here is Snyder demonstrating that with careful joinery, poetic lines will hang true without punctuation. Out of this decision would emerge a style. In later books, Snyder used warmer, more elaborate, and more direct or literary approaches, but his reliance on compound adjectives and article-free diction remained in his poetry—so, too, did adjectives without commas. It creates a hustling, spoken sound, one that is deeply American. In one poem, he writes of a "long old chorus" and in another of "high wild notes."

Perhaps this is one reason why Snyder is so good at writing about work. This book features one of the best poems he'd ever write on labor, "Hay for the Horses," which recounts a day the poet spends bucking hay alongside a farmer much older than he. "He had driven half the night / From far down San Joaquin / Through Mariposa, up the / Dangerous mountain roads" to simply get there to be able to work. It helps that Snyder clearly respects work and workers. He knows the rhythms of a day, how delicious a pause is when you've worked hard, and how talk then takes over. "At lunchtime under Black oak / Out in the hot corral, / —the old mare nosing lunch pails, / Grasshoppers crackling in the weeds—'I'm sixty-eight,' he said, / 'I first bucked hay when I was seventeen.'"

What a pleasing music these lines make, how much they mimic the feeling of what they're describing. "We stacked the bales up clean / To splintery redwood rafters / High in the dark, / flecks of alfalfa / whirling through shingle-cracks of light." Has there ever been a more balletic description of a body in motion? Like songs, Snyder's best poems and translations can be read and read again in close succession and deliver the same pleasure. You can hear the influence poetry from the East had on his ear. "A hill of pines hums in the wind," he translated Han-shan's words in *Cold Mountain*. Even rhyming couplets seem natural, not like a music box but rather a part of the elemental music. "In the thin loam, each rock a word / a creek-washed stone," he writes in *Riprap*. Because there are no ideas pressing down on the verse, we can simply observe with the mind's eye what Snyder wishes us to witness. At sea, where so many poets railed against the void, Snyder simply looks up at the starry sky and sees evidence of "the universe as playful, cool, and infinitely blank."

Snyder had come to Chinese poetry through Ezra Pound, who had popularized Ernest Fenollosa's critical text, *The Chinese Written Character as a Medium for Poetry*. It was a favorite little book of Ginsberg's. Fenollosa's ideas, though not in favor now, were hugely influential on the poets of his time. Snyder was one of the only ones to learn Chinese and Japanese well enough to begin translating these languages to the extent that he did. In another lifetime, he would have simply been a translator, and judging from his Han-shan renditions, he would have had a long and fruitful career doing just that. The best thing one can say about a good translator is that they are at least as good a writer as the lines require. Snyder is that and then some. Like all good translations of Han-shan, the poems re-create both the voice and the stillness, the poise of the line and their dart into paradox: "I've lost the shortcut home, / Body asking shadow, how do you keep up?" Placed side by side with his own work, *Cold Mountain* reveals Snyder ever more to be the hermit, but never does he presume to be the elder sage Han-shan was in his time. The music of the place is eerily similar, though. Pine trees sing in the window. Off the Cold Mountain trail, "Sharp cobbles—the icy creek bank. / Yammering, chirping—always birds. . . . Whip, whip—the wind slaps my face." These translations, begun in a Berkeley graduate seminar classroom, must have made a lot more sense to Snyder after his time in Yosemite, but they also begin to walk him toward a practice of the ecopoetics of coexistence. When the natural world speaks to Han-shan, the existence of the poet is drawn to a finer point as part of a wheel of living beings, of simultaneous fields of life—all of them interdependent.

> When the moon shines, water sparkles clear.
> When the wind blows, grass swishes and rattles.
> On the bare plum, flowers of snow.
> On the dead stump, leaves of mist.

As in the shorter poems that Snyder has written, the clean page allows the spare palette of elements to shine, especially water in all its formations. Rain, clouds, snow, mist, even tears move through the book as if drawn down by gravity, moving—as water does—down through the terrain.

Snyder had a running start to hearing this well. He grew up on a farm between Lake Washington and Puget Sound on the land of the Snohomish people. His family kept animals, and not far out his back window were second-growth Douglas firs. As he writes in *The Practice of the Wild*, "My usual pastimes were watching the migratory waterfowl in the sloughs along the Columbia River or sewing moccasins." Retreat into the wilderness isn't, for such a person, a retreat so much as a return to the wholeness within which he was raised. Snyder is simply unusual in his time in that he understood it as something worth returning to.

The Practice of the Wild seeks to repair the impoverishment of our alienation from nature. To Snyder, this condition affects our forms of government, our capacity for joy and pleasure, our language, our sense of home, and our ability to share and tolerate our neighbors. Addressing and repairing this condition is not, for him, simply an act of stewardship of land and the biosphere in which we live; it is a spiritual and psychological restoration that must be brought about too. "The depths of mind, the unconscious, are our inner wilderness areas," he writes. "We need to make a world-scale 'Natural contract' with the oceans, the air, the birds in the sky. . . . Take back, like the night, that which is shared by all of us, that which is our larger being."

Snyder is a skilled etymologist, and he frequently breaks down words—from *nature* to *wild* to *cultivate*—locating in their roots a greater complexity than their everyday usage suggests. Reading these essays is like watching a deeply informed preservationist of language replacing diminishing words with enlarging ones—and with enlarging categories. Instead of a nation or state, Snyder talks of bioregionalism, so when he addresses the compact he has made with the land on which he lives in the Sierras, it's important to point out that his part of the Sierras shares a lot of qualities with the Pacific Northwest where he grew up. Why are they different states? Meanwhile, *within* states you have great variety, and this variety—not an idea, let alone a flag—creates a kind of unity, one enforced by need. Take the California

Sierras, which are dry on the eastern side and required the Native people of that side to trade with the Miwok and Maidu of the western side, Snyder reminds. "The two sides met and camped together for weeks in the summer Sierra meadows," he writes, "their joint commons. . . . There are numerous examples of relatively peaceful small-culture coexistence all over the world." In his pages, one feels the loamy idea-soil of the movement to live and act locally taking root twenty years before it would become a meme.

Yet travel has been an essential part of informing Snyder's commitment to Native cultures, to the power of storytelling and teaching, and to being—as Barry Lopez was in his own way, too—a land bridge between literatures across the globe. Other sections of the book chronicle Snyder's travels in Inupiaq lands in the Alaskan Arctic, learning from language preservation movements and telling poems. So many writers of Snyder's stature would have traveled through with an idea of perhaps giving service. Instead, Snyder sees ever more clearly the values of the country whose passport he holds:

> American society . . . operates under the delusion that we are each a kind of "solitary knower"—that we exist as rootless intelligences without layers of localized contexts. Just a "self" and the "world." In this there is no real recognition that grandparents, place, grammar, pets, friends, lovers, children, tools, the poems and songs we remember, are what we think with. Such a solitary mind—if it could exist—would be a boring prisoner of abstractions. With no surroundings there can be no path, and with no path one cannot become free. No wonder the parents of Eskimo children of the whole Kotzebue Basin posted the "Inupiaq Values" in their schools.

On Gary Snyder

The Practice of the Wild is an unusual book, for it invites us to consider radical shifts in how we may live, but Snyder never presses his case with the petty despotism one can find in a guru. He simply beckons us into communal spaces from which he seeks to tease out lessons. Admittedly, they are the kinds of places most of us will see rarely, if ever, in our lifetimes, from the dogsled teams Snyder rides from house to house in Alaska, pausing on arrival to feed the howling animals fish stew, to a monastery outside Kyoto, where Snyder studied in the 1960s. He never presents these experiences with breathless access, though, or with self-aggrandizement; always it's in the tones of someone who has simply been allowed to do something with a history much older than himself.

He also takes pains to translate these experiences into everyday form. "It is as hard to get the children herded into the car pool and down the road to the bus as it is to chant sutras in the Buddha-hall on a cold morning," he writes. "One move is not better than the other, each can be quite boring, and they both have the virtuous quality of repetition." It is so unusual for a writer so restless, so prone to moving around the world, to reference the domestic space as a baseline reality for reality itself. Not for nothing is one of Snyder's finest poems—outside the ones discussed here—about giving his son Kai a bath. "The truly experienced person, the refined person," he concludes in *The Practice of the Wild*, "*delights in the ordinary.*"

How refreshing for a man whose lifeline overlapped with publications such as *Green Hills of Africa* to turn away from the models of masculinity—of detachment, of domination, of delegation—that Hemingway and others demonstrated to great popularity in his time, at least here on the page. Snyder's vast work is full of such surprises today. It remains the decent, the open invitation it was back in 1959. To read it, to wade into its lines, is to feel the shock of its necessity, in an era when our habitat's emergency is felt in every season, when every Californian is becoming a fire lookout, as Snyder once was with his friend Jack Kerouac on Desolation Peak. This work, so bracing, so still, invites us now to awaken the wild within us, to recognize it without, and to do this in the way that it can last—together.

ON KAY RYAN

Contemporary poetry is a bit like visual art. Much of it makes you grab your chin and nod in stumped appreciation—but you wouldn't want to live with it. Kay Ryan's work, however, hangs well no matter where it goes. Clouds, calendars, time, birds, jackrabbits. Everything her eye falls upon takes on a brisk, polished clarity. Her tidy lines disguise an enormous intelligence and tonal glow—a ferocious capacity for finding the essence of things.

The Best of It: New and Selected Poems reveals that right before our eyes Ryan has become a classic American poet. This should hardly be a surprise. Even though she is often compared to Robert Frost, and for good reason, her work here is a revelation. Beginning with new poems, *The Best of It* is the work of a pastoral poet, comfortable with her own counsel but keenly aware of the cost of self-sufficiency. "No unguent / can sooth / the chap of / abandonment," she writes in "Polish and Balm," a poem about the mystery of a dead woman's objects. "Who knew / the polish / and balm in / a person's / simple passage / among her things."

Few American poets have used the thin line so well, to such mournful effect. James Schuyler's poems concealed within their narrow aperture a lyricist's longing heart; more recently, writers as various as Amit Majumdar and Atsuro Riley have recognized in Ryan not just a stylistic muse but a philosopher on the same level as T. S. Eliot. Here, we are in different territory altogether. Turning each corner of a Ryan poem, the eye drops to the next solid, well-planked surface, as she guides us closer to the point where collapsing complications are swiftly subverted. The last lines of "Shift" perform this inversion with brutal efficiency.

>   It's hard for us
>   to imagine how small
>   a part we play in
>   holding up the tall
>   spires we believe
>   our minds erect.
>   Then North shifts,
>   buildings shear
>   and we suspect.

Poems like this, with their unfussy symmetries and patient alliterations, give the lie to all the bloodless revolutions that have occurred in American poetry in recent years. Theories are often mere fancy-dancing. To matter, you need to have something to say, wisdom, a point of view. That's an uncomfortable idea in many circles, especially as poetry is so often mistaken for high-priced aphorism, a simplifying wedge. True wisdom, though, never simplifies but rather sees complexity with an unsettling clarity. This is why, when we describe poems by Frost or Dickinson, we reach for the word *eerie*: They don't leave us anywhere to hide.

One of the great reliefs of Ryan's work is that she brings us to this point of disturbing clarity without telling too much about, well, herself. There are many poets whose intensely candid investigation of the self forms their strength—Sharon Olds, Mark Doty, C. K. Williams,

Aria Aber—but Ryan's steely privacy is rare. She gives us access to a different sort of intimacy, an intimacy of the mind. We watch her puzzle and torque, gain purchase on an idea and then let it go with the athletic finesse of Zen thinking. In "Emptiness," she packs centuries of thinking about the American West into eight brief lines.

> Emptiness cannot be
> compressed. Nor can it
> fight abuse. Nor is there
> an endless West hosting
> elk, antelope, and the
> tough cayuse. This is
> true also of the mind:
> it can get used.

Each line sets up the next, which arrives with a satisfying sense of inevitability because of the repeating internal rhyme (compressed / abuse / endless). As in so much of her work, Ryan keeps it simple. We are not caught off guard or struck dumb by where she has taken us. Plainspoken and clear-eyed, she tells us something we didn't know we knew until we get there ("It can get used"). And all this in eight lines. Few poets know how to compress thought so swiftly, while simultaneously keeping their lines so seemingly loose and conversational.

Here we have also entered distinctly western territory, where the fact that Ryan was born in San Jose, raised across the San Joaquin and Mojave, feels worth mentioning. She does not write the kind of poems in which landscape figures, but an inner landscape exists, is hinted at in this work, and it's one in which the entire history of clearing the West of its residents, its wildlife, can be named. She doesn't, you get the impression, think very much of it, this so-called civilization built on the land. "Much of this / apparently tenacious / earth is fairly slick," she writes in a later poem, "Things That Have Stayed in Position."

The Best of It, unlike so many selected collections, does not contain a shadow autobiography. In fact, Ryan is so sure-handed that the book is consistently good, her preoccupations reassuringly perpetual. She loves to study the fallacies of the mind; to watch the eye make mistakes; to pay tribute to the spooky mystery of nature's whole bestiary, from zebras to serpents to osprey; to atomize any kind of transformation into its purest elements.

Spending time with this book can alter the mind. The brevity and sobriety within Ryan's lines have a contagious skepticism to them, leaving us to emerge from her poems feeling not cleansed but quieted. That intense slowing is poetry's secret purpose, how it gets us to see. We slow down enough to learn a new language; we learn, all over again, how to see everything from the passage of days to the blur of a hailstorm, which Ryan describes as "A maelstrom / of ferocious little / fists and punches, / so hard to believe / once it's past." Eventually, this too shall pass, *The Best of It* reminds us, like everything.

VIII
EXPLODING FANTASIAS

INTERIOR CHINATOWN

by Charles Yu

Film and television have made narrative hijinks so common that it's a wonder so few novelists avail themselves of these techniques. How about a story told backward (*Memento*)? Or a past that's erased upon request (*Eternal Sunshine of the Spotless Mind*)? What about a narrator who is actually dead (too many to count)? Or a family that is trapped in a multiverse (*Everything Everywhere All at Once*)? The models are all there.

In film, from the beginning, even the hallowed position of the viewer has been turned on its head. Actors have been breaking the fourth wall since 1918, addressing the audience directly. "The key to faking out the parents is the clammy hands," Ferris Bueller told us seventy years after Mary MacLane turned to the camera in *Men Who Have Made Love to Me* and said: "A lot of people will tell you that a good phony fever is a deadlock, but, uh, you get a nervous mother, you could wind up in a doctor's office. That's worse than school."

This device works for one primary reason. We're all stuck in roles, some more than others, many of us playing ourselves. Almost twenty years ago, when he was still a lawyer, no doubt playing a role to some degree, Charles Yu published a short story that pounced on this feeling called "My Last Days as Me." In it, a twenty-two-year-old man acts his sixteen-year-old self in an ongoing reality drama in a kind of filmic purgatory, like an endless Groundhog Day:

> That last season was the best in the history of the program. Me and My Mother averaged nearly fourteen Tender Interactions a week. Ratings for Family were at an all-time high. My Mother cried Pitifully almost every episode. She had Large Problems. It was beautiful to watch her Suffer. A true professional.

It's a great gag, yet there are depths to be explored. Acknowledging what is expected of the mother as an Asian American woman, the story gestured toward an entire field of roles that are hard to break out of because culture reinforces them. *Interior Chinatown*, Yu's 2020 National Book Award–winning novel, takes this opportunity and runs with it.

Set in a fictional Chinatown, in which a family plays a set troupe of characters, it expands the world of Yu's earlier story into a deep satire of America's idea of race, as well as of film itself, of the roles Asian American characters are given by both and the way those tropes are internalized, making some absolutely hilarious jokes along the way. It is one of the saddest and funniest books you will ever read and an astounding breakthrough in how Asian-ness is talked about in the American novel.

The story begins with a simple statement—one that is repeated throughout the book, gaining new, different meanings each time: "Ever since you were a boy, you've dreamt of being Kung Fu Guy." Told in the second person, set in a restaurant, and laid out on the page in the format of a screenplay, the book immediately thrusts us into a paradoxical place: intimate estrangement. The second-person voice forces us to become the character, and the setting demands that we play a role.

"You," we soon learn, is Willis Wu, an actor growing up in a

Chinatown SRO (single room occupancy) hotel whose residents are also actors. There is Old Asian Man, Older Brother, Delivery Guy, and Emperor, among many others, living in small apartments above a Chinese restaurant. Willis has spent a life learning from his father, once a virile kung fu master, now Old Asian Guy. Willis struggles to accept the fact of his father's aging.

To take his mind off what is staring him in the face, he works. He has been trying to rise as an actor, but the names of his recent roles capture his predicament: Disgraced Son, Silent Henchmen, Guy Who Runs in and Gets Kicked in the Face. And Generic Asian Man. There have been others who have briefly transcended these roles—Older Brother, his own father—but in a series of dazzling montages, the novel reveals how little of themselves were captured by even the best roles they got. It is one of the most acrobatic feats of narrative in twenty-first-century American fiction. Looping through the scene, Yu manages to simultaneously indict a storytelling system and find spaces in its cracks to tell a meaningful tale. In many of these moments, the "you" he writes to becomes a plural you.

"Poor is relative, of course," he writes in one such moment.

> None of you were rich or had any dreams of being rich or even knew anyone rich. But the widest gulf in the world is the distance between getting by and not quite getting by. Crossing that gap can happen in a hundred ways, almost all by accident. Bad day at work and/or kid has a fever and/or miss the bus and consequently ten minutes late to the audition which equals you don't get to play the part of Background Oriental with Downtrodden Face. Which equals, stretch the dollar that week, boil chicken bones twice for a watery soup, make the bottom of the bag of rice last another dinner or three.

As the action opens, Willis is stuck in a police procedural called *Black and White*, in which a white woman and a Black man enter a crime season to find an "Asian Man" (played by Willis) already dead. Interior Chinatown, as the title suggests, is both an interior world and a world's interior viewed from outside—as by a camera's eye. Or an outsider's eye. Either way, as the novel begins, Willis is both figuratively and metaphorically dead, reduced to a body with a few identifiable qualities. In this sense, *Interior Chinatown* is the story of his resurrection.

One of the book's many liberating qualities is how quickly it moves from one posture into another. *Black and White* is an example—what begins in earnest noir-like tones soon devolves into a kind of sketch comedy of the form, riffing on all the ways that crime dramas like to set up a tale, play their actors off one another, and slot the audience into type based on which character appears largest in the ads in your neighborhood. The confidence with which Yu slips out of the straitjacket of the form produces a feeling closer to what it feels like to encounter story. That giddy sense of familiarity and collusion and resistance. It feels like a person both telling a story and looking over his shoulder at the ways it matches up with what is supposed to be told.

Keeping all this straight on the page is not as hard as it might sound. It quickly becomes clear that when narration enters the screenplay form on the page, people are playing a role, either in *Black and White*, the story of which runs the course of the entire book, or within their personal lives, which occasionally fall into dialogic pattern. In this way, Yu neatly thinks on how projections of being—Asian-ness, for example—quickly become internalized. They can create scenery. They can decorate a room. "The idea was you came here," he writes at one point about Willis, living in the SRO surrounded by people who have worn masks long enough to become their masks, "your parents and their parents and their parents, and you always seem to have just arrived and yet never seem to have actually arrived. You're here, supposedly, in a new land full of opportunity, but somehow have gotten trapped in a pretend version of the old country."

When the book falls out of the screenplay form into something that more closely approximates narrative prose, we have then entered true interiority—a world in which Willis's role is his to be designed, even if he has imported forms of self-loathing or limitation. As *Black and White* morphs and becomes a romance, a Western, a crime caper, even a courtroom drama, the prose sections tunnel ever inward. There are touches of lyricism and poetry. The gap between whom Willis plays and who he is expands. He meets a woman, falls in love, and is reminded that to be in love means to stop playing a role. He becomes a father and then faces a choice—whether to keep living in the world where he accepts the space given to him.

Interior Chinatown resembles some great books. It wrestles with representation with the daring fury of Paul Beatty. It argues with itself like the work of Dostoyevsky, but in so many ways, it is utterly its own creation. What else could be simultaneously this silly and orchestrally controlled? Is there a novel that manages to describe so well the way fantasy becomes reality? And yet, the novel is not here to come to conclusions: It moves with a unique and restless desire to interrupt even its own interruptions of culture memes. In the final courtroom drama, Older Brother describes Willis as being "guilty of wanting to be part of something that never wanted him." Defending him, Older Brother quips, "I've never defended someone for self-imprisonment before."

In one of Yu's previous books, *How to Live Safely in a Science Fictional Universe*, the author plays a version of himself, a kind of narrative technician, entering and sapping stories so that people can safely go back in time again. Though not autobiographical, *Interior Chinatown* feels like a sister project of intensely relevant design. It applies the actual Yu's prodigious gifts to spotlight a narrative danger that can change lives, can even end them. How not to be trapped in reflections and distortions of the past. It is a book of extraordinary power.

CITIZEN

by Claudia Rankine

For the past century, teenagers in the United States have been given Walt Whitman's poems the moment their imaginations kick up a thrumming like cicadas in August. The bearded bard's barbaric yawp in "Leaves of Grass"—"I am large, I contain multitudes"—has been treated like the libretto to America's proclaimed ideals: the concepts of freedom and liberty, equality and the right to happiness, etched into the nation's founding documents. Yet right alongside these great notions—in the three-fifths compromise, which counted slaves as a fraction of a human being—live some other ideas. Namely, those of exclusion, white supremacy, and justice for some, not all.

 The history of the United States is the story of how these competing ideas clash, creating a racial space—a contested field where the fantasies, projections, myths, and fears produced by this collision enact themselves. What it means in this context to have a self is a very different thing depending on where you are placed (or place yourself) in this racial field. What is defined as singing? What does it mean to have a body? To celebrate? To make visible—and what needs to be made visible? All of these questions power the work of Claudia

Rankine. Drawing from the worlds of theater, visual art, popular culture, and poetry, she has fashioned a way of exposing these questions that is unique, powerful, and so vital that it feels as if America finally has a bard not just for its ideals but for the reality in which we live.

For most readers, Rankine's voice emerged in 2014, the year she published *Citizen*, a lyric essay, featuring artwork from her partner, John Lucas, that collages together tales of racially charged encounters, told in the second person, with imagined or edited accounts of recent shootings of unarmed young Black men. The mixture of the second-person's collusion requirement—in reading, you, the reader, become the you who speaks—and the distance required to look at the various images creates a dynamic reading experience. You cannot simply regard the book and its ideas without confronting the assumptions you bring to it. Are the exhaustion, fury, sadness, and constant vigilance that the "you" voice describes new to you? Is it a relief to hear these feelings aired aloud? All too familiar, infuriating? Do the images Rankine collects and curates accept or refuse where you wish to place them?

Citizen was originally published after the long, hot, soul-sickening summer of 2014. Eric Garner strangled by several police officers while protesting, "I can't breathe." Michael Brown shot on the streets of Ferguson, Missouri, by police officer Darren Wilson, his body left there for hours. All of these images and more were played and replayed, as if simply being exposed to Black death was enough for those (mostly white) bewildered by this carnage to understand it or their place within it. These performances of white shock were not enough to stop the killing. (More unarmed Black men were shot in 2018 than in 2014, at a rate of five to one compared to whites. The flagrant murder of George Floyd in 2020 ignited a summer of pandemic-defying marches, historic ones in terms of scale and duration, and yet, in the mid-2020s, the trend of killings is higher still.) One of the reasons Rankine's book struck such a chord then, and still does now, is that it acknowledges this terrible ongoingness and also its invisibility to whites. But it also reveals how these most lethal forms of racism are the tip of an iceberg of often unrecorded encounters—microaggressions—that every nonwhite American will be deeply familiar with, interactions (sometimes even daily ones) that make the recipient feel destabilized, highly visible, embarrassed, hurt, less than, degraded, or depressed.

The setting and format of these interactions, as Rankine depicts them, make it impossible for many middle-class liberal white readers to opt out of the problem. This is their world, the universe of organic salads and of academe and of elite-status seating arrangements of airlines. Even if people of color are entitled to such spaces too, whiteness comes with the presumption of policing access to them, an entitlement *Citizen* makes clear. One of the many questions a reader of this book must ask is, Where did you put yourself in these situations? Was the ripple of threat a surprise? For the you who narrates *Citizen*, these settings are always a charged arena. "Because of your elite status from a year's worth of travel," goes one segment, "you have already settled into your window seat on United Airlines, when the girl and her mother arrive at your row. The girl, looking over at you, tells her mother, these are our seats, but this is not what I expected. The mother's response is barely audible—I see, she says. I'll sit in the middle."

The variety, intensity, and volume of these experiences lend *Citizen* the feeling of a reckoning; the way Rankine writes this into the body gives it visceral force and poetic power. Just prior to this incident, the book describes how such encounters lodge in the throat.

> Certain moments send adrenaline to the heart, dry
> out the tongue, and clog the lungs. Like thunder they
> drown you in sound, no, like lightning they strike
> you across the larynx. Cough. After it happened I was
> at a loss for words. Haven't you said this to a close

friend who early in your friendship, when distracted,
would call you by the name of her black housekeeper?
You assumed you two were the only black people in
her life. Eventually, she stopped doing this, though
she never acknowledged her slippage.

Rankine is a writer who finds so much of what defines us in those slippages—in the silence of you, in the friend's inability to (or desire not to) acknowledge what was just revealed. In this regard, she has not changed much in thirty years of publishing. From the very beginning of her work, Rankine demonstrated what is often called a restlessness with form—but what ought to be called a distrust of stable narratives, of familiar plots, of nostalgias, and of gazes that are assumed to be somehow indivisible. Even when they turn out to have come from her own life.

Rankine's debut collection, *Nothing in Nature Is Private*, is over thirty years old. "American Light," the volume's first poem, announces a major voice, one in control of its effects, asking big questions about what of the world can be seen.

In the lit landscape, in its peeled
back places, making the space
uncomfortable, representing no fault
in the self is a shadow
of a gesture of wanting, coveting
the American light.

A shadow on ships, in fields
for years, for centuries even, in heat
colored by strokes of red, against
the blue-white light—and in it
I realize I recognize myself.

Rankine's eye has always been attuned to light and perspective; her poetry asks why certain things are put in the foreground while others in the background. Hers is an art historical eye, an eye tuned to the figure, to patterns in representation. In this poem, she draws herself into a scene shaded by the context of slavery, then is surprised to find herself belonging there. A feeling of being arrested into history recurs across *Nothing in Nature Is Private* as she inhabits other personas, tells stories in creolized language, writes on love and lovemaking and moments when the world reduces her into a single feature of her body, its color. One poem reads like an outtake from *Citizen*. "This morning when the doorbell rang / and a man stood outside my door, / I thought he must be official . . . he looked past me / in search of—I'll use his words—/ I need to speak to your employer, / to someone who lives here."

Rankine's interest as a writer has been to reveal the layers of experience, then to tilt and renovate it from within. If *Nothing in Nature Is Private* performs this excavation through history and the prism of a family's journey, *The End of the Alphabet* burrows inward; it makes a quarry out of these impulses to uncover. Told in stark, brief sections, stutter-stepped by swift, interrupted attempts to make similes—the words "as if" repeating like a failed schematic—it chronicles an experience with pain so great that the self breaks down. Language, pulverized by anguish, becomes a seeking, broken instrument, forever suspended in its labors.

The End of the Alphabet is a difficult book to read, not because its style is impenetrable, but rather because it achieves an overwhelming intensity and then does not relieve us of its pressure until the very last page. Sentences run together, uncapitalized, like a voice spoken from within: "rip the mind out. go ahead." Will this directive unplug the source of pain? Not here. The internal dialogue is taunting, pleading, descriptively cruel. "You. you are defeat composed." Gradually, though, turning and pivoting on the endless task of describing from within what feels to come from within and without, relief arrives. "Laughter has the house to itself." It may be simply that the lungs come to the rescue of the mind, but the release of pressure is immense, and the book eddies toward peace. The effect of the book's arc is harrowing.

Pain and laughter are conjoined in Rankine's work. In *Just Us: An American Conversation*, published in 2020, which begins as an attempt to try to talk about whiteness with white men, her encounters ricochet with destabilizing laughter—sometimes at the absurdity of patently unfair situations. In other works of hers, the sound of a moan can break into cackles, as it does in *Citizen*, or an idiocy can produce disbelieving guffaws, as in her play *The White Card*, in which a white benefactor is perplexed by a Black artist's lack of joy when the benefactor unveils his latest acquisition, Michael Brown's autopsy report. Here is the body responding to stimulus: expelling air. Breath. Here is the body as a system of hydraulics that produces meaning that can cut through projected fantasies, falsehoods. It is a system that can even propel a sign of resistance to the forefront when the gears of language have ground to a halt. Humor turns the gears of many scenes in *Plot*, a book-length meditation on pregnancy, childbirth, creative work, and coupledom. Liv and Erland are expecting a child, and *Plot* charts the changing landscape of Liv's body, their space together, Erland's attitudes. At times, their collective bafflement at the changes of child-rearing—their highly intelligent dialogue about her going from one self to a vessel for two—reads like a form of feminist intellectual sitcom.

Not long after becoming pregnant, quoting Virginia Woolf, Liv feels "herself as beached debris," thinking, if she were an image, that she'd ask: "What kind of log is that?" As their child grows, she feels displaced and, also, simply baffled at the mechanics of it. "How to separate an interior out? / How to keep from polluting one in the other? / How to stay in and out of it?" In a late poem, "The Ouch in Touch," about making love while nearly due, Rankine describes perfectly the way these dilemmas often animate a woman's life, from mundane moments to her most intimate. The question they produce: How to experience "the reflected emotion surmounting the real, surviving it."

We live in a mediated world, and Rankine's breakthrough arrived with the method of collaging registers of language, reading them closely, and using this stop-motion study to show Americans seeing ourselves being seen. All while meditating on the forms of projection and using forms of lyric address to create disquieting and intimate effects. This breakthrough began in her 2004 book, *Don't Let Me Be Lonely*, the first of a trilogy, which continues through *Citizen* and concludes with *Just Us*. Taken as one continuous movement of thought, the trilogy is as tremendous a chronicle of living through an era of rising violence, spectacle, and unraveling public truth as this nation has had to date.

To return to *Don't Let Me Be Lonely* is to appreciate how rapidly America's media environment has evolved, at least technologically, since the early 2000s. The book opens with an image of a television set stuck on interchannel fuzz. It's a symbol of what follows, wherein the signal of a message or communication is often distorted, and in that way, the book redefines watching as a form of trying to see around one's misunderstandings—or limitations. The poet finds her father, forlorn on their front steps, the day his mother died. He says not a word, but his posture tells her everything she needs to know. A few segments later, the speaker—now writing as "you"—calls a suicide hotline, wondering: "Am I dead?" Moments later, an ambulance attendant turns up. "By law, I will have to restrain you," he explains, with firm delicacy. "His tone suggests that you should try to understand the difficulty in which he finds himself. This is further disorienting. I am fine! Can't you see that! You climb into the ambulance unassisted."

Much of *Don't Let Me Be Lonely* is about the gap between seeing things and being inside them, between knowing a thing and remembering it. Friends of the speaker begin to die of cancer. Another develops Alzheimer's, clinging to his dignity by writing out a sentence, "THIS IS THE MOST MISERABLE IN MY LIFE." Meantime, Bush wins the second election but cannot remember basic details about the horrific dragging death of James Byrd Jr. in his home state of Texas. How, the book wonders, do we live in states of relative pain, where some of it is invisible and forgettable, while other pain is intolerable? The book is a kind of psychopharmacology of unseen pain: of drugs and remedies, of sayings and repressed feelings, quietly shared confessions among people of color. Of breakdowns.

In many ways, this is the world of unseen suffering that finally surfaces into a specific, acute description in *Citizen*. "Sometimes 'I' is supposed to hold what is not there until it is," Rankine writes in *Citizen*. "Then what is comes apart the closer you are to it. This makes the first person a symbol for something. The pronoun barely holding the person together."

On the basis of *Citizen*, Rankine was awarded a prestigious MacArthur Fellowship, the proceeds of which she used to help fund the Racial Imaginary Institute in Manhattan, the point of which is to study the ways our lives are being affected by people's understandings and misconceptions of race. Whiteness—often neglected in conversations about race that are driven by whites—is at the heart of its project. What props up whiteness? What beliefs does it hold dear? Why is it not seen so often by those who live within it? These are the questions Rankine is most obsessed with today. As the Black artist Charlotte tells the older white benefactor in *The White Card*, "your imagination, like mine, like everyone's, is a racial imagination, except you don't really think of yourself as having a race and being shaped by the belief of that race."

Just Us concludes Rankine's trilogy with the author in the role of questioner, confronting assumptions of whiteness as they happen. Why must a man, with whom she has been having a pleasant transatlantic airline flight chat, punctuate the moment of their greatest comfort, her finally letting her guard down, with "I don't see color"? Whereas in *Citizen* Rankine often describes the effect of these interactions on her, or "you," she starts conversations in *Just Us*. In this particular moment on the flight, she replies sharply to her new acquaintance, and later, he writes her a letter, excerpted in the book with his permission.

This is one of more promising interactions, in which the highlight Rankine places on a deflective move leads to a continued conversation. Others are less so, and they often have to do with whiteness exercising one of its most intricate privileges: the ability not to see itself. To step outside what it is declared to be. Leaving a party, for example, Rankine is "paused in the hallway in someone else's home when a man approaches to tell me he thinks his greatest privilege is his height." At a play in which the fourth wall is broken and a Black actor asks white audience members to come onstage, the white person with whom Rankine has attended stays in her seat. "My tension begins to couple with a building resentment against my white friend. I feel betrayed by her." When the play is over, she says to her friend: "I didn't know you were black."

One of the most thrilling aspects of Rankine's trilogy is watching the way she begins to deploy herself—not only her life and her history but herself as a kind of actor—in scenarios, and how this risk in the work has borne unexpected fruit. In this theater scene, for example, the way that she wields a rolling series of questions is similar to the interrogations the speaker has of herself and interactions in *Citizen*. Two pages after she announces her feeling of betrayal at the play, Rankine continues,

> Is my friend's refusal to move, to be seen moving, a move she needed to make? Is it a message, a performance of one? Is she telling the black audience, you all don't get to look at me. You don't get to see me as a white specimen. This is fucked up, the man behind me had said. The unconscious, as I understand it, can lose context or perspective. Maybe my friend cannot bear to be told what to

do, and how that started and where it will end has little to do with her whiteness or everything to do with her whiteness. My perception of a blind spot around racial dynamics could lead to a larger discussion of white feminism and white entitlement.

Those questions and thoughts usher in the one she eventually asks out loud: Why didn't you go onto the stage? Rankine's friend's response, "I didn't want to," both is and isn't an answer. When Rankine writes up this experience, she hands it to the friend, as much to be sure she hasn't misrepresented the event but also, possibly, as a provocation. It works. The friend replies and acknowledges her dodge of what had been an invitation to feel a segregation that exists in their minds, whether they like it or not. "And then she did something I didn't expect but that explains why we are friends," Rankine writes. "She sat down and wrote."

Just Us invites white readers to share in this burden of America. The isolation in *Don't Let Me Be Lonely*, which is carried through *Citizen* as a burden of vulnerability, emerges differently in *Just Us* as a burden to carry alone the weight of American history—and what it means to come from a nation that is founded on genocide and slavery but says that all people are created equal. As Toni Morrison reminded in the dedication to her masterpiece *Beloved*, "Sixty Million and more" perished as a result of transatlantic slavery, which depended on an idea of race that ranked whites higher than Blacks. Without it, slavery would have been unimaginable. The founders of the United States couldn't imagine their way out of the imprisoning fallacies of their new creation of race. Rankine's work is a piercing example of the ways it is yet possible to try.

VOYAGE OF THE SABLE VENUS

by Robin Coste Lewis

Just over a half century ago, Chicago mayor Richard Daley asked Gwendolyn Brooks to write a poem. The occasion was the unveiling of the "Chicago Picasso," a monumental steel sculpture designed by the Spanish artist and installed in what's still called Daley Plaza. On August 15, 1967, the work was unveiled before a crowd of thousands, and Brooks delivered her poem, capturing the public's unease. (One alderman joked that he'd have much rather had a statue of Ernie Banks, the late, great Cubs first baseman and shortstop.) "Man visits Art, but squirms," her poem begins. And then, just as she does in so many of her poems, Brooks folds a universe of complex feeling into the next line. "Art hurts," she writes. "Art urges voyages—"

You'll find this part of the poem near the end of Robin Coste Lewis's breathtaking debut book of poems, *Voyage of the Sable Venus*. Lewis's collection is an exhibit of exhibits, an ode to Black joy, and a meditation on the metaphysics of the Black body—in particular, a Black woman's body. At its heart pulses a stunning found poem fashioned from the titles, catalog language, and plaque descriptions of art in which a Black woman appears, from sculpture that dates to 38,000 BCE to photographs from the present day. The paintings, objects, and sculptures Lewis refers to live in collections in Copenhagen, Rome, Melbourne, Rio de Janeiro, Zanzibar, Khartoum, and Washington, DC. Talk about a journey.

The real journey, though, is how far so much of this art has to travel to even begin to approximate the feeling of life, the thrum of joy, the warmth of, say, motherhood or erotic pleasure in a Black female body. And so Lewis does not begin with this piece. Instead her book begins in the poet's own body with the most inclusive word in the English language: "And."

> And then one morning we woke up
> embracing on the bare floor of a large cage.
> To keep you happy, I decorated the bars.
> Because you had never been hungry, I knew
>
> I could tell you the black side
> of my family owned slaves.
> I realize this is perhaps
> the one reason why I love you.

"To be in love," Brooks wrote in her great poem "To Be in Love," "Is to touch with a lighter hand." Lewis writes like a poet who lives in the possibilities of this wisdom. In the first section of the book's title poem, she writes with infinite tenderness, using a grip so light it can touch the weightiest of matters—like motherhood and dignity, like the history of slavery and how it has made bodies—and juxtapose gestures of care against the scale of enormous pain.

Lewis's eye is curious and visual, and it comes imbued with her own art historical method, a framing of deliberate design. Bodies do not feel separated from personhood in her poems—quite the opposite, even when what's being described is activity done in silence. "The

Mothers," for instance, describes a brief shared moment of togetherness between two mothers getting dressed.

> No need to articulate the great restraint,
>
> No need to see each other's mouth lip
> the obvious. *Giddy*. Fingers garnished
> With fumes of onions and garlic, I slip
> Back into my shift, then watch her hands—wordless—
>
> Reattach her stockings to the martyred
> Rubber moons wavering at her garter.

What would the history of art look like if such moments of radical queer love were not secreted into margins but celebrated with luminous clarity? Lewis's project appears to be, among others, asking that very question, posing it in poems and glimpses of how a body can tell many stories when it is not separated—by projections and violence—from the soul that possesses it.

The scale of this project is massive, epic. Although *Voyage of the Sable Venus* is a mere 176 pages, reading it feels like setting out on a quest. The hopscotch of its global settings adds to this sensation, as does Lewis's mastery of many poetic lines, from the long, thin, barely punctuated stanzas to the wavelike quatrains in "On the Road to Sri Bhuvaneshwari." The latter, one of the book's great poems, describes a night the poet spent on a narrow hillside road in the Himalayas, her passage blocked by a buffalo about to give birth.

> We wait with the whole tribe, wait with the whole night, wait
>   for her to stop bucking. Her hip bones
>   are as tall as my eyes. Her neck is a massive drum.
>   They do not force her, but they will not let her run.

The buffalo's calf is born dead, and she cannot be allowed to move until she sees this, understands, as Lewis puts it, "what has happened to her." Across this book, Lewis keeps shining this question toward women around her—in the history of places she has lived, and also in the particulars of her own journey.

Here is the alternate, perhaps ironic meaning of the book's title. Lewis has reclaimed from the sweep of historiography and art history the ability to voyage, the entitlement to regard and to see and not simply be seen. "Self Portrait as the Emerald City Nairobi, 2009" begins with these memorable lines:

> Is there a street that can anticipate
> our tenderness? A corner or a curb
> that stands still waiting for me?

In the book's title work, we get a glimpse of the many reasons the poet must pose this question. A series of poems built from lines in which figures are often described and erased simultaneously. "Female Figure with Child Kneeling . . . Young Black Female Carrying / a Perfume Vase with Necklace." "Rope / Head and Shoulders Girl / Portrait of an Unidentified Girl." The effect in montage is deeply disturbing, more Picasso than Picasso ever was.

The depth and nuance to the patterns Lewis has found in plain sight are sharpened by her use of juxtaposition. She presents us with bodies in supplication; bodies as utilitarian objects; bodies wearing masks; bodies writing; bodies missing parts of themselves; bodies used to tell stories; bodies that withhold parts of stories; bodies that are virginal; bodies that are owned; bodies that cannot be possessed, no matter how flamboyantly they are named; Black Madonnas; the Venus of Compton; bodies.

> Clapping Christening Cleaning
> Club Women Cooking Class

at the Benjamin Banneker!
The Green Chair People in a line.
Queens of the Boat hear animals dancing,
wrapping it up at the Lafayette:

Swerving between abstraction and figuration, from the names of institutions to monikers for Blackness—so many of them lit by the fantasias produced by whiteness—Lewis vividly captures the degree to which the images of Black bodies exist within an atmosphere charged by desire and history.

Managing this sequence requires a contradictory set of skills. Layering words together like this, in borrowed brushstrokes, demands a superior feeling for syntax. It means that a poet must begin with sonics. Lewis does this and more. Drawing us through the centuries, from sumptuous brocades to the slogans on posters of the civil rights era, Lewis creates a soundscape of the racial imaginary. We feel its percussive beat, the repetition of melodies made from dreams.

When we return to the poet's life in the final section of this book, Lewis muses on the lesson such images taught. Drawing us to her young eye, looking at the image of Dr. Martin Luther King Jr., shot, figures in the frame pointing up to his fallen body, she writes:

> Every year these four photographs
> taught us how English was really a type of trick math:
> like the naked Emperor, you could be a King
> capable of imagining just one single dream;
> or there could be a body, bloody
> at your feet—then you could point at the sky;
> or you could be a hunched-over cotton-picking shame;
> or you could swing from a tree by your neck into the frame.

Voyage of the Sable Venus shatters this choice by pointing it out and then presenting us with a variety of other options. By making a map of "Lost landscapes within the body—haggard and lush terrains— / North and South Poles suspended between pleasure and understanding," Lewis excavates her family's past to find these nodes; she peels the hard container-skin off the fruit of myths; she lingers where bodies are held by one another. She brings art to her lexicon of images, not the other way around.

Has there ever been a more apt rededication from one poet of another poet's lines? In speaking of her poem in 1969, Brooks told an interviewer that "those of us who have not grown up with or to [art] perhaps squirm a little in its presence. We feel that something is required of us that perhaps we aren't altogether able to give." While Brooks's poem was an invitation to take the journey to art, it was also—fundamentally—a beckoning for art to take a voyage to her. Brooks, and Lucille Clifton after her, altered the American racial imaginary by drawing art to them, to forms of Black interiority and Black joy they experienced. In her own book, Lewis takes this journey one step farther and brings it all the way home by way of Nairobi via New Orleans, to Compton, and beyond.

BARBARIAN DAYS

by William Finnegan

There are 840 miles of coastline in California, some of which you can surf. Stretches of it are simply legendary. Rincon in Santa Barbara. Trestles in Orange County. Mavericks and the gnarly waves at Half Moon Bay. Beach Boys songs aside, these are the reasons, if you live in the state, people back East ask: *Do you surf?* Duck into a bookshop, though, and you'll be hard-pressed to find literature as spectacular as the lore. So what happens between the ocean and the land that escapes the page? Why is an activity that is so enchanting and popular also so indescribable?

Barbarian Days: A Surfing Life, William Finnegan's memoir of his lifelong relationship to catching waves, is a hugely enjoyable corrective to this gap between the immense pleasures of surfing and the need for a better literature of it. Drawing on the author's journals and experiences over fifty years, it reveals startling complexities to an activity so often associated with beach culture. Indeed, *Barbarian Days* is to the board what *Moby Dick* was to the whale: It is, among other things, a quest, a lexicon, a travelogue, a bildungsroman, a knowing colonial exegesis, a history of the activity, a tale of male friendships, a study of whiteness, a love poem to the ocean, and a frank portrait of a man grappling with his limits and the hint that beyond them is an incomprehensible void.

We begin this epic journey not in California but in Hawaii. A staff writer with the *New Yorker* for more than thirty years, Finnegan can spin a mise-en-scène opening with the best of them. Thus the book starts in 1966, our hero and his family freshly arrived from Los Angeles in Honolulu, where Finnegan's father, a TV production manager, works on a variety show program. Despite the teasing, mild torture, and occasional abuse as one of the few *haoles* (white people) at school, Finnegan—three years into his lifelong surf fever—is in heaven.

Starting here says so much about Finnegan as a writer, and also about why *Barbarian Days*, published in 2015, will stand the test of time. From the beginning, Finnegan approaches surfing as an outsider, a student, and a strong observer. He instinctively knows that this fever that possesses him and others stretches back a long way and into many other cultures.

Surfing, after all, emerged from the Pacific islands, and some accounts go as far back as the fourth century CE. When Hawaii was conquered by Europeans, surfing had religious import. In one of the book's few historical interludes, Finnegan reminds us that the Calvinist missionaries led by Hiram Bingham were determined to eradicate the activity. They didn't succeed, and "from this terrible history modern surfing is descended," Finnegan writes, "thanks to the few Hawaiians, notably Duke Kahanamoku, who kept the ancient practice of he'e nalu alive." After winning a gold medal for swimming in the 1912 Olympics, Kahanamoku put on surfing demonstrations around the world. The activity notably caught on in postwar California.

We learn this ancient history and the backstory of how Finnegan, before moving to Hawaii, jumped on a longboard and learned to nose-ride ("scurrying . . . to the front of one's board—hanging five, hanging ten, defying the obvious physics of flotation and glide") on the scrubby shore of Newport Beach, California. He was ten years old and as skinny as a stork. Surfing wasn't a sport then, taught in school, judged in the Olympics. It was just an outsider activity, a kind of path. It made you weird.

In Honolulu, young Finnegan finally meets his tribe, a few in what turns into a series of friends who are wave-life gurus too. *Barbarian Days* tells the story of what these friendships draw out in him, from childhood all the way to late middle age. In Hawaii, from Roddy Kaulukukui and one of his friends, Ford Takara, whose parents own a gas station, young Finnegan learns how to navigate life in and out of the water. How to respect pecking orders. When to back down, when not to give quarter. How to claim his own style. Later, when his family returns to Los Angeles, to Woodland Hills—where he attends William Howard Taft, the neighboring high school to the one Paul Beatty attended— a fine-tuned attentiveness travels with him.

This hyperawareness comes in handy on the water, where Finnegan spends more and more time. It allows him to assess, to judge, and to know when to act in a dynamic world. "Wave judgment is fundamental," he writes in one memorable section, "but how to unpack it? You're sitting in a trough between waves, and you can't see past the approaching swell, which will not become a wave you can catch. You start paddling upcoast and seaward. Why? If the moment were frozen, you could explain that, by your reckoning, there's a fifty-fifty chance that the next wave will have a good takeoff spot about ten yards over and a little farther out from where you are now."

Fair enough: This all sounds straightforward—until Finnegan continues in this vein to break down, in brief, what elements and experience this calculation has been made from:

> your last two or three glimpses of the swells outside, each glimpse caught from the crest of a previous swell; the hundred plus waves you have

seen break in the past hour and a half; your cumulative experience of three or four hundred sessions at this spot, including fifteen or twenty days that were much like this one in terms of swell size, swell direction, wind speed, wind direction, tide, season, and sandbar configuration; the way the water seems to be moving across the bottom; the surface texture and the water color; and, beneath these elements, innumerable subcortical perceptions too subtle and fleeting to express.

As *Barbarian Days* progresses, living outside this realm of intensity becomes less and less tolerable for Finnegan. The 1960s have bled into the 1970s; where is he going? One by one, he drops his attachments to square life. He skips his high school graduation in favor of travel—surely, he realizes in retrospect, a source of worry for his hardworking Irish Catholic parents. He ducks out of daywork to become a brakeman on the railroad. The pay is good, and the stakes are high. You cannot stop paying attention.

The money he saves on the job ends up funding an epic round-the-world trip in search of the ultimate beach, the far frontier of experience. In Maui, Finnegan had made a friend named Bryan after spotting the big *U* of Joyce's *Ulysses* in his hand. Later, they reunite for this endless search. Finnegan admits his own vision of what he was up to: "I wanted to learn new ways to be. I wanted to change. I wanted to feel less existentially alienated, to feel more at home in my skin, as they say, and in the world."

Finnegan is aware of the figure he casts across this book, especially in his youth as a seeker. The middle-class white kid from LA determined to see the limit of the world or die trying, to maybe meet some exotic women, as he puts it, with an emphasis on the patheticness of the phrase. Going broke in parts of Southeast Asia and on some of the islands in the South Pacific where residents would kill to have some of the privileges he'd thrown away was offensive, and it became more so in retrospect. Finnegan deals with this awareness in reflection and self-deprecation. "Being a rich *orang putih* in a poor brown world still sucked irredeemably. We, that is, sucked."

Traveling away from the United States, Finnegan also begins to relearn a way of being masculine, a shift that emerges from his exposure to the ocean and the people he meets. Something changes after he travels through the Pacific islands and sees the desperation of some women there, their vulnerability before traveling pleasure-seekers. Later, in the northwest part of Australia, for example, where the distance between towns is marked in tinnies—as in how many tins of beer one drinks while driving—Bryan and Finnegan pick up two female hitchhikers on their way to a feminist commune. Finnegan immediately falls in with one of them, and he makes the unwise move of visiting her at the all-female retreat after their affair has ended. He gets an earful and is thrown out by police. He admits, "I hadn't respected her boundaries. . . . I couldn't argue with that."

Barbarian Days is a model, in many ways, for how a book written by a white man who undertook such a journey, and was changed by it, might look and feel, how its author can see around himself and also see himself at the same time—without rewriting the past. For instance, as Finnegan's travels take him far from the United States, and he awakens politically and ethically, more and more attention is paid to the context of where he has landed, the realities of life as it is lived there, and the figures that he and Bryan cast in the late 1970s.

Nevertheless, inexorably, sometimes feverishly, the hunt for the wave continues. Drawing on the journal he kept at the time, Finnegan describes the breaks he surfs at Grajagan, in the Indonesian province of East Java, as "big and sectiony and mushy up top," and another spot in Fiji is so sacred that he and his buddy won't even mention it to each other by name. Watching better surfers thread barrels and learning whom not to accidentally fade into a wipeout, Finnegan earns his MFA in attention and precision, the increasing risk driving home lessons. "The key to surfing Kirra was entering the wild section at full speed," he writes in another salt-sprayed passage.

> surfing close to the face—pulling in—and then, if you got inside, staying calm in the barrel, having faith that it just might spit you out. It usually didn't, but I had waves that teased me two, even three times, with the daylight hole speeding ahead, outrunning me, and then pausing and miraculously rewinding back toward me, the spilling lip seemingly twisting like the iris of a camera lens opening until I was almost out of the hole, and then reversing and doing it again, receding in beautiful hopelessness and returning in even more beautiful hope. These were the longest tube rides of my life.

This is a very different kind of MFA than one that can cost $120,000 these days. Finnegan didn't have a checking account, he relays here, until he was thirty-one years old. For most of his travels in the Far East, he lived hand to mouth, often working in kitchens with working-class people. It's not clear in his and Bryan's relationship who is Dean Moriarty and who is Sal Paradise, but by the end of their travels the model falls apart, as Bryan heads back to Missoula, Montana, and Finnegan continues on to apartheid-era South Africa.

Here, the scope of what Finnegan has seen on his travels catches up to him. "There was simply no escaping politics, and I found no common political ground with any of the surfers I met," he notes. For almost eighteen months, his board is a second fiddle as he teaches English and religious studies to teenagers in a township. It is the 1980s, and the general strikes led by high schoolers, among others, are just beginning. On one weekend, he hitchhikes to the coast with an eighteen-year-old activist who is hand-relaying key information to the city of Durban. The experience not only leads Finnegan away from surfing but draws him toward reporting.

In 1983, when Finnegan returns to the United States, Reagan is in office and AIDS is beginning to devastate the city where he has landed, San Francisco, a fact that draws right up close to Finnegan and people he knows. What does surfing mean in the context of risk and power? In one of the book's last major sections simply about surfing, Finnegan hews close to the power of destruction, and obliteration, describing the monster waves that pummel San Francisco's Ocean Beach in the winter. The waves are sometimes so big a bus could fit in the barrel. The water is so cold that after just thirty minutes, Finnegan's hands are too numb to unlock his car door. A wild and flamboyant doctor who has been studying the breaks there and their patterns like an urban Thoreau urges him on. Yet, Finnegan finally admits, maybe he has hit his limit.

Still, though, there is more surfing to come. *Barbarian Days* reveals that an endless passion doesn't—necessarily—have to lead to an end, as it does for some truly possessed surfers. Finnegan begins to downshift, traveling more to Portugal and other places where the breaks don't snap necks, and he directs more of the risks he takes as a reporter to covering life in places where power isn't measured in a wave but in a gun, or in a government often crumbling before one. It's hard not to marvel at the distance Finnegan has traveled by then—and at the fine alteration he braids into his language when he shifts from the lore of the board to where it took him, to the stakes for citizens in a country where he has come to witness the breakdown in civil order.

Like a surfing *Portrait of the Artist as a Young Man*, *Barbarian Days* is a chronicle of the moral changes that unfold inside its author as he grows up. It takes place not in a classroom but where the wind tacks this way, then that, then suddenly there is the ocean standing up in crests, tall as cathedrals. Here's a story of what happens when you run toward such beauty and try not to blink.

IX

THE SUBURBS

HOLY LAND

by D. J. Waldie

Being made of myth and materials, the suburbs are a hard place about which to tell stories. In the last century of American literature, only a handful of good novels unfold there. Even fewer plays and poems. Shaped by restrictions, built on erasure, the suburbs seem tailor-made for horror films. Tales that turn the racial covenants and landscape destruction, which also made the suburbs, inside out—these stories typically speculate through monsters about what all that control over the suburbs is meant to keep at bay.

There is, however, at least one great book to have emerged from the suburbs. It is *Holy Land: A Suburban Memoir*, D. J. Waldie's slim 1996 homage to the town of Lakewood, the planned city of eighty thousand in Los Angeles County where Waldie worked for the city from 1977 until 2010. Unfolding in 316 short, numbered sections, Waldie's book recounts the town's founding, his family's story, and the urban history of the West, mapping each upon the other with harmonic grace.

The effect of this weave is mesmerizing. It's also one of the rare instances in writing—Evan S. Connell's *Mrs. Bridge* might be another—of psychogeography finding a narrative form that makes sense in America. Writing in 1955, the French situationist Guy Debord described psychogeography as "the evident division of a city into zones of distinct psychic atmospheres; the path of least resistance which is automatically followed in aimless strolls . . . gives rise to feelings as differentiated and complex as any other form of spectacle can evoke."

Regimented, planned, and patterned so obviously as to become (cheaply) synonymous with boredom, the suburbs might seem the least conducive environment for such pipettes of thought. The genius of *Holy Land* is to find a way to be flâneurs through Lakewood without approaching this task literally. So we begin almost abstractly: "That evening he thought he was becoming his habits, or—even more—he thought he was becoming the grid he knew." This "he" is our guide in *Holy Land* as we tour through Lakewood. Our narrator, who is sometimes "I," sometimes "he," sometimes simply a transmitter of information, is a kind of one-man oral historian, collecting the stories of his neighborhood, the sensory details—dogs barking, jacaranda trees blooming—of living through seasons. In this way, he becomes a conductor of time, which permits him to move freely within a highly contained world.

And regimented it is. Laid out on a grid at right angles, each lot in Lakewood measures fifty by one hundred feet (the minimum size allowed by the County of Los Angeles). Each house occupies eleven hundred square feet. In front of each home, a fifteen-gallon tree must be planted. None of the species that wind up here are native to California. There's a numerology and comfort to these patterns that is almost religious. "The sidewalk is four feet wide," Waldie writes. "The street is forty feet wide. The strip of lawn between the street and the sidewalk is seven feet. The setback from curb to house is twenty feet. This pattern—of asphalt, grass, concrete, grass—is as regular as any thought of God's."

The liturgical qualities of such passages are not an accident. Waldie, who grew up Catholic, is watching a world be born and created so rapidly that you almost expect the developers to rest on the seventh day. There is a Genesis-like poetry to the assembly of materials, of people. The poetry of shingles and bundles, two-by-fours and tar paper, chicken wire, stucco, scaffold jacks, and concrete pours.

All this destruction to the earth, yet each house has a foundation no deeper than a few feet. Add to that hollow walls—stucco on the outside, barely an inch thick—and one staggers at the temerity hidden within such an enormous construction. The builders didn't have time. First homes went up in 1950, sold for $695 down and a mortgage of around $50 a month, more if the purchaser wanted to finance appliances, which many did. No one had any money. Built by veterans for veterans and others in the shadow of the bomb, Lakewood was a place made so close to a trauma, it feels impossible to be called a dream. Looking at pictures Waldie has collected, aerial shots of the land, which had previously been bean fields, it's hard not to think of sister images of Hiroshima after the devastation.

It's another unaccidental echo. Douglas Aircraft was then the area's biggest employer. While it was a Boeing B-29 Superfortress (the *Enola Gay*) that the US used to drop the bomb on Hiroshima, killing about eighty thousand Japanese people instantly and many more in the days and weeks to come, Douglas made its own medium-range bombers, including the twin-engine A-26 Invader, which was heavily deployed in the Pacific theater. Surely, some of the town's residents would have flown on one. Maybe even watched it rain fire on ships, island, people. But how much wants to be remembered?

Moving in counterpoint to the assumptions of constructions, Waldie paces the story of Lakewood's historic development—the biggest planned city in the world, the biggest shopping center of its time—with anecdote upon anecdote of erasure. Some of the residents, named by an initial to protect their identity, go mad. Douglas gives the city a fighter jet with a blue-eyed Native American, possibly

Navajo, depicted on the side of the aircraft. The Korean War memorial in town has only the names of the city council members. Other monuments obscure the identity of the original builders of the town.

These juxtapositions drive *Holy Land*, one of whose counterpart themes must surely be a riff on the desire for Zion. The three builders of Lakewood were Jewish émigrés. One, Mark Taper, came to California from Poland via England, where he made his first fortune in shoe stores and real estate. He was old enough to have survived the first blitz of World War I, when his father was injured in a zeppelin raid. The other two, Louis Boyar and Ben Weingart, came to Los Angeles from San Francisco and Kentucky, respectively, putting up $15,000 of their own money. It was this investment, as well as many borrowed millions, that allowed them to band together with Taper in 1949 to buy the land that became Lakewood.

And here the historical ironies begin to treble. Looping back to Los Angeles history, Waldie reminds us that the city was founded by the royal order of Spain in 1781—and the city was purposefully separated from the San Gabriel Mission. The priests insisted on the separation, he writes. "They feared the effect of the secular town on their Native American converts." Felipe de Neve, the first colonial governor, carried a map to the nonexistent city from Mexico City. "The book prescribed the exact orientation of the streets, the houses and the public places for all the colonial settlements in the Spanish Americas. That grid came from God."

One wonders, reading *Holy Land*, whether three Jewish men, standing on a landscape nearly razed of trees, made any connection to this long-ago map or to the state of Israel, which was coming into being at the same time several thousand miles away—not in a land without a people but in one where some seven hundred thousand were about to be displaced from their homes. Did the three of them hear the echoes between these two dreams, or between their regimented project in Los Angeles and its name and the right angles and regiments of

Birkenau, which means "birchwood"? It, too, was built on farmland, and each shed on the land was, Waldie says, making the connection overt: "36 feet wide and 116 feet long. Each had been built to house 550 prisoners."

This is an astounding juxtaposition. If a reader was feeling cramped by the idea of these houses, side by side, the barbarity of that housing measurement used during the Holocaust puts the project to build housing for the many (quite a few of them Catholic) into stark perspective. One that would have no doubt been at the forefront of these three builders' minds in 1949. Indeed, Taper had dedicated parts of his then fortune to bringing hundreds of Catholic and Jewish children out of Nazi Germany.

While a short film, *Suburban Memoir*, has been made of Waldie's book, it's not clear why a full-length movie hasn't, because Waldie leaves plenty of space for a screenwriter and director to imagine their way into the space between this period and what is reported here. For instance, Taper, Boyar, and Weingart bought the land from Clark Bonner, the nephew of the founder of the Montana Land Company. As Waldie writes, "The Montana Land Company made it very clear in its promotional material that the lots were protected by 'restrictions of an all-inclusive nature.' Written into deed covenants, these restrictions prevented the sale of lots to Negroes, Mexicans and Jews."

In other words, the three Jewish entrepreneurs were building a development that they wouldn't be able to live in. One wonders if they had conversations at the time with the association of musicians and World War II veterans assembled to make Crestwood Hills in West Los Angeles—originally planned to be a multiethnic utopian housing experiment. Some of the homes, many of which still survive, were designed by A. Quincy Jones. Pressure from nearby Brentwood residents caused the makeup of the association to change. Still, many of the cooperative members were Jewish, and the idea of living collectively was the goal.

As Waldie points out in *Holy Land*, even if tight quarters and shared spaces were design features in Lakewood, isolation became the norm. Mixing his family's story with those he encounters at the city office, he describes people slowly going mad, digging bomb shelters beneath their garages, telling on one another in a constant low-grade war of NIMBYism. Writing personally, no doubt, he says one of the saddest things ever said about his suburb: "You almost never hear the sounds of love." It's a testament to the way Waldie shapes his narrative orbitals that such details do not entirely define "his city," as he calls Lakewood. There are, of course, moments of unexpected social grace—the naming of three parks after Latin American freedom fighters—and of sheer wonder at its existence at all, at the success of its founders. After all, William Willmore, who founded the utopian racialist experiment that became Long Beach, failed and wound up dying poor. When Weingart died, he was worth over $200 million.

How to live ethically in proximity to such history is one of the questions *Holy Land* raises without ever really providing an answer; rather, through example, it offers a mode of holding the impossibility of an answer. The book is in many ways a demonstration of the power of counternarration. Diverting through education and more, naming the mission projects so many California kids were made to do growing up, *Holy Land* does not let its readers forget what was erased for Lakewood to exist, without ever making the presumption of claiming that what has been erased can be retrieved.

Part narrator, part time captain, Waldie is the mournful poet of his palimpsest city, striding through it figuratively the way Guillaume Apollinaire once did Paris. "If you lived in the old days, you would enter a monastery," Apollinaire wrote of himself. Waldie, whose own family went partially into the cloth, has a similar aura. Meditative, archival, but possessing of a prose that feels written on foot, he has drawn an eternal book about a changing place. In this living map, he chronicles so much. The construction of his city, the unbuilding of his own family: first his mother's, then his father's death from heart disease. Then his own peculiar afterlife in the dry quietudes that live adjacent to grief. "You and I were trained for a conflict that never came," he says, addressing all the other children of the Cold War. Oh, but there were others.

MEAN

by Myriam Gurba

A great writer doesn't have a style: She *is* her style. The words she chooses, the rhythms she arranges, what music her prose makes. In the highest realms of art, where the act of storytelling is essential to survival, these are not alsos: They are the reordering, the choosing of a written body. In a world where so many bodies are at risk, one does not have to think hard to ponder the importance of this task.

In her powerful and darkly comedic memoir, *Mean*, Myriam Gurba gives us an electrifying, front-row seat to the high stakes of forging a style. It is to the memoir what *Paris Is Burning* was to the drag show. Ribald, poetic, broken into shards in some moments, as lucid as a California sky in others, the book shows how complexity asserts itself in stylistic variety and under the pressure of trauma. It also demonstrates how powerfully humor can deflect the clutches of preconceived emotions.

As soon as you know this is a memoir about rape and survival—which becomes clear on page one—a host of tones and expectations begins to boot up. Gurba is having none of them. This little book is also stippled with puns (has a writer ever enjoyed saying "cum laude" so much?), fart jokes, brilliant riffs on Japanese poetry, California lingo, and some of the best descriptions you will find of history and anthropology professors. "He looked ready to dig or raid a tomb," Gurba writes about one of her Berkeley teachers.

As a made object, *Mean* is a magnificent thing. The book unfolds in many short chapters, which ripple out from evocative titles like "Wisdom," "The Unbearable Whiteness of Certain Girls," and "Aesthetic Boners." Some chapters move like miniature stories, others like vignettes, others still with the yoked repetitive rhythms of a Sylvia Plath poem or a Sonia Sanchez piece. Throughout, Gurba writes in short, staccato sentences that detonate musically.

The overlaying of these chapter titles and Gurba's inimitable prose produce the sound of her voice: unfussy, unpretentious. It invites collusion. It speaks, you listen—and follow. "Let's become that night," Gurba writes in her opening incantatory passage. "We're November's darkness. We're the baseball diamond's sediment. We host Little League games by daylight. By dark, we become an Aztec altar."

The passage is lustrous and terrifying, and by making her readers the night, it places us everywhere and nowhere, like ghosts. The idea of possession will appear and reappear throughout the book. As readers, we lurk unseen around events that will haunt Gurba for many years. Meanwhile, she is tormented by what she describes in her opening pages: a true-life crime in which a dark-haired Mexican girl was brutally raped and murdered, her body left behind. The papers called her a transient. Gurba tells us her name was Sophia.

One of Gurba's strongest skills is the transition. Out of this true-crime opener, we're tipped abruptly into an almost pop-art depiction of growing up in Southern California. The child of a Mexican mother and a half-Polish father, Gurba is raised speaking one language ("English and Spanish"), frequently defending (or refusing to explain) what she is, where she is from, how she got here (she's always been here). Already she is full of the attitude that is worth quoting in full:

> We act mean to defend ourselves from boredom and from those who would chop off our breasts. We act mean to defend our clubs and institutions. We act mean because we like to laugh. Being mean to boys is fun and a second-wave feminist duty. Being rude to men who deserve it is a holy mission. Sisterhood is powerful, but being a bitch is more exhilarating. Being a bitch is spectacular.

The "we" here describes Gurba and her friends at the time, but it also reaches out, inviting others in, and stakes out territory. A space of queer rebellion, a place for survivor realism, for mess and solidarity. This we isn't always, exclusively brown, as throughout Gurba describes her curiosity about and love for (certain) white girls, beginning with her friend Ida. "When she came over to my house, she slurped Mom's pozole instead of asking 'What is this?' in that supremely bitchy California-girl accent some white girls reserved for interrogating my mother's hospitality."

As we follow Gurba into her friendships, childhood, and teenage years, the assault and murder from page one and the graphic images with which she describes it linger, seeping into the book's descriptive DNA. The games Gurba plays on the playground she describes as rehearsals of sexual assault; her aunt, we'll learn, regales her with tales of *violación*; molestation is a fact of life. A boy named Macaulay gropes Gurba in history class, kicking off one of this book's continuing meditations on what history means. ("Some of us use rape to tell time," she will later write.)

Again the image of a possession comes back, layered this time and filtered through a Catholic prism. After a baseball coach is found to have assaulted many of her boy classmates, Gurba writes: "If molestation is a circle, a circle of life, then isn't the hand of every molester working through the hand of every other molester? It's fair to say that

Mr. Osmond's hand was working through Macaulay's hand just like the Eucharist is no longer bread during Mass; it's Jesus coming at you through a cracker."

The structure of *Mean* is an elegant, subtle score. The book begins with Sophia, and we don't hear about her again for fifty more pages. All along, Gurba's descriptive lexicon of assault has created an exquisite foreshadowing. Will what happened in childhood be it, or will she escape? A reader is apt to wonder, until Gurba writes, "You never know what spaces might turn into graves," adding, "Sometimes my concerns about the history of violence taint everything. . . . I was allowed to escape. I was allowed to walk away from that spot. Sophia was not. Guilt is a ghost."

Here is the ghost that most haunts this book. After all, we are not watching Gurba's childhood but witnessing her retelling of it, from adulthood: a time during which, we soon learn, she experiences a profound rupture. Looking back, everything that will happen to Gurba on a street in broad daylight at age eighteen filters into the telling. She becomes a writer, so the book is eminently concerned with words, language, definitions, and wordplay. She will fall in love, so the telling also studies the first burning of desire, the construction of solidarity, the role—if any—of safety in eros.

And she will survive an assault—miraculously—by the man who killed Sophia. Telling this story from the present, Gurba produces mounting tension leading up to that day, which she approaches and backs off from, explaining her hesitation. Warning us, telling us why she will hold back. That she will ultimately keep some details to herself. And then she tells what she can, and it's both matter-of-fact and terrifying.

As a memoir of trauma, *Mean* is acute, powerful, and full of descriptions survivors will recognize. Gurba recalls her waves of reaction—how she began to study like a machine, working out obsessively. She gets a 4.0 and impressive muscles; she immediately sets new, harder goals.

Eventually, her faithful body-raft breaks down under the weight of what it must hold. Passing out, sprawled out on the floor of a Berkeley bathroom when it finally gives out, wrapped in a blanket, she still makes a joke: "'I am a bean burrito,' I thought."

Gurba went to Berkeley to study history, because she wants to understand it, but also literature and art, because she is drawn to them. In those classes, she suffers through—as many of us did—Gertrude Stein. *Mean*, in many ways, is Gurba's brilliant deviation from her lesbian forebearer's example of writing prose undergirded by the aesthetics and theory of visual art. Proceeding in its later part with stories, personal registers, lists, found poems, and even a 911 transcript, *Mean* is a glittering example of the possibilities of collage: a stitching where tears in the reality reel occur.

The book's descriptions of what the posttraumatic state does to the mind are vivid and distressing. Gurba's own mind, continually under assault by the assault she just survived, works overtime. One day, she believes she sees *him* in the supermarket, then realizes her mind has put "that face over this homeboy's face. It blended them into one composite." And then, fashioning a joke to a serious observation, as she often does, Gurba adds: "The posttraumatic mind has an advanced set of art skills."

They are not just its skills, though. They are Gurba's skills uniquely. One of the triumphs of *Mean* is not to parlay the familiar narrative of overcoming adversity, nor to circle a lugubrious morbidity, which would be, of course, understandable. Instead the book is a celebration of the creator herself and her mind, and the friends and family who enabled its (and her) survival. That mind is part semiotician, part stand-up comic. Believer in ghosts, fighter for their rights. Maker of new rituals.

In one of the book's moving later passages, Gurba travels with her parents and a new girlfriend to the site of Sophia's murder to make an offering. Her father can't bear to get out of the car. Before the mists of meaning can descend, Gurba quips, "What a dick," then corrects herself, the voice's irreverent tone coming as ballast. "I didn't think of him as a pussy—he hadn't earned that compliment." And so they go out and walk among the shadows on that baseball diamond—where so many haven't a clue they are standing on a grave—unsure what to give, what to offer. As if this extraordinary, essential book isn't enough.

ELSEWHERE, CALIFORNIA

by Dana Johnson

California is where people from elsewhere wind up, the state's settlers and their descendants like to tell themselves. It's a powerful myth in a state of broken myths operating in plain sight, one made more resonant by the brute fact of migration. Every day, people arrive in Reseda, in Turlock, in Sacramento and San Diego at the end (or in continuation) of remarkable journeys. But within the state, every day, a related voyage is undertaken by millions too, one you might put this way: There are elsewheres within California. Indeed, there are elsewheres within single Californian cities. From South Los Angeles to West Covina, the LA suburb where the narrator of Dana Johnson's debut novel grows up, for example, stretches a distance of just twenty-eight miles. In reality, the gap between these two neighborhoods is so vast in cultural and racial stakes, it gives Johnson's heroine a lifelong case of vertigo.

Elsewhere, California is Johnson's brilliant map of the questions this journey poses for an artist, especially if she wants to make art out of where she is from. How far back does she go? What language does she use? Whose values matter, and how does she begin to portray the ways that people's imaginations create roles she can try on, or even live inside? Reject or take comfort in? Reading *Elsewhere, California* doesn't so much answer these questions as drive us past them in different shapes and forms, dramatizing their demand to be asked and posed anew, to never be taken for granted—even if the woman asking them appears to live the good life, as Avery Arlington, the novel's heroine, does.

All maps need to start with scale; it's how we appreciate distance. Avery's starts with her parents' lives as this map's legend—where they came from, how they thought. "My parents were not playful people," the book begins, as if to signal that Avery's life of choices, that her anxiety about the direction her life has gone, is already a significant deviation from their own modest beginnings. The Arlingtons came west in the great migration from Tennessee, "all the way from Africa," her father liked to tell her as a kid in one of their games. "I'm not from any of those places," she'd reply when goaded into listening to tales of hardship. "I'm just from California."

The universes that live within that four-word sentence is the territory this book sets out to chart. To do so, Johnson draws on all the first-person sounds of revelation, and some of the details of her own life. Like her heroine, she was born in South LA and moved to West Covina at a young age. Johnson has thought a lot about the particulars of the class journey to becoming an artist. *Elsewhere, California* was miles ahead of the obsession with autofiction that reared up, the world over, in the first part of the twenty-first century.

Elsewhere, California is too dramatic, too uncontained, and ultimately too invented to be classified as autofiction. Its setup evokes the vertigo of a noir film. As the book opens, a sense of unease and fraudulence has crept into Avery's life. She lives in the Hollywood Hills, married to a wealthy Italian builder, trying to paint. Unhappiness has sent her to a therapist, then onward to a hypnotherapist. Avery's grown brother, who we later learn works at UPS and still lives in the San Gabriel Valley, where they grew up, scorns his sister's pain. "My brother Owen said that my main trauma was that the house I was living in," Avery quips, "was too big for me to clean all by myself." Not that long ago, their mother cleaned houses, so Avery's brother's choice of insult has its barbs.

A Dana Johnson fan might be forgiven a bit of déjà vu. This state of affairs is where Johnson's debut collection, Break Any Woman Down, left off. The collection began with Avery moving into a new school and developing a crush on a white classmate. It ended with Avery grown up, looking after her mother, drinking too much, and confused by her relationship with Massimo, a strong-willed Italian man determined to spoil her.

Although they share characters, Elsewhere, California is very different from the collection that precedes it, for it proceeds from the uncanny fractures that develop out of simultaneity—within the person. After its opening scene, the book splits into two threads, one taking place in the present tense, as we build to an exhibit of Avery's paintings that she plans to host, the other happening in the past. The two sections unfold in different languages: the present Avery narrates in the voice she has learned to speak in through practice and education, the kind of voice that is from nowhere or *elsewhere*.

The voice of the past Avery is told in the vernacular she spoke as a child. The one she learned not to speak, most of the time. The kind that embarrassment teaches her not to use. "It sounds like theres a whole bunch a people somewhere that I have never even met and they watching me," Avery says, recalling a night she was scolded by her father for cursing at a white neighbor's house. "They disappointed in me because they all taught me better than what Im doing."

Over the course of the book, these two languages gravitate toward each other, intermingle and infiltrate the imaginaries each section creates. This movement is supremely well handled. It's like realizing that the melody of each sound has not begun in one place or another, but emerges only in the conversation between the two. It's not, after all, as if Avery's parents didn't encourage her sense of migration, of elsewheres, through example. When friends from their old neighborhood come over and are too loud, Avery's father says, "Dash need to stay his ass on 80th Street," referring to South LA.

Elsewhere, California sheds light on the paradoxes of this upbringing, in which Avery is reminded to remember where she's from, *but not too much*. Like so many parents, hers send her to the kind of school that will reinforce this lesson. Gradually attending to how white women at school speak to her mother, and how white neighbors encourage her to speak, Avery begins a process of watching herself from the outside. As she falls in love with the Dodgers, and delights to Fernando Valenzuela's high leg kick, as she drops to the ground to practice earthquake preparedness, another part of her is always watching her performance for flaws.

Johnson traces the costs and consequences of this double consciousness in Avery's life, revealing how an ability to adapt turns into a sense of distrust when her adaptation succeeds. After they meet at a bar, Massimo plying Avery with flattering lines but an even more flattering sense of restraint, he takes her on a date. They pull up to a great big house in the hills, and he comes around to open her car door, a gesture she has seen only on television before. "I had always hoped that one day, a boy would take me out on a date and treat me that way, the way Massimo was treating me, and yet when he . . . reached for my hand, I was embarrassed. I thought he was making fun of me."

Elsewhere, California is full of such intimate moments, wherein the contradictions of a journey—you are here, you have arrived, and yet you never do—are drawn carefully out in the weave of life, then heightened by their juxtaposition to the past. We learn how in the beginning of their relationship, Massimo was fascinated and turned on by Avery's dark skin, pleased to see it against white sheets, against his lighter skin. Around the same time, narrating from the past, Avery shows us how she learned to be around white people. She develops crushes on white actors and singers. A source of shame and worry for her mother, of ridicule by her cousin Keith.

Unlike so many novels about artists, *Elsewhere, California* has given its heroine an oeuvre you actually want to see hung in a gallery. In addition to portraits and paintings, Avery has done a series in which she paints well-known white celebrities in blackface, first tarnishing their shiny images with blobs of paint here and there, then suddenly rendering them entirely in blackface. The effect of these works—and other pieces described herein—is potent and destabilizing. They are not easily categorized by like or dislike, but rather by weight and pressure. Like the colors Johnson uses throughout the novel—this story is saturated in Avery's eye for shades, for the gradations within gray and white, in blue—this artwork applies pressure to the plot and creates states of mind in the reader that are vivid and complex.

Her dedication to capturing life in its most robust state enables Johnson to honestly portray a relationship that has tensions, power dynamics, and sexual anxieties interwoven with its sweetness. Massimo worships and desires Avery, wants for her to enjoy her art, but he contains contradictions. In some moments he thrills to her shaved head, strokes it in ways she likes; in others, when, for example, they are pulled over by a police officer who addresses Avery as "Sir," he is appalled and embarrassed—mostly for himself—by the fluidity of how her gender is interpreted.

As *Elsewhere, California* progresses, it dramatizes how in any state of existence we can be at least two things, often more. Brenna, Avery's best friend growing up, has never totally left where they grew up and is a supporter as much as a heckler. Similarly, even though Keith, Avery's cousin, wound up in prison, he has not departed into the past either, reentering her life in abrupt and sometimes frightening ways like a haunting. It's a persistence that lingers like desire, but it has as much to do with shame as it does with love.

Where is the road map for navigating such treacherous relationships? Avery seems to ask at certain points in this sumptuously thoughtful book. Where is the guide that says, this is how you live this? *Elsewhere, California* is both the record of that question and a hopeful act of creation which posits that asking it well enough can be a kind of answer.

THE BARBARIAN NURSERIES

by Héctor Tobar

Some novels are so teeming with energy they seem to contain whole cities. Noisy, wondrous, irritating, pulsing planets full of sons and daughters: hucksters, winos, wisenheimers, and lost souls. Without the dimension added by these imaginary communities, our real metropolises would be impoverished, reduced to their simplest myths and glossiest images.

No city in America has needed such a book quite like Los Angeles. Its long boulevards and metal-gated shotgun houses, its water thieves and hustlers and Mexicanos have been occluded in fiction. Héctor Tobar's second novel, *The Barbarian Nurseries*, brings them all sharply into view in a book so vast you can get lost here. It tells a grand story, bulging with dozens of minor characters and one unforgettable heroine.

At the center of the family is not a mother or a father but a Mexican live-in domestic named Araceli. She works six days a week for $250 for the Torres-Thompson family, cooking, cleaning, and watching over their three children—Brandon, Keenan, and fifteen-month-old baby Samantha. Araceli was once one of several undocumented immigrants from Mexico working in the home. Now, with Scott Torres's investments tanking and his wife, Maureen, determined to continue as if nothing has changed, Araceli's daily burden has become immense.

But her role balloons one morning when she wakes to discover that after an explosive argument, both Scott and Maureen have fled their home, leaving Araceli alone with the two Torres boys. She waits, she frets, and then, when it seems they have been abandoned—Maureen, must have taken the baby—Araceli packs a bag and sets off on foot with the two boys in tow, in search of their estranged Mexican American grandfather, whom neither boy has seen in two years. All she has is a photo of the old man and an idea of where he used to live.

Araceli's bold move will later prove devastating for her and the Torres-Thompson family, but it is the moment when *The Barbarian Nurseries* begins to soar. Like Odysseus's endless journey home, Araceli and the boys' trek across town is full of strange and almost mystical encounters. They travel through the wasteland of Los Angeles's rail yards, its hauntingly decayed Union Station. They are taken in for a night by a Salvadoran woman and spend July 4th at a posh barbeque in Huntington Park, surrounded by young women with perfect American accents who attend Ivy League schools.

Tobar, who won a Pulitzer Prize in reporting for the *Los Angeles Times*, has a prismatic, relentless eye for the many layers of Americanness at work in Southern California, often within the same person, and uncomfortably so. The man hosting the barbeque looks down on his fellow immigrant neighbors, who have not yet saved enough to buy their own homes. A Mexican American border guard, whose story threads briefly through the novel, finds no contradiction between his background and his job.

Reporters who write novels are often a little heavy-handed with themes, and Tobar is guilty of this throughout *The Barbarian Nurseries*. But he is so confident in his ability to enter his characters' minds that this leftover scaffolding falls away, again and again. While Araceli marches across town, embracing a responsibility she never wanted,

Tobar tracks Scott and Maureen in their respective flights from responsibility. Scott holes up at a coworker's house and plays video games for two days; Maureen has taken baby Samantha and goes to a spa.

As awful as their negligence sounds, Tobar spends such a sizable section of the novel's opening depicting Scott and Maureen's parental and financial exhaustion that one almost understands their instincts for self-pampering and escape. Araceli might be rescuing the boys, but she is no saint, either. One of her petty vanities is intellectual pretension. Even while people are helping her—and later defending her—she judges their fashion, their accents, even their cooking.

In the novel's closing pages, Maureen and Scott finally return home, discover the children missing, and file a missing persons report, turning their private drama into a public one. The media frenzy over the mangled and manipulated story of the maid who left with the children—maybe fleeing for the border!—provides enough accelerant to bring this huge story to a roaring climax. As readers we are at once voyeurs and participants. We know why Araceli left, and we've witnessed what the boys have seen. It is their Los Angeles, the city that has been all around them and invisible, until now.

DIGITAL DYS/UTOPIAS

THE GOLD COAST

by Kim Stanley Robinson

In 2022, in San Francisco, I rode in a driverless car for the first time. I am old enough both to have watched *The Jetsons* and to then see some of their technologies come to pass. Video conversations. Drones. Smart watches. They've all become part of day-to-day life. Flying cars always seemed a bit much, but the way no one had to drive in *The Jetsons*? As a Californian who once commuted, *that* I could get behind. In a way, though, we've been there for a while. Most planes fly on a computerized flight plan. They basically take off and land themselves, a commercial airline pilot told me. When I learned this, I wasn't the least bit surprised—or worried.

By the time new technology arrives, it has often already so thoroughly altered our consciousness, our culture, and our way of being that to observe its arrival is impossible. That goes for more than gadgets. We are all enmeshed in a vast array of systems, especially ones we don't see. Many of us in the United States do not ever witness an animal slaughtered; some of us don't interact with the person who delivers our food; the scenes of factory life where so much technology is made barely graze us. And so convenience—in the modern sense—is created invisibly.

When "Griffin" pulled away from the corner of Mason and California, drove up Nob Hill, and slowed to a complete stop at a dark crosswalk, I was only briefly unnerved. It was a good driver. The steering wheel turned with handless precision. The stops were perfect. Within a minute or two, I'd begun, as in many car rides, to gaze out the window and daydream. I'd been prepared for this moment by years of technological advances. A phone that was a camera; a refrigerator that self-regulated; a coffee machine that woke me up with coffee already made. There was no rupture here. The last time a schism really occurred was in the creation and use of a nuclear weapon. The ability to destroy every living thing on earth is the most transformative technology humans have ever made, even including agriculture or iron work.

In the late twentieth century, Kim Stanley Robinson wrote a trilogy of novels about life in California in the future, each imagining a different outcome. One, *The Wild Shore*, is a nuclear holocaust frontier novel; *The Gold Coast*, which is the second, is a near-future social realist book; the third, *Pacific Edge*, is a story of a green utopia and its possibilities. For all their can't-blame-them flubs—answering machines? Texas Instruments still a thing?—they get two major things right. The first is that nuclear technology threatens our very existence. The second is the recognition that technology often has already changed us before we adapt to its values.

The Gold Coast is the darkest of the three. It revolves around the dilemma of how to live ethically when the systems of our—particularly men's—lives, and the ways one copes with those systems, have produced a fundamental disconnection. In the novel, set in the year 2027, a group of men, many of them loosely or directly attached to the vast network of defense contractors in Orange County, live dissolute, somewhat malaise-driven lives. They ride in driverless cars that move on tracks; they take hallucinogenic drugs through eyelid dropper; they toil to produce ever more effective weapons of killing, on time, for maximum profit.

The Gold Coast is a chilling portrait of the world made by this disembodied life of convenience and mass murder. Every bit of land has been developed or turned into freeways. The only growth seems to occur in a densely packed area of glass skyscrapers, "a crystal city of weapons procurement." Dennis McPherson, who works there on a supersonic intercontinental ballistic missile defense system, feels himself "coming out of automatic pilot . . . whenever he goes out into the world and advocates for stopping weapons by building even more weapons."

Throughout the novel, machines are a metaphor for life. Talking to an air force general in charge of procurement, Dennis jokes about his son, Jim. "He's a strange one. A brain without a program." Twenty-seven-year-old Jim is "a part-time word processor for a title and real estate company, a part-time night school teacher" at a community college. Essentially, however, he's a poet who hangs out with his friends— Tashi, a surfer who lives off the grid; Sandy, a drug dealer; and Abe, an EMT who patrols the freeways in a tricked-out 1,000-horsepower Chevy van, which runs on gasoline and pulls people off the wrecks that keep occurring because of the driverless cars.

At times, as Abe, Tashi, Sandy, and Jim orbit one another's lives, *The Gold Coast* feels like a necrotic, futuristic *Dharma Bums*. Jim is drawn ever closer to a mysterious figure named Arthur. While Arthur is no Japhy Ryder, the character modeled off the poet Gary Snyder in Kerouac's novel, he has a similar dedication to clarity, a monkish singularity. At night, Arthur plasters Orange County in posters encouraging people to wake up, and eventually mentions to Jim that he is involved in planning direct action—read violence—against the defense industry.

It's worth pausing here to say that most of the novel would almost certainly fail the Bechdel Test, the rubric set up by the brilliant comic book artist Alison Bechdel about asking whether the female-identified characters in a book are defined entirely through their relationship to men. That is absolutely the case here, but the gender dynamic depicted might be on purpose, a subterranean commentary on the social relations produced by its technologies. Of Robinson's trilogy, *The Gold Coast* is the most filmic, and all of its characters have been shaped by visual culture and especially pornography. "Video saturation has trained Jim, like everyone else, to a fine appreciation of the female image," Robinson writes acidly in one scene before Jim and friends pile naked into a Jacuzzi.

Jim, his father, and their friends are not that old trope of boys in need of a soft touch to be civilized, but men absolutely caught in a world of machinist masculinities. At work, Stewart Lemon—Dennis's boss—has learned that the only way to truly motivate his underling is to threaten and bully him. To jack the most productivity from him by igniting his anger. Abe has learned to prowl the highways like a soul-smoked Highlander, packing away the part of him that feels or has empathy so that he can saw through metal, sometimes cutting off limbs in order to free victims of the machines men have made. He's more robotic than the robotics that assist him. At night, among the friends, he drinks more than most.

Jim, wavering between the world of his father, Tashi's earth-loving ways ("The less you are plugged into the machine, the less it controls you"), and the promise of vengeance by Arthur, is the character who reflects on this state of existence the most. He sees it and wants to do something, but doesn't know how. He can't escape the questions this way of life provokes, the commodifications it encourages, even in what he might call pleasure. In one memorable scene, he and his "ally" (lover) Virginia pair off from one of their hot tub get-togethers to have sex. Robinson's future depicts all sex as mediated, to the point that most people plug into an elaborate system of cameras and projections so they can watch themselves as they have intercourse. To go to bed without this viewing is almost unthinkable. In the middle of Jim and Virginia's session, however, the system breaks, and instantly they stop. Catching a brain wave, Jim drags a huge mirror into the bedroom, and at last they're able to finish: "Jim can't help grinning lasciviously at himself. The image is different also, the video's softness and depth of field replaced by a hard, silvered, glossy materiality, as if they've got a window here and are spying on a couple in some more glassy world."

The Gold Coast reflects the glass aesthetics of its time. It unfolds with the rolling dolly shots of *Miami Vice*, Michael Mann's breakthrough 1984 TV show. It is a feast for the eye, constantly showing us things and how people live, cutting cinematically from character to character as Jim is drawn into an actual plot to attack a defense contractor, and not just any contractor but the one his father works for. As a writer, Robinson is keenly attuned to the way a scene in the old sense is not just a moment of drama but a tableau—a spectacle.

But he can shift gears, and throughout *The Gold Coast*, in interstitial chapters written by Jim, others drawing from different characters' memories, he moves into a high poetic register. One of the most unexpectedly radiant chapters is the briefest, which unfurls in the mind of Jim's uncle Tom, who lives in a sprawling retirement community called Seizure World. After Jim visits and then leaves, Tom enters a kind of reverie and remembers playing in the orange groves that once plunged off in every direction in Southern California, the area around each tree perfectly symmetrical, a symbol of the manipulation of nature's design.

"We ate the oranges too, choosing only the very best," Tom recalls to a mind's-eye Jim. "The green and slightly acrid sweat that comes out of their skin as you peel them, the white pulpy inside of the peels, the sharp and fragrant smell, the wedges of inner fruit, perfectly rounded crescent wedges . . . odd things. Their taste never seemed quite real. . . . No one could imagine that all the groves would be torn down."

A lesser novel would have let this bygone world and its emotional utopias stand. But *The Gold Coast* is a novel, among other things, about the way utopias always proceed from destruction. So a few chapters later, in Jim's voice (or that of another; it's not entirely clear), the novel reminds us that all of this land was stolen by the Franciscan missions and ethnically cleansed of peoples whose connection to it had lasted thousands of years before it was renamed as a different utopia: Orange County.

The Gold Coast asks, Is there such a thing as the last needed brutality? Bathed in California light, are Robinson's men just another group bent on a new totalizing violence? And has technology made decimation and starting over the only way we can see change? It has certainly gone that way for Dennis, the weapons manufacturer, driven by his abusive boss. Dennis can hardly be surprised when his son turns to violence, as he does. Jim "dreams of a cataclysm that could bring this overlit American to ruin, and leave behind only the land, the land, the land."

It took another novel for Robinson to offer an alternative to this cycle, one drawn out in the green utopia, *Pacific Edge*. Would that we were closer to that reality. Instead, to read *The Gold Coast* today is to experience an uncanny familiarity. Bombs made far from the consequences of their dropping; people tuned in to screens to distract them from what they know. Encountering this world on the page is like stepping into a car without a driver, or paying for an object with a telephone, or seeing one's own face in a mirror without expecting it and finding—for a brief moment—a blankness, or lack of recognition, because so often when we look at ourselves, we aren't really looking.

THE EVERY

by Dave Eggers

"California is spectacular," so many newcomers have told the rest of the world. But not all of them. Saul Bellow took a grim view of what the state's magnetic force drew. In *Seize the Day*, he wrote that "in Los Angeles all the loose objects of the country were collected, as if America had been tilted and everything that wasn't tightly screwed down had slid into Southern California."

Another great Chicago writer has taken better to the Golden State—Dave Eggers, who arrived in the Bay Area several decades ago and hasn't left since. Unlike Bellow, who was fascinated by people but didn't like them very much, Eggers adores people and appreciates California on an elementary level. As he wrote in his memoir, *A Heartbreaking Work of Staggering Genius*, the state's everyday scenery staggered him in his early days, the way California can. Driving on the highway, he steers "past the surfers, through the eucalyptus forest before Half Moon Bay, birds swooping up and over then back, circling around us—they too, for us!—then the cliffs before Seaside—then flat for a little while, then a few more bends and can you see that motherfucking sky? I mean, have you fucking been to California?"

I still remember the moment I read this sentence, a Californian rotting away in a New York City winter. Every cell in my body wanted to come home. Eggers had a different conditional reason for that barbaric yawp of receptivity. He'd arrived in California after the tragic death within months of his two parents, with his younger brother to raise. *A Heartbreaking Work* tells the story of how they fared and how out of loss, or desire, the feeling of being alive, which can emerge in grief, we create utopian structures to hold us. They can be a family, a friend group, a magazine. (Eggers starts two during the book, *Might* and *McSweeney's*.)

Ever since then, as he expanded to an astounding array of genres—essentially all of them but poetry—Eggers has continued to write about the ways we create Valhallas. Why we need them, what possibilities and pitfalls they hold. In his books, these structures take on a variety of shapes: families (*Heroes of the Frontier*), boondoggles (*A Hologram for the King*), imaginary tribes (*The Wild Things*), and even parks, like the one at the heart of his Newbery-winning book, *The Eyes and the Impossible*.

Shaggy-dogged, grand and full of hope, sometimes sinister (as in *The Parade*), these utopian dreams are the engine of organization behind Eggers's books. They create the indelible pockets of pressure between outside and in—the space wherein an attempt to live up to ideas collides with people and their limitations. Not for nothing are three of Eggers's best-known books portraits of seekers and survivors: *Zeitoun*, *What Is the What*, and *The Monk of Mokha*. How his books narrate that negotiation, the feeling of dreaming and of being let down, is a big part of their appeal.

Of course, California has been at this arcadian business for years—not just providing a home for communes, planned communities, of which there have been many, but also dreamlands. It has in fact built the world's biggest, most far-reaching utopian experiment in human history, and that's the internet and all the associated businesses that have sprawled across every scintilla of human life, offering us not simply life itself but *more* life, sometimes a replacement for life, a betterment of it through its abstraction, and prosthetic tools (like generative AI) with which to engage in the real thing. Or the parts we'd rather deal with at a remove.

The early 2000s were a gold rush for space on an infinite plane, as companies conquered territories by type of service (flower delivery, antique shoes, basketball stats) and were, in turn, gobbled up by other sites, bigger retailers. In the past dozen years, that model of the web has been retooled by the consolidation of power within the hands of a few tech giants, several of whom touch us (and we them) through their social media products. In this transition from users who buy products or view media to people who are the product (through the data we create by using the internet) and the media we produce, a fundamental shift occurred. As digital pioneer and futurist Jaron Lanier put it, "As the internet, the devices, and the algorithms advanced, advertising inevitably morphed into mass behavior modification."

In the mid-2010s, this march toward behavior control became ever more entrenched, as disinformation, political phishing, and deep fakes entered the American political space on an industrial scale. With none of the algorithms of any of the major tech companies transparent, it is still impossible to understand who was pulling what levers in this huge system of information distribution. By some accounts, just the ads paid for by Russian bots reached over a quarter of the electorate alone. During the pandemic, each one of the major platforms became clearinghouses for fear-triggering information about COVID, vaccines, and who was behind them, with some of these falsehoods being spread by the most powerful man on the planet, the president. With the second Trump presidency, the forces behind all of the major platforms entered the White House, with part-time Californian Elon Musk—who donated over $200 million of his nearly half-a-trillion-dollar fortune—taking on an unspecified, seemingly unlimited role to refashion what government is and how it works.

How did we get here? In the future, if anyone wants an answer, they will need to turn to Eggers's two novels *The Circle* and *The Every*, which unfold during this transformative period as well as the near future. (I reviewed the first when it came out and edited the second in my current job at Alfred A. Knopf, where it was the first book I worked on.) *The Circle* revolves around Mae Holland; her parents need extensive health care, so she holds her nose and takes a job at the new tech giant, a company called the Circle, that has parked itself in the Bay. On her first day, she is struck by the building as if it were a mirage: "My God, Mae thought," Eggers writes, "it's heaven."

The Circle was a novel of its time—the era in which tech giants were considered gods and ultimately good. Magazines decorated their covers with portraits of their founders. Mae is not, in this sense, a dupe for becoming seduced by the Circle and its technology—all of us were. Who didn't buy an iPhone in this period and stroke its screen and marvel at how soft it was, how silken? But inside the Circle, life was somewhat different. What begins as a highly automated workplace starts to seem like an insanely robotic one—if workers don't receive enough likes, they are demoted. If they aren't going transparent or allowing their life to be viewed at work all the time, they are regarded as secretive. Keeping up with this, Mae steadily drops values that have been essential to human life—balance, privacy, belonging. Very quickly, the work family she develops inside the Circle replaces her actual family, and she begins to mimic the needs and values of the corporation.

The Circle landed in 2013, the year of the National Security Agency Prism scandal, in which it was revealed that one of the US agencies had a secret spy program looking at domestic activity. In this sense, the novel might read like a thriller, but it touches a different genre we are all familiar with—the corporate exposé. Most of the moral dilemmas, as experienced by Mae, are entirely about her employment at that corporation. The corporation is the villain, and whether she bends to it or not—to help her family—gives us the dramatic tension of that story.

Inside the Circle, we get to see how a company like that operated, what it tried out (in software and policies) on employees, what it made them reframe. "SECRETS ARE LIES; SHARING IS CARING; PRIVACY IS THEFT," Mae says at one of the all-office meetings, which are like megachurch performances. The applause is thunderous.

In *The Every*, Eggers navigates the world these mega–tech corporations have wrought, rolling out this type of behavior modification on the users themselves. It is a world in which every experience, every object—photos, sandwich makers' backgrounds, old clothing, people's entire wardrobes—is hoovered up and owned, ranked, and possessed by one company. To keep us involved, all the tools used inside the Circle by Mae (frowns, likes, PartiRanks) have been let loose on the population at large, and these analytics have created a mob of people furiously turning to the cloud for signals of how to live and act, and then battling one another with ever more fury to enforce those signals. It's a perfect circle of everyone looking at everything and trying to parse (or sometimes police) every utterance, every interaction, every node of existence.

As we begin, Mae has risen so high up into the Circle, and the Every—the corporation that has gobbled it up—that she's something of a phantom. Everywhere and nowhere. Word is she might be pregnant, but in everyday terms she exists as the voice in the onboarding software, welcoming new hires. Caroming into this behemoth is Delaney Wells, whose goal, it quickly becomes clear, is to take down the company from within. She'd started this effort a long way back and even, strategically, wrote her college thesis on the folly of an antitrust measure against the Circle, coining the phrase "Benevolent Market Mastery"—a great euphemism for dominance. During her job interview, she plays the part of an aspiring corporate drone, while meanwhile her body is in full revolt. "Delaney marveled at how quickly her armpits became dank swamps."

If *The Circle* sometimes feels like a corporate exposé, *The Every* has all the hallmarks of corporate espionage. At times, it reads like a slapstick version of *The East*, Brit Marling and Zal Batmanglij's edgy 2013 thriller. Delaney and her roommate, Wes, live like radicals in a part of San Francisco known for its off-the-grid restaurants and high concentration of Trogs (short for troglodyte, people who refuse technology's vision of the future). Wes has been raised by two mothers and is prone to wearing significant T-shirts. (One of them depicts the assassinated Swedish prime minister Olof Palme.) With Wes's irony-heavy technological savvy and Delaney's acting skills and conceptual power, surely they can make a dent in this corporation by mimicking its worst aspects back to it.

One would think. But every time Delaney floats a new idea meant to tackle the company, the Every absorbs the notion and it becomes wildly popular. How about an app in which friends can rate their friends? Done. (It winds up with the name AuthentiFriend.) It's not a far cry from the fictional apps people are already using, like OwnSelf, which atomizes every aspect of the day—from steps, to how much time one talks to a kid, to the kinds of language one uses—and judges and rates and parcels it out. In one scene, Delaney is interrupted mid-conversation by an urgent ding from her colleague Winnie's computer: "'Sixteen minutes. Time to move around,' she said, and then she began marching in place, her knees as high as she could manage while wearing snug denim. With every fourth step, Winnie did a kind of twisting motion at the waist, with her elbows high. Then she returned to marching. Delaney had not been invited to join, so she simply sat and looked into the rafters."

At the start, most of this is, as in *The Circle*, somewhat recognizable. Who doesn't want to get a few more steps in and make better use of time? Who doesn't wish their photos were better organized, maybe even had more captions? Bit by bit, though, more life is fed into the Every and its assorted apps, and byte by byte, the lives of all the characters in the book begin to be regulated by it.

Eggers seems to have spent some time inside a tech company, or he's very, very good at imagining their cultures. One of the best recurring set pieces includes Dream Fridays, where a motivational-speaker approach is taken to all employee gatherings that showcase new innovations. In one of them, an earnest technologist has started a VR app called Stop+Lük, in which travelers can book virtual trips to places led by actual tour guides. "Sweet lord God, Delaney thought, she hadn't seen the umlaut coming."

Here's where *The Every* really sinks its teeth into us. For who doesn't want to reduce carbon? Who doesn't want to reduce the harm we wreak on the planet? This worry, this frisson of fear of sheer existence, is the true quarry of this novel, as, led by Delaney, regulations and restrictions proliferate across the Every. Wes gets a job there and using hashtags manages to make bananas verboten (Bananaskam, he types into a public chat board in the lunchroom, mimicking the Swedish word for *flight shame*). The algorithms have already been set loose on books, juicing down the classics into their most essential words. AuthentiFriend is sped up, and Wes and Delaney set loose ten other ideas just as bad.

Once the novel has its engine up and running, the scenarios of ridiculousness proliferate and implode. So many of these inventions speak to "leering and shame" as a form of culture and control. There are people called Sams and Samaritans, who watch what others do and comment on and report on them, and an app that channels their ratings called DeputEyes. An app that regulates what people say called TruVoice. There are a few remaining anything-goes areas—a part of San Francisco known for its lack of surveillance has the vibe of a western frontier. Meantime, online, a Twitter-like feed in which anything goes called Blech launches and is instantly a hit. So many of the book's inventions draw on the engines of our digitized world, AI and facial recognition, and many of them are logical leaps forward from the inventions that power and stud the action in *The Circle*.

As the value of offense takes over all other values, every single interaction becomes traumatic. Watching elephant seals mate on a company trip turns into a catastrophe about which attendees need counseling. Delaney gets demerits from her colleague for not watching a video the colleague shared with her fast enough. A new interface for decision-making arises called Are You Sure?, which rates all possible moral vectors of decision-making—from buying a rug to making orange juice—making anything not funneled through it seem insane and reckless. Pets are banned on campus. It is inhumane to treat animals like pets.

So many of the inventions that proliferate in Eggers's universe are at war with pleasure. With uselessness, with meandering, with what cannot be controlled. Of course, a group of wild mammals on a beach going through the natural cycle of birth and rearing would be overwhelming and terrorizing to the Everyones (which is what the employees are called) who go to see them. In many ways, *The Every* feels like more of a San Francisco novel than *The Circle* does. Following Wes and Delaney to and from work, as they walk their dog, Hurricane, around the Bay, you burst the bubble that was not often pierced in *The Circle*. You feel the surf crashing and the wind, and watching a dog enjoy it with great, uncomplicated abandon makes Delaney and Wes's determination to undo this death star seem reasonable.

As a heroine, Delaney is such a different protagonist than Mae. She has to be. She grew up with the Circle as a familiar orienting point, with journalism as a historical artifact. Instead, she grew up with screens, with elsewhere being here and here being the abstract thing. She's a compelling mixture—very bright, skeptical, funny, and determined. Her plan is also generationally apt: How many young people now, irate at the world they inherited, want to take down the institutions they believe are destroying us or spreading toxicity through the culture? How could anyone blame them?

If anything, the young today have seen a world made by gluttony, and *The Every* pulses with this value word: The word *every* appears so often in the book that it becomes like a shining, shimmering fish, swimming in the rapids of the plot. It can be every as in aggrandizing, every as in greed, every as in all of us, every as totalitarian, the Every as in a company that—while the Circle replaced the family—replaces democracy. (The Every gets involved in taking out candidates when needed, something tech billionaires have already tried to do in America.) In this way, Eggers has written his book's eponymous corporate name into the very language of the book, underscoring how its power lingers and vibrates beyond scenes that take place there.

And so we wind up in a world not unlike our own. The conflagrations of commentary that occur at the Every, however righteous—one of the employees calls a corridor of cattle farms on Highway 101 Trigger Valley for vegans—also wind up serving an insidious purpose: distraction. While people watch and monitor one another, more and more wealth is being amassed by a very small group of people. Wealth and power on a colossal scale. During the first five years of the 2020s, just four people—Mark Zuckerberg, Elon Musk, Bernard Arnault, and Jeff Bezos—saw their wealth skyrocket by nearly a trillion dollars. Most of the rest of America were in such dire straits that the $1,200 check the government sent out during the COVID-19 pandemic was desperately needed relief. Eggers's portrait of the vampiric values of startup acquisition is so arresting and disturbing. How companies are fattened up to be bought and killed, or harvested from the inside. How dangerous it is for living that this practice has such lucrative incentives. It leads us to one or just a few big companies, swallowing everything. Every idea.

Battered, betrayed, Delaney doesn't have a chance with a company the size of the Every. It's not that it can't be brought down; it's just that there is nowhere to grab. There is a plot in which Delaney tries anyway, and Eggers follows this plan speedily to a breathless mountaintop conclusion. Ultimately, though, as with any dystopian thriller, the idea at the heart of *The Every* is the main character, and here, that character is riveting. It's an idea posed as a question: What if we have created a perfect panopticon in which to modify human behavior with metrics and shame? Where does that lead humanity? How does it feel to live in that world? How do we change it? Why do we find choice so enervating? Some of the questions this leads to in *The Every*, as fascism doesn't just knock but *bangs* at a great many governments' doors, are disquieting, to put it mildly. There are several kinds of utopias out there, after all. One is a world in which all people are free; another is a world in which all decisions are made from above. One of the chilling points made by *The Every* is that we may have already made our choice in this matter.

THE CANDY HOUSE

by Jennifer Egan

It was a long twelve years between 2010, when Jennifer Egan's *A Visit from the Goon Squad* landed, and 2022, the year Egan published its prismatic cousin, *The Candy House*. A technological revolution happened: smartphones, social media, disinformation, deep fakes, the Arab Spring (launched on Facebook and Twitter), memes, surveillance capitalism, Donald Trump and his forty thousand public lies, a global pandemic, a genocide in Gaza—all this and more tumbled into our lives. These things sped up, fractured, and reinvented time and, as a result, our experience of consciousness too.

Egan has always been after what the poet John Ashbery once called "the experience of experience." In her earlier novels *Look at Me* and *The Keep*, she wrote into the changing present like a stylish twenty-first-century Balzac or Colette, her *comédie humaine* a study of people desperate for connection but caught by forces—image culture, gaming and its models of human competition—destined to make them ever more isolated. Like novelist Robert Stone, whose scalpel-sharp prose style hers often recalls, Egan wrote so smoothly, and so neatly mapped her tales onto familiar forms (the roman à clef, the gothic), that it was possible to miss how radical her books were at heart.

With *A Visit from the Goon Squad*, it seemed as if Egan had decided finally to choose a form as tornadic as these forces she was circling—death, desire, the way we build cultural rituals like rock and roll—to contain our awareness that life ultimately ends. So much has been written of that novel's virtuosic use of point of view, of its new modes of storytelling, of how it evoked the passage of time with a *Canterbury Tales*–like structure. What's less often said is that the book is a devastating study of love and regret.

A deep and languid sadness melodizes *A Visit from the Good Squad*. It lurks in all the crumbled relationships that mushroom from the rocker turned producer Bennie, from the way some of its characters spin out into drug use and mental illness, longing to retrieve the youth they'd spent, the youth they'd burnt. Set between the 1980s and 2010, this was not the if-you-remember-it-you-didn't-live-through-it era of American life. It was the period that brought us Harvey Weinstein, milk containers with missing kids, crummy casual coke use. You see, to some degree, how much heavy lifting the music has to do. Or maybe that's just the music industry.

Rather than linked by narrative, the tales that make up *A Visit from the Goon Squad* are connected by love and regret, at the core of which is time—not time as a mineral or a unit but *lived* time. Time as marked by tree rings, by carbon decay, by aging, by the retreat of memories that are distorted by that aging. The book is heavily dominated by the actions of Bennie and the way his midlife nostalgia defines, or at least enacts itself onto, the world of the book. Clustered around him like islands in a newly created archipelago, quite a few characters in *A Visit from the Goon Squad* do things they wish they could undo, and experience ruptures—a drowning, an assault in a park, treating a lion like a media op rather than a wild animal—that will mark them for years. Rereading that novel now, it's hard not to interpret it not only as a morality play about the consequences of time but also as an elegy for the way we lived then, even when that way of life was destructive or, as we now say, toxic.

The Candy House, in the wake of these events, catches up with the characters who were spoked around Bennie in the earlier book: his assistant of many years, Sasha; his ex-bandmate Scott; Bennie's ex-wife, Stephanie, and her brother, Jules; and more. The book fans out into their afterlives but also into those of their descendants, those who had no choice in the matter but to be born into a world in which technology is the dominant prosthetic for connection—not music, not sex, not even skin.

The melody here is not love and regret but a cycle of longing and unsuccessful replacement. "I have this craving," says tech mogul Bix Bouton, lying in bed, exhausted, next to his wife and child, "just to talk." Anyone who has had a life run away with their time, who has loved ones they want to spend that time with, will relate, but what they may not relate to is that, rather than talk, Bix decides to solve his longing with yet more technology, a new invention.

At the center of *The Candy House* spin a series of inventions Bix's company, Mandala, has unleashed. All of them depend on externalized consciousness and a total capitulation to the data greed of tech giants. For example, one system, called Own Your Unconscious, makes it possible for people to both preserve and extract their memories, then upload them to the cloud in exchange for the promise that their grasp of the past will be improved by the unattributed scraping ("gray grabs") of everyone else's uploaded memories.

As with some of the inventions described in Dave Eggers's *The Circle*, this world is so close to ours that we might as well call this genre hyperrealism. Indeed, given how much users post on social media and how much the internet operates like a hive mind owned and manipulated by a few companies, all of them in California, the outsourcing of memory has long since begun.

The Candy House is a terrifying, sometimes very funny study of the destruction that this reliance on outsourcing memory wreaks on the inner lives of its characters. In the book, an anthropologist whose seminal work *Patterns of Affinity* is the model for this process tries to warn her daughters. "Nothing is free! Only children expect otherwise, even as myths and fairy tales warn us: Rumpelstiltskin, King Midas, Hansel and Gretel. Never trust a candy house! It was only a matter of time before somebody made them pay for what they thought they were getting for free. Why could nobody see this?"

Egan's use of simple chronology does much of the work here. By this point, we are already a third of the way into the book, and most of its characters have exchanged living—of being present and all that entails, whether boredom, terror, or fear—for escape. Wisely, for a book about technology, *The Candy House* doesn't always point the finger at technology but instead at the culture, the assumptions that technology promotes. Namely, that pain is intolerable and productivity can be infinitely maximized. In one chapter, a man's life is detonated by his creeping dependence on stimulants, as well as the Valium he takes to come down, which leads to more consumption, which nearly puts him in a death spiral.

The structure of *The Candy House* is even more sped up and elliptical than *A Visit from the Goon Squad*. We begin with Bix and his new invention and close with them, but in between, there are dozens of characters: a neurodivergent young man trying to game the odds of getting together with a woman who has a boyfriend; a researcher collaborating with a man whose public screaming is a kind of performance art, meant to wake up people from the way they perform their lives; children growing up in the shadow of selfish, chaotic parents and trying to surf the waves of hurt these relationships have spun into their lives; a woman in a kind of video game living her life as a spy. "You are one of hundreds," the story tells her, "each a potential hero." Pacing the lives of her characters with technology, Egan boldly shows how much that technology evolves to provide us things our emotional lives lack.

Perhaps for this reason, addiction is a major force in the lives of many characters in *The Candy House*. Theirs are not the rock and roll addictions you can try to glamorize. For every casual pot smoker, there are several heroin addicts, methadone users, people whose lives become honed to the service of a need. It's hard not to read a warning in these portraits: that the cycle of retreat and escape, if it becomes dependency, turns into a reflex. One that retrieves less and less from the flight into oblivion, nothing but another trip on the flight.

In technological terms, the difference between drug addiction and tech dependency in *The Candy House* is in how the culture at large treats these phenomena. In Egan's world, those who are opting out of the new memory enhancements are treated like anti-tech activists. In the book, these resistors unite around a nonprofit called Mondrian and its founder, Chris Salazar, the son of Bennie from *A Visit from the Goon Squad*. In one memorable scene, Bennie refuses to eat at Chris's abuela's house because of the uneasiness he feels about her owning an uninsured Mondrian painting, a piece of art she bought with the proceeds of her cryptocurrency speculations. She tries to throw off would-be burglars by serving food on tacky Mondrian-themed plates. "No one who owned a real Mondrian would ever acquire such crap she would say."

Egan mysteriously and pleasingly strings together these callbacks to her previous book across the several dozen tales of *The Candy House*. These recurrences feel like life, in which some events are uncanny, some things happen on purpose, and some other incidents just can't be explained. They just become memories. It is tempting to apply the low-grade tools of pattern recognition we all increasingly rely on to this field of events, but daringly, Egan resists the instinct to make a story that can be gamed in this way. Even when she hands some of the book's blinking themes regarding technology and connection, memory and selfhood to characters who are academics or researchers, the move is more of a feint than a lamp in the thicket of narrative.

There are simply too many moments in *The Candy House* to make any one of them definitive or to make any character's life representative. Even Bix is swallowed by his creation. At the beginning of the book, he goes undercover to a meeting of questioning academics, some resistant, and brings with him a prop, a copy of James Joyce's *Ulysses*, so he can appear to be what he is not: a questing student, a searcher living under that book's famous last lines. The move—however inauthentic—ignites a series of interactions that lead to a thought that will make him rich all over again. Years later, though, at the end of this bracing and sobering novel, he is estranged from his son, a lifelong resistor who *actually* believes in reading. Bix holds up his tattered copy of *Ulysses* as proof that they have things in common, unaware that by having turned the book into a gesture years ago, he has nearly evacuated it of value.

How do we rescue ourselves from this maze of self-referential drivel? The question veers through *The Candy House* like a siren. For all her narrative technology, there is in Egan a Victorian belief in the power of beauty and a kinship to their dedication to bringing society to life in their pages. At the core of her novel is a value they too were obsessed with exploring: love. Toward the book's end, there is a moving scene—so reminiscent of the end of *Wuthering Heights* one wants to shout for joy—in which Egan offers us a glimpse of how connection isn't just possible; it is the law of nature, of all we emerged from. That this disquieting book can also gently argue that honoring this unity in the world is what we are here for is just another reason it dazzles so brightly in a time of darkness.

XI

RUPTURES

STAY TRUE

by Hua Hsu

On the heels of a tragedy, it's understandable to want to filibuster reality. To talk, to remember, to try if not to stall the truth then to at least ask it some questions. Find out how a disease developed, what made a driver sleepy, why a person chose a darkened street as a shortcut. Or which way the wave broke. Reverse engineering the march of fate this way can make it seem less impersonal. Doing so, however, cannot seal a rupture in time, especially one the size of a missing person. Someone beloved. This exercise in reality maintenance may slowly accustom the bereaved to the new world in which they find themselves. But it can also have the side effect of rendering the remaining image of the departed too much from the shadows of their absence. As if all of us are merely souls arrowing toward our particular destination.

I write this because I came to such a conclusion in grief, as I suspect you have, too—living in a world where those we love are taken from us. So, too, did Hua Hsu. In 1998, when his friend Ken was murdered, he faced a choice: to chronicle the effect of death on himself or to remember his friend as he was before his life was taken in a brutal carjacking. In *Stay True*, as the title suggests, Hsu has chosen the latter way, and in so doing, he has written an exquisitely poignant book about friendship and growing up in California. The book is a Gen X anthem and a meditation on Asian American identity. What a gift it is to anyone who has known a friend.

It begins, as so many California stories do, in the car. "Back then, there was no such thing as spending too much time in the car," Hsu writes, and just like that we're tooling around Berkeley toward College Avenue in a hand-me-down Volvo, Hsu at the wheel, trying to control the music that will be listened to on a drive to nowhere or to the grocery store: "the one that took about six songs to get to." The car as rolling jukebox. The car as secondary apartment. It's all here. Hsu lists some of the friends who'd ride along, the way they scrabble for shotgun.

Stay True moves like a pop song with six choruses, moments in which harmony is defined and redefined in a variety of situations, each featuring a new array of people. In the book's second section, we meet Hsu's family, who are part of the East Asian diaspora in which millions of people from China, Taiwan, Korea, Japan, Mongolia, and more traveled to the United States for a better life. Hsu's parents came for graduate school from Taiwan, met in Illinois, and had him. His childhood, briefly sketched, brings him to California in the late 1980s and early '90s, when Asian grocery stores, shopping malls, languages, and life are no longer entirely in the margins of Silicon Valley. Even if Asian Americans aren't always fully accepted, Asian-ness simply exists, and Hsu grows up within and without it.

Music would come to be the heart of Hsu's life, but grudgingly at first. It was originally his father's territory. The records Hsu's father buys, listens to, and keeps undinged in their clear plastic wrappers have the appeal of so many dads' bait and tackle for weekend fishing. It all seems a bit much until Hsu hears Nirvana's "Smells Like Teen Spirit" on the radio and a pilot light inside him clicks on. He begins to make zines because he's heard it's an easy way to get free music. He prowls the import sections of record shops, searching out bootlegs. Later, it occurs to him that he was part of the final stage of that culture.

"Maybe those were the last days when something could be truly obscure," he writes. "Not in the basic sense that a style or song might be esoteric. But there was a precariousness to out-of-the-way knowledge, a sense that a misfiled book or forgotten magazine could easily be lost forever."

The same is true of people in a world in which technology has yet to leapfrog distance. When Hsu's father finds better work prospects back home in Taiwan, he moves there, and arranging long-distance calls proves so difficult and tricky that Hsu's family buys two fax machines, and Hsu and his father conduct their relationship by fax. "California's sunny day also influence the 'thinking and behavior,'" the older man says once to Hsu. "Make people thinking 'bright.' Do you think so?"

There are so many things to admire in this book: its poise, its wonderful evocation of self-consciousness, its shape and marvelous design. Key to all of them, though, is Hsu's sure-handed touch with quotation. How tempting it must have been to include more. Instead, quoting lightly and just enough, Hsu conjures his father as a man equally keen to have a relationship with his son as he is simply to know him. A definition of love and friendship Hsu later expounds on.

What a glorious ballad to friendship this book becomes when Hsu arrives at Berkeley. To those who attended college in America, so much of this will be familiar—achingly so. The feeling of dread over who your roommates might be is perfectly described. So, too, is the epochal nature of time when you're eighteen. How endless a year is, and then how quickly, when things go well, you fall into patterns with friends. How you begin to define yourselves against yourselves, as if staking out roles in a sitcom. In Hsu's life, that means living with his close high school friends Paraag and Dave in the dorms. It is almost by accident that he meets Ken.

Sarcastic, shy, committed to straight-edge values, as defined in punk subculture, Hsu could not have been more different from Ken, who is Japanese American and projects the comfort of someone whose family was always here in America, or at least a little longer than Hsu's. When they first meet, Ken is bounding up stairs, at ease in his skin, comfortable with his voice, possessing good manners, like someone who has no beef with reality. Meanwhile, Hsu is years into an aesthetic of defining himself by what he does not like. Somehow Hsu winds up helping Ken move his things into the dorm.

What luck these two met, because despite differences, they become fast friends. Ken leans toward fraternity life, Dave Matthews, and girls; Hsu burrows ever deeper into thrifting his clothes, Marxist thought, and the early mazes of the internet. They meet in between for cigarettes, long conversations, and the kind of low-grade pranks college life is fueled by. In one of the more amusing scenes, Hsu describes Ken coming home from a party and the two of them assuming alternate identities to participate in an early right-wing conservative chat room on AOL.

While their friendship grows, Hsu is discovering the power of intellectual thought as if for the first time. Pausing to pull out Derrida, who wanted to disrupt our ideas of dichotomies, Hsu builds the theoretical foundation for why this friendship between supposed opposites works so well. Drawing on Derrida's ideas of recognizing oneself in the other—and knowing that friendship is temporally marked—Hsu reveals himself and Ken gleefully, sometimes desperate to make a mark against all odds. They wanted to be inserted in the record of time. "We sought a modest kind of infamy," he writes, describing how in a library beneath the painting of an old white man "we would write our names on slips of paper and sneak them into empty spaces underneath him, wondering how long it would take before someone noticed us."

Ideas are the melody of this book. Postmodernism crashes into Hsu's life and quickly becomes so ubiquitous in his classes that it can simply be reduced to that which is "weird." Deconstruction as a literary method is so heavily used that it nearly turns Hsu tone-deaf to reading altogether. Here is the tailwind of political correctness and the rise of the right-wing backlash that continue to this day.

Stay True is particularly strong at revealing the ways an idea can be felt communally, especially when it assumes the force of culture or policy—like Proposition 209, which ended affirmative action in California in 1996. In the wake of this body blow to campus life, Hsu becomes politically involved, volunteering for a Black Panther, mentoring underserved kids in the East Bay, spending time at a prison writing workshop, and editing an Asian American literary journal called *Slant*. He still loves music, but he also has a new way of defining what he is against.

When Hsu is with Ken, though, most of what they talk about are passions—music, food, friends, ways of being. What rise through the waves of this book are these passions, lovingly rendered, from songs and albums to books and works of sociology. The songs, through their repetition, take on the power of a soundscape. Of all these, the Beach Boys' "God Only Knows" is the most lasting, with its repeated phrase "God only knows what I'd be without you." Moving liquidly through Hsu's own harmonic narrative arc—as an Asian American, as a college student, as a friend, as a political activist, as one of those left behind—the song appears and reappears, washing over the events and people he describes with the layered meaning of a ceremonial piece of music.

The song also lends an eerie note of foreshadowing to the murder to come. How do we live in a world we don't fully comprehend? Early on in *Stay True*, Hsu recalls trying, in his nerdy late-teen way, to approach this problem by itemizing reality. By becoming an expert in his corner. But once Ken is killed, he resists the urge to deal with this question about how to fathom the world by imagining that life had gone a different way. The other questions he faces are too grave to do that. What if he had stayed at the party where Ken spent his last minutes with friends? What if? Words Hsu's father once sent to him by fax echo down the line of years, giving if not comfort then a certain degree of pathos for the difficulty of living. "That's the dilemma of life," Hsu's father told him back then. "You have to find meaning, but by the same time, you have to accept the reality." The genius of this sweet, sad, and also joyous song of a book is how it does both.

TELEPHONE

by Percival Everett

One needn't have lived on a California hillside to grasp the essential nature of entropy. Decay and unraveling are as much a part of nature as death, as landslides, as tornadoes, yet our way of grasping the world is accretive. Accumulative. Or so it seems. Take libraries, for example, which are formed through subtraction as well as addition. Stacks be damned. The scriptorium at Alexandria once held nine volumes of poems by Sappho. Today, we are left with but one.

Living in a world built on erasure and entropy—on loss—creates in us powerful desires for cohesion, if not permanence. One way to address these longings is in stories. But can we trust them? Here's the existential dilemma at the heart of Percival Everett's *Telephone*, a moving love letter to the reader and to anyone who has ever had to tell a person—say, a child, anyone beloved—truths that were untrue. *You're going to be OK.*

How easily this book begins. On the surface, it feels familiar, as so many Everett books do in their opening pages: sometimes a Western, sometimes a satire. Then slowly the form erodes to reveal something less stable, something mutable. An inner pulse. Thus we begin here in the garb of a campus novel. Zach Wells, our narrator, is a paleobiologist who teaches at a Los Angeles university. He is bored, his dog is growing fat. Zach teaches his courses half asleep. He and his wife, Meg, have begun to drift apart. Their daughter, Sarah, is the brilliant glue keeping them together.

Whereas most writers' books escalate, Everett's mutate, often right before our eyes, creating a dreamlike feel that is both pleasant and off-kilter. In addition to writing stories and novels, and like Meg in this novel, Everett is a poet, so his prose books also make full use of language's most uncanny capabilities to produce effects. Repetitions, montaging, and echoes of words across *Telephone* create a field of sonic possibility. Into this charged zone spill seemingly tiny occurrences. Zach finds a note written in Spanish in a shirt he bought on eBay. His daughter flubs an easy move in their near-daily chess game. He has dreams of strange import.

Zach's professional area of specialty involves the bones of dead birds found in caves. Using tools of study to measure rates of decay and the size of species, he can tell stories about what life around a cave might have been like, what would have lived there, and why. Snippets of his field research break into the book's narration in the opening chapters like a darkly alluring overheard chant. These snippets simultaneously desensitize and resensitize us to encountering words in their most primal, categorical form: malleable units of knowing, detached from what they refer to.

Eventually, this patterning of incident and language creates a rich enough psychic plane that the reader—like a dreamer—must begin interpreting. What is this all about? What is it that will grab this melancholic, somewhat detached man and make him act? Gruff, sometimes laconic, and only recently awoken by the birth of his daughter, Zach is continually reminding us that he is a poor guide, even to his own emotions, which, as a scientist, he regards with a mixture of skepticism and shame, even when the worst possible thing is happening. "I suppose anytime someone is seeing a pediatric neurologist," Zach says when an eyesight problem plaguing Sarah becomes hard to define, "it is a given that there is an abundance of anxiety, and so our wait in the outer area was notably brief."

An abstract description of the hospital is typical of Zach. As *Telephone* progresses, though, and Sarah's illness becomes real, his slightly pedantic register breaks down. He cannot hide his own feelings with intellectual games, especially when he and Meg face an almost unbearable question: What do they tell their daughter when a diagnosis comes? Almost prideful about his directness with hard facts, Zach faces the choice of whether or not to lie. Surely, sometimes, a lie is a better story than the truth?

In recent American fiction, there are few books as perceptive, as agonizingly right about the weight of illness on a family as *Telephone*. When Sarah's medical condition becomes clearer, the stress of it dilates the intimacy between Zach and Meg: Sometimes they touch; sometimes he drives downtown to drink alone in a skid row–adjacent dive bar. Sometimes he talks about his feelings. Sometimes he holds them in so that Meg doesn't also have to carry them.

Telephone is more than a chronicle of their family, though. Read slowly, it captures another praxis in living: that of choice and randomness. To put it in terms of genetics and phenomenology: If our bodies are formed in code, what shapes our actions? Are we not also enacting the mixture of programming, biological and social, to which we've been exposed? In the novel, Zach, a former US Marine, finds, at first, that some manifestations of his former training allow him ways to battle back his grief: a bar fight, defusing a snake encounter in the desert.

But violence will not save their daughter, nor will heroics or prayer—and besides, as Zach puts it, God doesn't care. So what can Zach do? It depends, in a way, on what he has done. Three versions of this book exist. Each set of decisions leads to a slightly different book, a slightly different set of possibilities, a different meaning of the title. In this way, the novel is a little like the game of telephone, in which, as a message is passed from listener to listener, at each stage it becomes something else.

Late in my version, Zach has decided that there's a way to benignly redirect this linguistic mutation—entropic or otherwise—by intervening in another catastrophe: the one hinted at by the strange message he found in his shirt, and others that followed. It does not spoil the book to say that the predicament he finally uncovers involves a girl in a situation just as dire as the one facing his daughter. "When she was much younger," Zach remembers earlier in the book, "Sarah wondered aloud whether we could climb into the fog and clear it away like cobwebs." Who would say no to such a question?

GOODBYE, VITAMIN

by Rachel Khong

I once had a friend who measured his life in dogs. Winding down a long meal, he often said things like, *I'm five dogs into a seven-dog life.* He wasn't alone. Recently, another friend, on hearing of an elderly family member's dachshund's passing, replied with knowing despair: *Oh,* she said, *poor thing, she's on her last dog.*

People measure time in all kinds of ways: children or trees, houses or jobs. Some take a step back and call it history. Others move one step closer and name it love. Time is our calendar, our walking stick, our call to prayer. None of us can escape it. We don't just live in its embrace, so we have to mark it.

Each of us does this differently, even within a family—which can lead to comedy or tragedy. Rachel Khong goes for both in her exquisite debut novel, *Goodbye, Vitamin,* one of the finest meditations in California writing on how families live among, make, and depend on memories, one word at a time.

The novel begins with a painful rupture: Howard, our narrator's father and a college professor, has recently been diagnosed with dementia. Owing to some erratic behavior, he has been sent home on academic leave, and Annie, our narrator's mother, has begun removing aluminum cookware—a possible source of the disease, she believes—from their kitchen.

Meanwhile, dumped by her fiancé, smarting with humiliation and a feeling of having failed to launch, Howard's daughter, Ruth, has returned home for Christmas. On December 29, she writes:

> Now Mom is asking if I could stay awhile to keep an extra eye on things.
> By *things* she means Dad, whose mind is not what it used to be.

Goodbye, Vitamin is told by Ruth, diary style, one day at a time, over the year she remains at home. Her tone is confessional, shocked, reality-thwacked. With one visit to the doctor, her family's world has been shattered, and she narrates like someone for whom even familiar things are seen too brightly, too well. Arriving home, coming down off a five-hour energy drink, Ruth says: "My street smells cold and familiar. All the grapefruits are hanging from trees like ornaments. It feels like there's a sun going down in my head. . . . On our street there is a squirrel that's been hit, not freshly, and now looks like smashed cookies."

She is not the only one with a diary, as it turns out. When not shut away in his office, Howard hauls out a diary he kept as a young father. In its pages, he recorded scraps of the accidental poetry Ruth created with her toddler questions. ("Today you asked me where metal comes from. You asked me what flavor are germs.")

Wending around each other, Ruth's and her father's diaries form a kind of double helix of parenting and daughtering, of grief and wonder. Of love's uneasy chronicle. It's a structure so complex and powerful that it can invert roles. As the days progress deeper into winter, Ruth hatches a plan with her father's graduate students to sneak her father back onto campus as if he were still a teacher; it's less clear who is the parent and who is the child.

During his years as a professor, Howard taught California history, and now he does it again, only in stolen classrooms, all the lessons out of chronological order. The Gold Rush and the migration from Canton, China, mixed together with the sixteenth-century Spanish romance novel that gave the state its name. Perhaps this is how history comes to us after all—out of order, a puzzle in need of reassembly. Baked by the oven of fantasy.

Goodbye, Vitamin is a deeply perceptive portrayal of how family history can come to us this way too. Slowly, we understand from Ruth that years ago she learned that Howard had had an affair, and the effects have eroded the riverbank of Annie's faith in him. Ruth has never faced these facts. It's why she finally admits that, until now, she wouldn't come home. "I wanted to preserve my memory of my perfect father," she says. "I didn't want to know the many ways he'd hurt my mother. I didn't want to have to pick sides."

Ruth has a brother, and he has chosen sides—their mother. For the first half of the book, Linus tracks the family gossip like a satellite, observing the action as if squint-eyed from afar, but never touching down. Ruth visits him in Santa Cruz, and he plies her for details but still won't come home. For all his perspicacity, as his relationship with a flight attendant melts down, he's totally oblivious to the ways he is living out his emotional inheritance.

Goodbye, Vitamin is a short book, but it manages to evoke a lifetime of a family's shared experiences shard by shard. We watch as patterns repeat and ripple. Ruth has to be aware that she drinks the way her father did, and that ultimately the costs of this obliteration will come due, even if each hangover makes a new day feel new. Meantime, Linus's refusal to address what has happened mirrors his mother's deflections.

Although Howard is at the center of this book, Annie is not overshadowed by him. She emerges here as a potent, amusing, and strong character. Reencountering her mother as an adult, Ruth is confused by her own behavior toward her. When Ruth thinks another affair is developing right beneath her mother's nose, she leaps into action trying to thwart it, provoking her mother finally to say, "You have no right."

If this were a play, there'd be a big shouting match at some point. But there are no big confrontations here because there can't be—instead, Ruth must haul these incidents up from her own memory and reexamine them. Yet, one morning in the present, Howard washes his shoelaces. One afternoon, he begs his daughter for no more crucified vegetables—trying to say *cruciferous*. He weeps.

Given how many of us have been or will be caretakers of elderly parents, it's shocking there aren't more novels about the task. *Goodbye, Vitamin* is one of the all-time greats about this grim but glorious period of life. It's all here, on the page, in Ruth's one-year orbit of the sun: the rage and bursts of regret, the alcoholic relief, the grunginess of shit, the cosmic moonshots of clarity's return, the endless force of the body's terminal velocity. Reprieves from the decline swift as passing comets.

Goodbye, Vitamin never batters you with its awareness, nor does it wallow in morbidity. Instead, it hones its sight on the strange loops of time, in which pitching in at caretaking makes a child older, a parent younger. Ruth's mother, relieved to some degree of her secrets and sometimes her housework, emerges flirtatious, young again in memories resurfaced.

These loops, and greater ones, take flight in Khong's epic second book, *Real Americans*, a novel that covers some eighty years in a Chinese American family's life, across three generations, from a futuristic Bay Area back to Beijing during the Communist revolution, a story I know well because I wound up as its editor at Knopf over the past two years. It is an old-fashioned Great American Novel, one that asks new questions about time: Who gets to treat it like a resource, and who gets to view it like a wage.

I love the book. I haven't read a novel that deals with the collision of entitlement and luck in American life quite like it. It feels like a sixth novel, not a second, for its confidence and craft, the depth of characterization, the way it reverses the order of a family saga, going from youngest to oldest and back again, like an accordion balanced neatly on a knee.

And still, I will always have a soft spot for *Goodbye, Vitamin*. Especially because I later learned this was not, as first novels often are, autofiction writing itself into a family story. Neither of Khong's parents suffers from dementia. She simply *imagined* it. This is a tremendous feat. As the book deepens, its form of address changes to become even more intimate. The diary, written for no one, begins to address Howard. The past that has been so painfully dredged up is allowed to sink back into the gloomier depths. Following a doctor's advice, Ruth and her mother—and Linus, too, eventually—decide to live more in the moment.

And so, rather than beginning each diary entry using the past tense, they start with "Today." "Today you told me that the Santa Ana winds are sometimes called the 'devil winds.'" "Today you and I sanded the patio." "Today you asked about my job at the hospital." And then, after Howard loses his temper and breaks every glass in the house, Ruth notes how their doctor informs them that "in a matter of days . . . it can go from being manageable to scary."

The worse Howard gets, the more he sounds like Ruth as a child. "This morning," she says, "Mom was making a sandwich and you said, Swiss cheese holes are called eyes. Your cheese watches you."

There are times when the world feels like a river of horrors. There are times when the world unfolds like a river of wonders. *Goodbye, Vitamin* imagines how, under great pressure, and with the fiercest love, these rivers are not always separate. In fact, they pour into one another, mixing, forever mixing, until they pour out into a much wider sea.

THE WRONG END OF THE TELESCOPE

by Rabih Alameddine

When it comes to enemies of art, some dastardly and unbearable villains can kill a writer cold. Assassins—both successful and would-be—spring to mind. For every Salman Rushdie who miraculously survives an attack, though, many have not—like Anna Politkovskaya, who dared to write truthfully about life in contemporary Russia; or Walter Rodney, the Marxist historian of Africa killed by a car bomb in Georgetown, Guyana; or Ghassan Kanafani, the Palestinian writer murdered over fifty years ago in Beirut by agents of Mossad. One thinks of the dozens of Mexican journalists killed doing their work in a narco-state.

It should not be incumbent on a writer to give their life, but that is sometimes the bargain. This risk speaks to how dangerous it can be to interrogate the sacred, to ask questions, to poke fun. Power structures everywhere would prefer us to deal with preconceived emotions, even when it is these very forces that lead us to conflict, because such feelings can be managed, deployed. When someone or some someones can be called an enemy, a terrorist, a freak, or less than human, you can exclude them. You can ignore them. You can go to war with them. You can kill them.

Few writers in America are as allergic to preconceived ideas—have as much fun with them, even when writing about the deadly serious—as novelist Rabih Alameddine. Drawing on vast reservoirs of wit, pathos, and storytelling dexterity, Alameddine often guides us laughing into tragedy and po-faced into the comedic. His 1996 debut, *Koolaids: The Art of War*, unfolds during the Lebanese Civil War and the worst days of the AIDS epidemic in San Francisco. Though bearing witness to both, it also manages to crack jokes about Tom Cruise, *The Waltons*, every single religion, and death itself.

This dark, cackling intelligence is operating at a dazzling peak in *The Wrong End of the Telescope*. Bearing witness, once again, this time to the terrifying reality migrants face upon arriving in Europe, fleeing war, Alameddine also manages to send up the empathy-industrial complex that has grown up around "the 'migrant crisis,' the object of much counterproductive virtue-signaling. Volunteers from Europe and America descend on Greece in hopes of helping, and also take a selfie with a real, live refugee from Syria."

Observing this clusterfuck is Mina Simpson, a Lebanese-born trans doctor. Sharp-tongued, Beirut-raised, vulnerable, and great company, she is a classic Alameddine heroine. As a narrator, she is a reluctant guide and like an outsider scans every room she enters, seeking exit. Upon arriving in Lesbos, from Chicago, she immediately begins differentiating herself from the Americans. "He was my people," she says, eyeing an Arab man at the airport, "kneaded by the same hand. He was on the shorter side, my height, not in the greatest of shape. His hair had less gray than mine but was the same shade of dark."

Before he was a novelist, Alameddine was a painter. Though he never worked figuratively, he is an exquisite portraitist as a writer. He gives the gift of sight to his characters and allows them to be seen seeing, judging, and making wrong assessments. The effect feels like something Proust's narrator describes in *Swann's Way* at the outset of that sublime novel: "Our social personality is created by the thoughts of other people," Proust wrote. "Even the simple act which we describe as 'seeing someone we know' is to some extent an intellectual process. We pack the physical outline of the creature we see with all the ideas we have already formed about him."

Can we truly see someone, especially a person whose life has undergone an almost supernatural transformation, such as crossing a body of water on a dinghy for their safety? Or crossing from one presentation to another? *The Wrong End of the Telescope* asks whether this is even possible and, if so, what one does with such sight. Being trans, Mina draws this question to an acute point, and being an outside observer who hasn't been home to Beirut in decades makes it poignantly confusing for her as she begins talking to migrants who have forfeited homes, livelihoods, and health to arrive on unfriendly, unglamorous shores speaking her mother tongue.

Doctors today call listening to people's stories *narrative medicine*, but it is also, for Mina—being Middle Eastern—simple hospitality. Time and again, Mina is shocked by the way ailing migrants are sorted not through decency and questions but rather through preconceived interrogations about political situations. On top of this, some volunteers would like to take their picture without truly seeing them. Many of those arriving are highly alert to these distorting lenses and refuse to play along. Among the early patients whom Mina coaxes into talking to her is Sumaiya, a Syrian mother who is clearly dying of some form of cancer. The scene where Mina deals with her is worth the price of the book alone.

Sumaiya's story forms one of the primary threads of the novel, but, as with all of Alameddine's books, there's so much more that winds around this central story. In alternating short chapters, we hear of Mina's own migration from Beirut to the United States, how along the way she finally recognizes she was meant to be a woman, even as she presented—in an increasingly politicized time—as a Middle Eastern man. The first time she falls hard for a woman, they experiment with S&M in one of the most tenderly erotic scenes of that ilk to appear in a novel in years.

The Wrong End of the Telescope thrives on such juxtapositions: Mina on the island, weaving through a mixture of tat (Barbie dolls given to arriving children) and tragedy (a young man from a village who wanted education so desperately, his family has sacrificed everything so he could study). Her consciousness is constantly layered by previous affectionate relationships, previous wounds, which Alameddine unfurls with monumental care. These scenes never explain. They simply channel moments of life that reverberate. The feeling of sleeping next to a sibling at age ten, the brute force of a mother's example as a paragon of beauty. Ultimately, Mina is, like so many Alameddine characters, deeply lonely. Her family eventually abandoned her. Like many queer people in California, scores of her friends died during the 1980s and 1990s from AIDS. The diva persona she wears is born equally of joy and defense.

It is this combination of longing and rage that leads Mina to a correspondence—real or imagined, it is not quite clear—with a figure who resembles the author of the book. Spliced periodically into the texts, his missives illuminate their recipient like a lyric poem, through inference. Like the real Alameddine, Mina's silent correspondent is a survivor, a Beirut-raised immigrant to America, a writer who tried—and hated himself for trying—to figure out how to write about migrants and their arrival in Greece.

One passage describes how a woman Alameddine met decorated her tent in a refugee camp with sequins. "She had studded her entire pantry with sequins, with results Liberace would have envied. You thought she must have spent untold hours gluing sparkles onto sheets of wood that would become a pantry to store nonperishables. Intricate and delicate, no spot left uncovered, so over the top that many a drag queen would kill for it."

The Wrong End of the Telescope is a secret celebration of drag. Of the spaces of care that made it possible for Mina to realize who she was, even if she balked the first time, drawn into a performance in Brazil by a friend in the 1980s. "They covered your face with so much makeup that you felt like a cadaver being readied for an open casket. But no, you were no cadaver; with lipstick, eyeliner, and a good foundation, they restructured your face, built another atop the one you wore."

Alameddine's novel would have been predictable had it merely poked fun at the selfie-takers. Instead, what it does once Mina has begun to see patients is explode as many preconceived emotions as possible about what counts as transformation. As Mina's self-consciousness recedes, we hear more and more stories from the migrants she meets and talks to, their arcs always interrupted by arrival, not unlike the syncopated tales told in Olga Tokarczuk's masterwork *Flights*, a novel about what movement does to a life.

As Mina's stay extends, she meets people who surprise, annoy, frighten, and delight her. She meets a trans person from Raqaa who responds matter-of-factly that they were able to treat themselves during the civil war by taking pregnancy pills. She hears of a doctor, Sitt Fawzieh, who cross-dressed during the time of Daesh rule in Syria so he could treat both men and women—donning a burka and entering homes as a female physician. "Once inside a home, he would take the niqab off and put it back on as he left. No one in the community betrayed him, of course. He was one of them. And so was she."

Disguises, especially those donned for safety, have a way of making the duped angry—as if something has been taken from them. Among fellow disguisers, though, a disguise or an evasiveness can feel like home. On the beach in Greece there are Iraqis, Syrian, Palestinians, and some people who seem to be masquerading, possibly, as migrants to hide some other reason for travel. Being there among them is the closest Mina has been to her family in decades, and Alameddine conjures the mixture of shame, relief, and confusion this familiar plethora produces. Ultimately, the brother she was closest to comes to visit her, and *The Wrong End of the Telescope* weaves musings on family with insights about larger tribes. What does it mean for someone like Mina to be of a *them* like the people she's treating—and why is she so willing to travel across the globe to help them, when she wouldn't even go home to her blood family?

It's hard to believe we are barely a century into the period of the passport. Depending on which United Nations white paper you read, the numbers of people the world over who will be migrating due to desperate need in the next fifty years will be in the billions. To put that in perspective, at the end of harrowing climate collapses in the Sahel, civil wars in the Middle East, a brutal Russian invasion of Ukraine, and Israel's genocidal assault on Gaza, there are a mere hundred million on the move today. In other words, in many of our lifetimes, there will be ten or twenty times the current number who are without a home. Too many for a selfie. Too many to live in a world that talks about walls, or us, or them. This groundbreaking, moving, and, yes, very funny novel asks the dangerous and daring question: How long are we going to keep looking at this condition through the wrong end of a telescope?

GOLD FAME CITRUS

by Claire Vaye Watkins

"The Mojave is a big desert and a frightening one," John Steinbeck wrote in *Travels with Charley*. "It's as though nature tested a man for endurance and consistency to prove whether he was good enough to get to California." By the time Steinbeck wrote this, man had long since *gotten* to California: The clue is in the desert's name. Mojave Indians, who go by the name Aha Makav, had been in the desert for at least two thousand years. White settlers only arrived in the early 1800s, and because the pathway to gold fields cut through the Mojave, some of them began to stay there, displacing Mojave people from ancestral land along the Colorado River. Cutting down trees. Armed conflict led to a one-sided peace treaty and, eventually, reservations.

As anguishing as this loss is, a bigger theft loomed. It would be committed years later, far away, in Los Angeles. At the turn of the twentieth century, city planners made Southern California habitable by taking from the desert—draining water from the Owens Valley and its aquifer through William Mulholland's vast, infamous aqueduct. "There it is," the hydrologist reportedly said in 1913, when water first arrived through his pipes in the San Fernando Valley. "Take it."

Within a few decades Los Angeles would grow from a mere 50,000 to some 320,000. An arid city was suddenly growing citrus, and its studio lots were manufacturing fame.

A former gold prospector on the Colorado River, Mulholland lived out the principle that you took what you wanted, and if you got there first, you kept power. How fitting that an imperial, autocratic-leaning president would sound like him when talking about California and the water issues its growers faced. But this experience also should have taught Mulholland (and Trump) something about finitude and consequences. The Los Angeles Aqueduct may have allowed the city to grow, but it quickly sucked Owens Lake dry. Paiute people who had lived there since the sixth century BCE were unable to support themselves on land they had been connected to for over a millennium. The desertification of the area created dust storms, the consequences of which were felt by people imprisoned in the Manzanar incarceration camp during World War II. Today the Owens Valley is a major source of dust storms that reach Los Angeles and send its air quality levels rocketing into unbreathable zones. And was it even necessary? "On top of all this," Marc Reisner wrote in *Cadillac Desert*, his classic book about California and water, "the Owens was a generous desert river."

Claire Vaye Watkins grew up in the Mojave and has a desert dweller's sense of how to accept what it gives. She also understands the steep consequences of taking what it does not. California has been rehearsing its destruction for decades in pop culture, but none of this phantasmagoria of guilt proceeds from a sense of the landscape and who has called it home as deeply as Watkins's novel *Gold Fame Citrus*. In this trippy and grave book, a nuclear incident and drought have brought California to its knees, shattered public order, and left people living on cola rations in small pockets, trading for blueberries and raiding abandoned homes and stores like bands of survivors in *The Walking Dead*. The West has been cut off from the rest of America as it is slowly swallowed up by an enormously expanded Mojave called the Amargosa Dune Sea—the descriptions of which will ring true to anyone who has ever spent time in the Owens Valley area today.

In the middle of this maelstrom is a family—a man, a woman, and a child, thrown together by circumstance, luck, and longing. Luz is an ex-model with Chicana roots, who doesn't speak Spanish; Ray is a soldier gone AWOL from the military, who has the independence of a surfer and the kind of survival skills one needs in an apocalypse; and Ig is a child the two of them meet in a fire dance ceremony at the beach (a way they blow off steam), a child they sense is being neglected at best. A group of bandits—picture the crowd Patrick Swayze's crew hangs out with in *Point Break*—ditch Ig with them, so Luz and Ray are not necessarily *taking* her; they're just not giving her back. They hustle the toddler, who swerves between preverbal sounds and complete sentences, back up into the Hollywood Hills where they've been crashing at the hillside mansion of a departed starlet. When their new child poops on the floor, they wipe it up with one of the actress's abandoned Hermes scarves. It's okay, Luz points out; there are hundreds of them.

Gold Fame Citrus is rich with this sense of useless former luxury. "LA had gone reptilian," Watkins writes, "primordial." The city is full of dried-up swimming pools, and during the baking hot days, Ray constructs a half-pipe from the cork that once lined the walls of the starlet's she-shed. If the world is over, why not skate? To protect themselves from the sand that strafes the city mercilessly, Luz has stuffed designer clothes into every cranny of the empty mansion. Cash is on its last legs, and Luz understands as a woman that there will be currencies after (and during) this transition that she'd rather not be a part of, but for the time being there are goods to buy.

> Enough money could get you fresh produce and meat and dairy, even if what they called cheese was Day Glo and came in a jar, and the fish was

molting poisoned and reeking, the beef gray, the apples blighted even in what used to be apple season, pears grimy even when you paid extra for Bartletts from Amish orchards. Hard sour strawberries and blackberries filled with dust. Flaccid carrots, ashen spinach, cracked olives, bruised hundred-dollar mangos, all-pith oranges, shriveled lemons, boozy tangerines, raspberries with gassed aphids curled in their hearts, an avocado whose crumbling tapped innards once made you weep.

Watkins is a stylish and canny writer, and she sculpts a sense of dread so palpable you can feel it drumming into Ray's and Luz's bones. Time is running out; they can't stay holed up in the hills forever, however much it feels good to play house with Ig. Pretty soon, people will come for the child, or to see what treasures the house might still hold. So the three of them pile into the actress's abandoned classic VW Karman Ghia, packed to the gills with supplies and extra gas, and drive toward the last remaining encampment of friends. They'd really like to escape from California without Ray winding up in jail or one of the prison camps rumored to cluster in Washington, Idaho, and elsewhere. A friend named Lonnie who is living on the beach might have a few inside tips. And thus they flee.

At this point, you'd think that *Gold Fame Citrus* would become your typical cli-fi disaster novel, wherein the destruction of the old way of life stokes the flames of the reader's awareness. No, not the Hermes scarves! Keep consuming and you too will live like this! The novel feints in that direction and then bends toward something far more radical, montaged out of the many disasters that have befallen the West since colonial exploration began. The novel is not so much a postapocalyptic road trip as it is a book *about* that genre of tale, a warning of what it is used for, a psychedelic remix, one part twenty-first-century

Odyssey, one part environmental tone poem in which the central character becomes the desert itself.

It takes us a bit to get there. First Luz, Ray, and Ig must visit with the aforementioned old friend Lonnie, who is cosplaying as a Mad Maxy guru on the coastline. "If I was going anywhere—which I'm fucking not, I'd go to the Amargosa," he says. And you can almost hear the bro-pocalypse tone when he adds almost as an aside, "There's supposed to be a town out there." So they drive toward the desert, dodging mile-wide sinkholes, beckoned along in spite of the destruction as if by magnetic pull toward the rising wave of sand on the horizon. At one point they peer into the distance and see it: "There was nothing cool or blue or airy about this calcium-colored crust capping the range. It throbbed with heat, glowed radioactive with light."

Warnings abound, some of them echoes from the past. At one point, we learn that Luz's mother, Estrella, died by drowning. Her father, a prospector in oil, has siphoned more than his fair share from the earth. Is she destined to be sacrificed back to a sand-born sea and to the land's wrath? Later still, we discover that as a child, Luz was considered one of the first babies born in a new era of time and American life, her existence marked as a kind of species ground zero. Baby Dunn she was dubbed, a doom-period celebrity, her childhood tracked in the public eye like the progress of human survival. Perhaps fame and doom were always this wrapped around each other. Picturing her in her borrowed Karman Ghia with her stolen baby and (not-husband) Ray, a hat on her head hiding the last of her cash, it's hard not to start casting, in one's mind, the actor who would play her in the film version.

Gold Fame Citrus is full of such cinematic moments, in this world where the Central Valley has turned to salt flat, and a wicked wind blows. In one of the most memorable scenes, they come across a yucca plantation. Trees stretch on and on to the horizon, at first like a beacon of hope: life! But when Ray and Luz approach them softly, they discover that the trees are utterly hollow, dead a long time from the inside out. There's no groundwater. The plantation is not a sign of life but a graveyard. It's when this book turns, wherein destruction is not reflected back onto Ray, Luz, Ig, and all humans, but destruction of nature itself is seen for the massacre it has always been. Not much later they run out of gas, and then Luz forgets to put the cap back on the gas can, and nearly all of the rest of their fuel dribbles out into the sand. Ray wraps up and heads out to seek help and doesn't come back.

When this happens, a whole new book begins. The desert rears up and surrounds Luz and Ig as they are slowly dying of thirst. As if to help us appreciate this fact, Luz's point of view fades to black, and as the book's middle opens up we are in a new mode—essayistic. Nearly factual. The desert can't be avoided because it is everywhere, "dunes upon dunes, the vast tooth-colored superdune in the forgotten crook of the wasted West." If this were a play, the scene would begin with "Enter desert," which Watkins queues up like a beast of yore. Experts, scientists, and travelers attempt to fathom it, and it is beyond all their capacities.

> Still came BLM and EPA and NWS and USGS, all assigned to determine why a process that ought to have taken five hundred thousand years happened in fifty. . . . Did they not realize that the dune now behaved more like a glacier, albeit a vastly accelerated glacier? Question: Were they aware that geologists had ascertained that the base of the dune—the foot, they called it—was rock? That it carved the land more than covered it? Question: Did they wish to comment on the fact that the buildings they envisioned, in which they had spent the entirety of their short lives—their homes, say, or their twelve-step club—had already been crushed, were now but fossil flecks in banded sandstone?

The dune, we learn, is considered international waters, a new frontier. When Luz and Ig flee the stalled Karman Ghia and awaken there in a school bus being tended by a woman named Dallas, it is as if they have left the US. They are out of the bosom of crumbled society and are at sea on a sloping, moving, shifting bedrock of sand. It's not clear where they are, or even when. But it's a world in which water is somehow in greater plenitude. It turns out that Levi Zabriskie, the commune's leader, whom Luz will soon meet, has a douser's gift, and as a result the people there treat him like a god. Ray may have "had the blazing prophet eyes of John Muir," but they are nothing compared to the deep, burning intensities summoned by Levi.

In one of the first pieces she ever published, Watkins wrote about her father's membership, one he ultimately rejected, in the Manson family. "My father first came to Death Valley because Charles Manson told him to," she wrote in 2009. "He always did what Charlie said; that was what it meant to be in The Family." Watkins has since written around this piece of family history in her feverish and bioluminescent 2021 novel, *I Love You but I've Chosen Darkness*, a novel that skates close to the facts of her life as a woman becoming a mother raised in the shadow of a cult. In *Gold Fame Citrus* she explores the ways that all colonialists and explorers are cult leaders in their way. That it is this tradition that unites the three elements of the book's title.

As she settles into a life of being taken care of, "Ig's back, round as a beetle against her," the ghosts of the explorers of decades past flit back in Luz's dreams as if to haunt her. She dreams of John Wesley Powell, Mulholland, Brigham Young. Her subconscious— or that of the land—is trying to awaken the cycle of taking from which she proceeds. Meanwhile, all the commune residents reenact the land thefts of the past. At night they light bonfires that burn with an odd sheen. Luz goes to find out why, and she discovers that it's because they've used the evacuation pamphlets, which read, "LEAVE OR DIE."

By the time Levi has started to seduce Luz, we know there's something off here. That for all the comforts of the commune, for all its safety, it depends on the very same hierarchy that brought Luz and her society to this brink. Dallas puts this quandary in intimate terms. "It's just. You spend your life thinking you're an original. Then one day you realize you've been acting just like your parents." How does one end such a destructive cycle? Not since Robert Stone's 1975 *Dog Soldiers* has there been a novel written about America's violent present that leans so surreally on hallucinogenic transformation to answer this question. Both novels suggest that some form of escape is not possible. Perhaps, like the coyote carcass Luz sees "gone wicker in the ravine" earlier in the novel, accepting the end is better than fighting it with partial measures. After all, Luz learns that one of the plans for the Amargosa might be to nuke the whole thing and use it to excuse the endless toxic waste the rotting American arms have created.

Earlier, before all this falls apart, Ray talks to Luz about modern-day Californians and how they brought this disaster on themselves. It's an attitude redolent of Steinbeck, but with a cruel punisher's streak in it. "California people are quitters," he says. "No offense. It's just you've got restlessness in your blood. . . . Your people came here looking for something better. Gold, fame, citrus. Mirage. They were feckless, yeah? Schemers. That's why no one wants them now." Everyone but the desert, and that's how this incredibly dark novel offers up an unusual form of solace: Eventually, it suggests, whether the land is conquered or not, its generosity is complete. It will welcome us all back into it in due course.

DEAD IN LONG BEACH, CALIFORNIA

by Venita Blackburn

Reality has been a fiction ever since we left the cave, but it has felt especially fictitious of late, and that is reflected in quite a lot of books that call themselves realistic. Even though most people live multiple lives now—digitally, professionally, internally—a lot of fiction assures us that thoughts typically come one at a time. That our selves are coherent, predictable vehicles that we have control over. That the internet interrupts our lives about as often as background noise.

In truth, hasn't reality become a little bit more tornadic in the past two decades? Thoughts and fantasies and projections and memes—in a world without privacy, of socially externalized selves lived online and offline—are all spliced together, projected and poorly hidden. And this leaking container/curated performance called the self? Surely it has several different identities and avatars, all lurking within it.

If this sounds at all straightforward to you, chances are you will feel that Venita Blackburn has written one of the first truly realistic novels of the twenty-first century. *Dead in Long Beach, California*, her sidewinding, immensely clever debut novel, moves like life—speedily, knowingly, metafictionally, and, still, poignantly. It's a book about how neither drowning in stories nor spinning them can protect you when they happen to you, as its protagonist, Coral, finds out in the opening pages of the book.

As we begin, Coral is gutted to discover that Jay, her beloved, annoying, doing-his-best-as-a-single-parent brother, has taken his life. She is bewildered. She had just seen him days earlier with his daughter, Khadija, for dinner. She'd texted with him. What could possibly have happened? Blackburn's novel is less concerned with the mystery of Jay's decision than its impact on Coral, who immediately begins to disassociate.

The first signal of this reaction is the book's narrative voice, which ebbs and flows into a first-person-plural chorus, a kind of emotionally cognizant gang of Siris who begin: "We are responsible for telling this story, mostly because Coral cannot." It's an astonishing opening because it manages to be compassionate and aloof at the same time, robotic and empathic, a register perfectly suited for the hinges this book will use to get in and out of hard truths, projected identities, fantasy, and heartbreak.

Blackburn was previously known as the writer of flash fiction and short stories. *Dead in Long Beach, California* changes that, thanks in part to her nimbleness at framing, manipulating time, and using tiny alterations in voice—essentially, all the techniques that made her great in smaller spaces—to move this story along. Her novel is also a marvel of interlocking structures. As a week ticks by, the past tiptoes back. Between sections of Coral's hit graphic novel, *Wildfire*, clues to Jay's final decision flicker into view, like a window into a life in the world of late capital, where every relationship is transactional, every aspect of identity monitored, every decision augmentable and changeable.

Coral, as a fiction writer, has lived in a constantly mutable world for a long time. When asked a question on a date, she lies, because why not? Who doesn't when it comes to their online profiles? This minute but pervasive bit of alteration is one of many instances in which the presentation of who Coral is accordions into a series of masks.

She is a hardworking freelancer, a writer who wants attention, a gay woman who has dated men, and a daughter who wishes she was treated less like a girl. Managing all the ways she is read and typed produces in Coral a deflective shimmer: a constant sense of living inside a story or a meme. Or maybe that's just modern life?

So it's not as strange as you'd think, when someone texts her brother, for Coral to reply from Jay's phone as him—kicking off a weeklong immersion in his life, full of painful improvisations and imaginative leaps and an odd bit of housekeeping. He has no digital footprint, so Coral must create one, complete with social media profiles, to cover up the lies she tells to put off dealing with reality.

A few books come to mind while reading *Dead in Long Beach, California*, most notably, Zadie Smith's *NW*, in which a woman's fracturing marriage leads her to skulk off into corners of the internet, while her everyday life takes place in northwest London. Returning to everyday life from the swirl of make-believe, Smith's heroine finds surfaces extrabright, strange, highly textured.

Dead in Long Beach, California unfolds in a similar time period, but it was written more recently. All of the book slides along made or fabricated surfaces. Projections. One of the novel's deeper points concerns how this habit of dissociating into narrative—in an era of crisis, which the book slowly paints—engineers our sense of others. Our sense of how to imagine them. Coral feels so capable of inserting herself into her brother's life that she even has a conversation with herself (over text) as him.

By this point, Jay has been at the morgue for a few days. But does this matter in grief? Blackburn's novel employs three time frames, and she weaves them to create the oddness of shock. One of these time frames is the week after Jay's suicide; the other reaches back to the life Coral shared with him growing up; and the third is life in America now, and on this front, Blackburn uses the peculiar magic of the choral voice to superb effect. Narrating Coral's life in a collective voice, the book frees itself up to comment at will on all the various trappings of modern life.

From debt to drugs, from online dating to the habits of work life and who gets to win the meeting, the emptiness and loneliness of modern existence emerge from this novel in halogen-lit clarity. Even with all the tools of surveillance and expression at her fingertips, a writer like Coral can't say exactly what she means in person, nor can she excavate what resists knowing.

The wrenching truth that underscores this novel is that Coral clearly feels that she didn't know Jay as well as she thought she did—otherwise, wouldn't she have seen this catastrophe coming? *Dead in Long Beach, California* asks us whether stories are all, in a way, a form of evasion from truths that cannot be summed up in an arc or a genre. As if to poke fun at this instinct to predict through storytelling, as we move from day to day, the chorus that narrates Coral's sections gives each set of memories a catchy genre title or two.

"The Clinic for Excavating Repressed Memories in Search of Solutions to Current Crises" is the moniker of sorts that kicks off the novel and its series of flashbacks from Coral's childhood, a childhood in which she was raised alongside her brother, more by her father than mother. "In the Clinic for Dying While Willfully Participating in a Poorly Thought-Out Cultural Trend" is the chorus's jokey name for a section that reads like an origin story, which validates Coral's lesbian identity.

The speed with which Blackburn moves around in these sections gives her novel a vibrant and deeply lifelike feel. Even as this book makes us laugh, it knows it has opened a window, a little one, between that expulsion of air and the knowledge that all of us live in a world of hard, inescapable truths. Some of us juggle this knowledge better than others. Some of us simply can't. The way that Blackburn acknowledges that this variety can exist within one person is perhaps the most dazzling aspect of all.

XII

WHO IS A CITIZEN?

THE MARS ROOM

by Rachel Kushner

All of Rachel Kushner's books have been about revolutionary scenes. From the tumult of Havana in the 1950s in *Telex from Cuba* to the group of experimental painters and motorcycle maniacs who animate *The Flamethrowers*, her novel about art and radical politics in the New York art world of the 1970s, to her latest book, *Creation Lake*, set in an eco-leftist commune in rural France where the 1968 generation and their fellow travelers go to drop out of society, the worlds in which her work takes place have often chosen their placement at odds with mainstream life. Their ideas and their antagonism and their art are their resistance.

What happens, though, when people aren't in charge of the changes that swirl around them? This is one of the key questions of *The Mars Room*, which unfolds in California in 2003 and some years before, capturing life within one of the country's largest carceral systems. Like everything in California, it didn't have to be this way; so, among other things, *The Mars Room* is a book about lost chances, and it makes us feel the ache of that through the telling of stories within stories about the lost souls who people its pages, mostly inmates at a women's prison, which Kushner's heroine Romy Hall is sent to for a crime we read our way toward.

First, there is talk, and much of it. The book opens with a bravura passage about inmates lumbering toward Stanville, the prison at the heart of the book, on a bus at night down a multilane freeway. They travel at night so as not to be jeered at, so as not to scare citizens. The views out the window, through which an amusement park roller coaster can be seen, and the rocking of the bus lend the ride the aura of a gothic field trip, and one of Romy's seatmates won't shut up. "My family goes back three generations in Apple Valley," she says. "Which sounds like a wonderful place, doesn't it? You can practically smell the apple blossoms and hear the honeybees and it makes you think about fresh apple cider and warm apple pie. The autumn decorations they start putting up every July at Craft Cubby, bright leaves and plastic pumpkins: it is mostly the baking and preparing of meth that is traditional in Apple Valley. Not in my family. Don't want to give you the wrong impression."

It's hard to think of another book this full of talk that feels this real, like a garrulous space made up of the people trapped there. The air filled to the brim with their digressions. The novel is not set only in the prison, though. There's so much in it about the landscape of the so-called Golden State; the scuzzy underwater world of San Francisco strip bars, where Romy worked; the dirty cops who drive around slid low in their seats mimicking the criminality they declare themselves prosecutors of. Kushner is our Genet and our new Dostoevsky, a stylist whose style doesn't enshrine her in hip self-regard but rather does something far more radical: She turns her readers' gaze back out to the world she has drawn from, showing it to us as the fallen place we so often pretend it is not.

That prison bus, which takes Romy to where she is going to spend the rest of her life, or at least the next thirty-seven years, is our boat across the River Styx. Kushner has volunteered doing human rights work in California prisons, and Stanville is clearly based on Chowchilla, in Madera County. It is one of the biggest women's prisons in the world, notoriously overcrowded with nearly four thousand inmates, and marked by scandal and violence. It is the only prison in California with women on death row. Heading toward a place like this, you can feel fear on the bus, but not from Romy.

That's because long before Romy wound up on her way to Stanville, she had spent her life adapting to the circumstances in which she found herself. Growing up in the Tenderloin in the 1980s, dodging creeps and muggers, taking beatings at school, she learned early to keep her head down and make sure she could roll with a lot of situations. This mutable, performed quality is what made her good at lap-dancing and sex-work jobs, and why when one of her customers began to stalk her, she was confused, unsure whether she should try to placate or to play the person who needs rescuing. She tried both, and that double act set up the conditions for the crime that led her to prison. But her alienation, Kushner shows, started long before that. To quote Erving Goffman, the pioneering sociologist of the 1950s whom Kushner herself has cited with regard to this book: "And to the degree that the individual maintains a show before others that he himself does not believe, he can come to experience a special kind of alienation from self and a special kind of wariness of others."

Romy ripples with wariness. She is wary of seeming weak and wary of trusting anyone, and there are a number of people in this book who claim to be trustworthy. Watching Romy silently deliberate over whether friendships in prison are worth risking the safety of dropping her guard is one of the most heartbreaking aspects of *The Mars Room*. Kushner produces these moments by submerging Romy in a sea of words—stories, other people's—which wash over and through her like a new kind of weather, now that there is no outside.

Kushner is an enormously gifted listener to American speech. Her ear turns toward the extra explanatory phrase, to the overoffered comment, to justification and ritual self-shaming, to projected weakness as a form of strength. In some situations, whoever gets the most sympathy wins. She also can hear when a voice sends longing across a contradictory emotion, like fury—the way sound travels over rough water. Her radical porousness is at its narrative best in *The Mars Room*, which introduces us to the women who will do time with Romy in Stanville, from a butch trans woman named Conrad to Sammy Fernandez, who has cycled in and out of prison all of her life. Both of them give Romy early lessons in survival. Sammy, for instance, teaches Romy how to pass items through toilets by flushing them—"Burritos. Twinkies. Cigarettes. Pruno in a shampoo bottle."

There is a kind of institutional novel genre—Ken Kesey's *One Flew over the Cuckoo's Nest* and Pat Conroy's military academy novel *Lords of Discipline* come to mind—but this is not what Kushner is making here. In her pages, we do not meet characters who hold neatly to their tropes but rather watch them assemble and reassemble their selves daily in a series of situations that also simultaneously assemble the prison itself. The prison is like a factory that makes itself daily, manufacturing hierarchies, economies, all while its inmates work for twenty-two cents an hour building things the outside world needs. Setting her cast into motion and allowing them to talk, to start trouble, Kushner creates a series of portraits of people caught in this hellish labor economy—of the self, of the body—people who are made by the place they're in.

Romy collects biographies early on when she thinks that's important. The fixed story. "Child Protective Services took Sammy away," she says at one point about Fernandez.

> She was in and out of group homes and wound up
> in Youth Authority, where she learned to fight.
> "You get a lot of skills there you'll need for prison."
> By twelve she was out of YA, back with her mom

and turning tricks to support her mother's habit. The men liked young company. Her first sugar daddy was a bail bondsman named Maldonado. She eventually got strung out herself, was arrested, took a narcotics number, a never-never number she called it, and had been in and out of prison ever since, on sales and trafficking charges. Her mother was long dead. Many people she'd been in YA with were here at Stanville. Her network was extensive. It was a lifetime of prison connections.

Over time, these biographies begin to dissolve, and what remains is a group of women who can either help or torture one another, sometimes both. Sammy's life, however, remains of particular interest to Romy, as she worries terribly about her son, Jackson, who was taken care of by her mother for a time, but that time has run out and she's about to lose him. Is this how he is going to wind up? At one point, Romy lands in a suicide ward after she is forbidden to know whether her son, who has been in the hospital, is okay. No longer his guardian, she has no rights. "'Please, Lieutenant Jones. Please.' It was happening. I was pleading with a sadist in a little girl voice."

Finally, she gets out of suicide lockup and faces what is very likely to be a lonely reckoning with her fate. As it enters this stretch, *The Mars Room* becomes one of the great American novels about time. Romy won't even have an option of parole until she is at least sixty. She has years to think about her life. In flashbacks we learn of Kurt Kennedy, the regular who began frequenting the club, and the ways Romy tried to manage his attention, his growing possessiveness, his watchfulness. This is quietly one of the best American novels on stalking. The buildup to the violent confrontation that leads to Romy going to prison is tense and shocking, and the way Kushner situates this story within the stories told by Romy's fellow inmates—some of whom are in prison for killing men—creates an overwhelming feeling of entrapment.

There are several rising questions that form tension here. Romy had a public defender, and the cop who arrested her was at best negligent. Kushner gives us just enough daylight to wonder whether Romy might be one of the rare lucky people freed for such malfeasance. There's also an escape plan being hatched, an unlikely one, but *The Mars Room* is just the kind of novel that might allow that sort of explosive ending—it is very much the kind of novel about prison that Robert Stone might have written had he spent time in Chowchilla. "There was a prisoner named Lindy Belsen who had been convicted as a juvenile and had her sentence commuted by the governor," Romy says at one point. "She was famous at Stanville. A team of volunteer lawyers had gathered around her. They built up her case as a story of human trafficking. She'd shot her pimp in a hotel room. He'd groomed her for prostitution from the age of twelve." As much as prisoners envy Belsen her release, they also resent the story for the way it reinforces the idea that undisputed innocence is the only means of gaining freedom.

As a killer who is also a victim, Romy knows she cannot hold the word *innocence* steadily in her hands. It tips this way and that, depending on the time, the room, the context. Maybe it's not a present-tense word. At one point she remembers something from a book one of her lovers used to read, *The Brothers Karamazov*. "At the end of [the book] Alyosha asks the children to . . . retain the innocence of the most wholesome feeling you ever had in your life. Part of you stays innocent forever. That part of you is worth more than the rest."

The Mars Room is a tale about the importance and impossibility of holding on to such innocence in a world where this kind of memory might destroy you. As varied and complex as are all the women Romy serves with, none of them will ever vote. Many will never see their families again, which for some of them is just fine. Quite a few may never have an address not attached to an ID number. Romy struggles to see deliverance here. "The lie of regret and of life gone off the rails," she cries out one night. "What rails. The life is the rails and it goes where it goes. It cuts its own path. My path took me here." *The Mars Room* is one of the only novels that ever shows you the rails, the knife, the path, the long bus ride in.

THE SYMPATHIZER

by Viet Thanh Nguyen

Empires have roles for all of us to play, whether we want them or not. Soldier. Barbarian. Refugee. Grateful immigrant. Suffering victim. Innocent taxpayer. Savior. Revolutionary. Terrorist. Villain. Politics is not the only theater in which these roles get cast: Memory, and all the cultural forces that keep it alive, is the other. Watch the news closely enough and you can see figures change roles as time and fortune turn. A revolutionary becomes a terrorist; a grateful immigrant becomes an innocent taxpayer. A terrorist, a quaking country's new savior.

Most people scripted into this loop have not opted for these changes: They are conscripted into them. Throughout the late 1940s, Ho Chi Minh was supported by the Office of Strategic Services, the predecessor of the CIA, as a revolutionary, a beacon to his people, whom he led to independence. Later, he began to speak of Communism, and he became a villain. Subsequently, the US war machine launched one of the most destructive wars in modern memory against his people, leaving more than three million Vietnamese, Cambodians, Laotians, Hmong, and Koreans dead. Thousands more continued to perish in the decades after from the effects of Agent Orange and thousands of land mines strewn across the region by US forces. Some 58,220 American soldiers perished in the process, and countless others died after they came home as veterans.

This explosion is the rupture that decided the direction of Viet Thanh Nguyen's life. But the way he uses narrative to refuse the roles given to him is what has made him a great artist. Model immigrant, grateful refugee. Perfect victim. Raised in San Jose, California, the child of refugees running a grocery store, growing up in the blast radius of the dream machine that creates the afterlife of so many imperial wars, he watched as his birth country's story was told back to him through the films made about the war his people called the American War and Americans called by his country's name, Vietnam.

Since the mid-2010s, Nguyen has rewritten the script he was given with an intensity and prolificness that feels like fury. In essays and critical work, books of creative nonfiction and short fiction, he has traced the way war is fought first on the battlefront and then in memory. Studying films and literature, the patterns of political thought and aesthetic philosophy, he has torn up the tropes that reiterate American innocence in the face of terrible violence, replacing them with subtler, more truthful forms of entertainment. And he has cast people like him in new key roles in those narratives.

The Sympathizer, his Pulitzer Prize–winning debut novel, was the first salvo in this raid on memory, on the way novels and films about this war have so often been propaganda masquerading as art. It is one of the most important novels of the twenty-first century, and it comes to us in an adopted guise. At first glance, *The Sympathizer* looks simply like a clever reversal of the cold war spy novel. Told in the voice of an unnamed narrator, it chronicles the travails of a Communist double agent tasked with following into the afterlife a cadre of South Vietnamese officers, chief among them the General our hero once assisted until Saigon fell.

The novel is told from the future backward—our hero has been captured, it's not clear by whom, and he is confessing his story. This genre of talk comes preloaded with pitfalls for our narrator, the bastard child of a French priest and a Vietnamese woman. Whose forgiveness is he to seek? God is out of the question for him—as a Communist sympathizer. A man of two faces, at least, whose sins is he admitting to, and which ones are mortal? Late in the book, he remains full of questions: "What was I confessing to? I had done nothing wrong, except for being Westernized." Surely, he is just doing his job.

Perhaps he simply does it too well. As a narrator, Nguyen's hero embodies to the point of mockery some of the spy genre's hero characteristics. He drinks scotch, marks time with cigarettes, and has all but memorized the critical text that bewitches all the American officers he comes across, Richard Hedd's *Asian Communism and the Oriental Mode of Destruction*. This weighty tome is gripped in the large hand of Claude, the General's CIA handler. The beefy American is an anomaly for Nguyen's narrator: He's a jock who reads. Claude is also the reason that he and the General and ninety-some other handpicked South Vietnamese make it out of Saigon alive on the last American cargo plane in April 1975.

Nguyen has so many skills as a writer that it's difficult to cover them all, but one of his best is key to a book like this: He writes violent action tremendously well. It comes in handy here. Fifty years on from that fateful day, Americans are still more apt to remember video footage of helicopters being pushed into the sea, as if the real victims of that war were machines. *The Sympathizer* takes its time setting up the long, chaotic rolling dolly shot of their departure from the air base. Sex workers, families, mistresses, American airmen, anyone who worked for South Vietnamese officers—thousands of people storm the runway desperate to leave, knowing that as bad as things have been, what's coming could be worse. It is hot and muggy and everyone stinks. The plane everyone has boarded comes under fire, and then, as they try to escape its burning fuselage, the survivors are raked with machine gun fire.

Nguyen's hero survives, as does his best friend, Bon—two of a trio who made a blood pact as teenagers to always watch out for one another. Bon's wife and child are killed, however, the first in a series of violent deaths that punctuate *The Sympathizer*, each one getting closer to the narrator. A bastard, he is marked by double vision from birth, preparing always in advance for how people see him. This learned defense was useful when he went to America for university and then wound up the key interlocutor between his boss, the General, and his American handlers. But this double vision fractures when he leaves Saigon. Bon, for example, is not a double agent: He is a true South Vietnamese believer. When his family is killed, surely Nguyen's hero's primary sympathy ought to be with him as a man, as a friend, who has suffered loss—not with the cause?

Nguyen situates this flicker of a thought perfectly in his hero's ethical peripheral vision. It could simply be a glitch of sentiment, of friendship. Besides, there is so much to come for him: escape to Guam, then California, where he will nominally remain the General's driver. Only, in California, the General and so many like him will also become akin to so many Americans: People who want to make money, experience some comfort. And now they live under drastically new circumstances. A man known as the "crapulent major" becomes a gas station attendant in Monterey. The General's wife turns to her greatest talent—cooking—and opens a restaurant. Meanwhile, the General opens a liquor store, skimming blended scotch off the top. All the profits from the restaurant supposedly go to the movement back home, but Nguyen's hero has his doubts.

Our hero has good reason to note all this with forensic clarity. Part of his mission is to report back to party leaders on the activities of the exiled South Vietnamese. While telling his offstage interlocutor his story, Nguyen's narrator is also reliving the letters he sent to the

Parisian aunt of his friend Man, which is how he smuggles information out of America. Nguyen expertly milks this assignment for a potent mixture of comedy and pathos. For all the bribes he took in Saigon, the crapulent major is also simply an older man with a family, trying to move on with his life when the narrator has him killed. The General ordered it, and to disobey would call the narrator's loyalty into question. Instantly, the man's ghost begins to haunt Nguyen's narrator—stirring up other ghosts who had been hidden in the background of the narrator's psychic space, such as his mother, who died when he was a young man. Surely, she imagined more for him than this, this life as a fixer, spy, and low-budget assassin.

All this might be easier to weather if straightforward revenge was possible, but *The Sympathizer* thwarts that easy rewriting. In the years immediately following the war, boondoggles shape-shift and take on new purposes—namely, to preserve the power structures that underwrote the war. On these fronts, the narrator also fails spectacularly. A US congressman makes a deal with the General to turn his soldiers into footmen for votes, and there's little the narrator can do to stop them. Separately, he gets himself installed as an adviser to a blockbuster "Vietnam War" film. Rather than stop the film's grossest distortions, he nearly gets himself killed.

And thus *The Sympathizer* takes its ultimate form—a modernist American comedy about war and ethics. The deeper into the morass of his assignment Nguyen's narrator sinks, the more American he becomes—a model success, a man who has adapted just enough. To his left and right are other Asian Americans who have made similar bargains, without being spies. Philippine and Korean American actors, Chinese American waiters, Thai revolutionaries. Misrecognized at every step, they, too, ply a double life, even as back where they've come from—as in Marcos's Philippines—terrible things are done to suppress life, in the form of torturing, detaining, even murdering their relatives.

In America, Nguyen's narrator finds one man or woman after another who have made this bargain—to simply change disguises—which leads to ironies within ironies. For example, when the General begins to round up his former troops on American soil to perform exercises, they do this work on stolen Indian land—like so many other American reenactors. A trained observer, Nguyen's narrator has the excuse to keep watch on all the people around him, one of the ways *The Sympathizer* constantly bursts forward in great gusts of hilarious description.

Nguyen is one of modern American literature's most dexterous phrase-makers, especially when it comes to describing people. One man "had the habit of speaking with his teeth clenched, gnawing at his words like bones." The longer the narrator's friend Bon stays in America, the more cynical he becomes, and the more he talks. "Usually Bon used words like a sniper," the narrator notes in one argument, "but this was a spray of machine-gun fire that silenced me for several moments." Do any of their conversations about life and home have any point? he wonders. "Did we salivate for sadness," he asks himself at an extravagant wedding where the General's daughter appears like a mirage. "These questions required either Camus or cognac, and as Camus was not available I ordered cognac."

What a way for a scene to transition. In one phrase, as Percival Everett has done with the Western or Charles Yu the Hollywood noir, *The Sympathizer* boots up and borrows a filmic genre's entire lexicon, and also makes good fun of it. Chapter by chapter, this novel creates and marshals "the humming, crackling AM channel of hearsay" among a society of political exiles, but it also turns its gaze fundamentally, crucially, on the country and people who for years have been telling their story. At one point, Nguyen's narrator goes with the General to meet with the US congressman and his attaché. The meeting takes place upstairs in a restaurant, a room in which he discovers that he "was in close quarters with some representative specimens of the most dangerous creature in the history of the world, the white man in a suit."

Just when you think this novel is overstuffed, it begins closing in on its shattering finale. After another piece of wet work for the General, Nguyen's narrator gathers too much heat to stay in the US, and he flies to Thailand, where he plans to hump to the Laotian border and reunite with exiled South Vietnamese, still planning resistance from afar. He winds up in Bangkok for a day, where at last he sees the blockbuster action film he imagined to have influenced. Sitting in a darkened cinema, legs bumping up against his neighbors, moviegoers talking over the sound, he is bowled over by the scale and power of the finished story. Despite himself, he has to admire the director, a man who probably tried to kill him on set.

As the credits roll, Nguyen's narrator starts looking for his name. After he passes "VC RAPIST #1" and "DESPERATE VILLAGER" and "CRAZY GUY IN WHORE HOUSE" and then all the animals and even the animal trainer, he realizes he will not appear in the credits either. That for all his effort to change the course of one slice of visible memory, he hasn't just failed, but hasn't even been recorded as trying. One of the most difficult questions *The Sympathizer* addresses is what he is supposed to do with this rage. If a man such as this one, a man so close to power he can even be handed its cigar to smoke, on occasion, cannot change a system from the inside, what is he supposed to do?

Nguyen's example as an artist has been to create his own means of production. *The Sympathizer* was an HBO series; surely, he had something to do with its mostly Vietnamese American cast. His children's books, like those of Toni Morrison and Sandra Cisneros and Junot Díaz, have all rewritten the script of how kids like he was can see themselves. One of Nguyen's most powerful books, his recent assault on the memoir as a form, *A Man of Two Faces: A Memoir, a History, a Memorial*, essentially functions as a postmodern biography of his mother, whose story his own life was to occlude, were he to agree to the typical model-minority script: They sacrificed so I could become a storyteller for my people.

The question in this activity remains, To whom or where should one's sympathy lie? Is it a betrayal to let it range widely, as Nguyen's narrator does here, seemingly against his own will? Broken but not beaten by a variety of losses, improperly reeducated at least twice, he must confront the fact that this instinct of his is both imperiling and essential. Those who are truly doomed in this magnificent novel are the ones who cannot stomach this numinous risk or follow it to its conclusion. The ones who have accepted the power of empire to choose roles and have decided to honor these casting decisions. Book by book, Viet Thanh Nguyen has been showing us there's another way.

THE OTHER AMERICANS

by Laila Lalami

In roughly the time it will take you to read this essay, someone in the state of California will be injured in a hit-and-run crash. Nearly nine people an hour, twenty-four hours a day, 365 days a year, are injured, according to recent data from California Highway Patrol. It's a shocking fact. Add to this about one hit-and-run fatality per day and it looks like the Golden State has an epidemic in coexistence. We are, indeed, vulnerable simply by living together. Walking the same streets. Driving the same roads. Driving two-ton SUVs or, god forbid, riding a bicycle. If we agree on rules applying equally and offering equal exposure, then perhaps a society works.

But it doesn't really work that way, does it, because the stress doesn't fall equally. Take this from the cast at the heart of Laila Lalami's *The Other Americans*, her 2019 novel, which begins with the hit-and-run death of Driss Guerraoui, a hardworking immigrant who had just begun to live a life in which he made choices rather than adapted to forces outside himself. "My father had often outrun disaster," his daughter Nora, one of the book's nine narrators, says. "The protests in Casablanca had moved him to California; the arson had made it possible for him to buy a diner. But now disaster had finally caught up with him." The arson mentioned here is one of the rips in the fabric of the community where *The Other Americans* takes place; the novel is set in the Mojave, ten miles from Joshua Tree National Park, in a town along Highway 62 where change has come and some are more comfortable with those social shifts than most. Driss and his family were part of that change, transplanted to California after the crackdown on protests in Morocco turned violent. And yet he thrived. Working diligently, buying a failing doughnut shop and renaming it Aladdin Donuts. Not long after his wife, Maryam, had been able to leave the business to help raise their kids, it was burned down. A retributive arson post-9/11.

For this reason, when Driss is killed, Nora's first thought is that what has happened to her father was not an accident. *The Other Americans* takes place mostly in the aftermath of this event, this uneasy question hanging in the air as the novel cycles through its large cast, all of them touched, in one way or another, by Driss's death, many of them with experience enough to have similar doubts. Efraín, a Mexican man who saw the moment Driss was hit, is afraid to come forward; when he reads the name of the victim, he realizes how close it is to Guerrero. How easily it could have been someone like him.

Lalami has in her earlier fiction written brilliantly about the perils that migrants must navigate. In *Hope and Other Dangerous Pursuits*, a boat carrying a group of Moroccans crossing the Strait of Gibraltar to Spain capsizes, and in flashbacks, we learn what conditions brought them to a dodgy raft on high seas. Her dazzling *The Moor's Account* narrates the journey of Estebanico, the first person of African descent to explore the New World—a journey full of peril and danger, from Florida to Mexico. Several times during the odyssey, Estebanico buys himself into freedom.

In her essay collection, *Conditional Citizens: On Belonging in America*, Lalami writes about her own path from Morocco to the United States and about becoming a citizen in a country where people like her—a woman, an Arab, a Muslim—often have to prove their innocence, even in the absence of a crime. This trajectory suggests that *The Other Americans* would become a kind of argument in the form of a fiction—but it is a far subtler book than that.

Whereas Lalami's previous fiction reveals the perils of surviving, *The Other Americans* deals with the problems of belonging. In the novel, Nora has a tattoo on her wrist of words in Latin that mean "a voice crying out," presumably a reference to "vox clamantis in deserto," which might be a shortened form of a quote from St. John the Baptist. Among the things that the passage addresses is the need to repent. But also—the power of a voice. Coexistence requires both—voice and listening.

The Other Americans is one of the only novels of its type that understand the necessity of both. Moving along its narrative wheel, Lalami's book reveals unexpected and moving parallels. Coming home to bury her father, Nora encounters Jeremy Gorecki, a onetime honors student like her whose life hasn't gone as planned. His mother died young, and into that rupture, he poured himself, covering for a father who drank. While Nora fled to become a composer, he fled into the army—and wound up in Iraq.

Of all the books featuring veterans that have been published in the United States in recent years, *The Other Americans* is among the best. While Jeremy's story is one of knocking down doors in the dead of night in Iraq, terrorizing families, he has other memories, other elements to his personality—and the book isn't distorted to acknowledge only his trauma. In fact, his experience of nearly being killed far from home has made him appreciate—all the more—what Nora's family has gone through, even before the accident. This sensitivity is rarely portrayed in veterans in fiction, who are often, for purposes of drama, written as damaged beyond repair.

In one of the most striking scenes of the book, Nora flees the excessive ministrations of her mother to a bar. Jeremy sees her crossing the street and decides to follow her in. She has a drink—he, a few years sober, a burger. They begin to connect, and then she asks a question that forces him to reveal to her—an Arab and a Muslim—that he fought in Iraq. The slow, understated way this confrontation happens, and its erotic aftermath, is one of the finest collisions in recent American fiction.

If *Hope and Other Dangerous Pursuits* and *The Moor's Account* deal with characters traveling toward and through a place, everyone in *The Other Americans* is, in some way or another, stuck in the environs of the Morongo Basin. For a swift if sprawling book set in the desert air, with a few hikes thrown in, the novel feels claustrophobic. People run into one another. People see one another doing things. Time is spent in cars and shabby shopping malls.

Narrating all this in multiple first-person voices—with one brief foray into second person, when we hear from Nora's sister—requires a fine-tuned musical register. Lalami has it. The characters in the book do not so much narrate as speak into the air. Somebody one day will make a superb play or opera out of this novel; a great deal of the work has already been done. One by one, characters emerge and speak, often quite briefly, for two or three pages at a time, each with different accents and habits.

The Other Americans exists in that gray space on the continuum between everyone speaking and everyone occasionally listening to one another. Only one character doesn't do so much listening—Anderson Baker, who has been in town the longest. He's the owner of a bowling alley, a father late in life, and his is a world of people like him and "the other Americans." "Some people say I should be grateful for the business that the newcomers are bringing to the town," he says at one point. "But the way I see it, they're changing this place and wanting me to be grateful for it. They didn't ask if we wanted them here, and they just came."

Ultimately, the narrative strategy of Lalami's novel becomes a kind of philosophy. Moving character to character, we are made to understand why it seems not just natural but right that people would compare their fates. Measure what one person had and what another person didn't. At the root of the mystery of Driss's death is a comparison of this kind made by a person jealous of what Driss was able to obtain; even if that envy didn't become a weapon, it was a form of violence.

Can an accident be a weapon? *The Other Americans* is one of the rare books to present one as such, across so many different meanings. It's by accident—nearly—that Driss misses a bullet in Morocco and lands in California; it's by accident that a detective working the case winds up in California and not back East, where she grew up; it's by accident that one of Jeremy's buddies saves his life in Iraq, a fact that makes Jeremy beholden to him, even though the man is a walking fuckup.

Gently, quietly, *The Other Americans* creates a portrait of life in an uneasy United States of the near present, where accidents are in fact the greater norm, the bigger uniter. The minority are those other Americans, the rare few who have not been brought low by an intervention of fate, by catastrophe. One of the most tragic truths at the heart of this important book is that even among the minority, there are those too proud, too grief-stricken, sometimes too bigoted to acknowledge that they, too, are waiting for a voice to cry out in the desert.

THE BACKYARD BIRD CHRONICLES

by Amy Tan

At least a billion birds migrate through California every year along what is called the Pacific Flyway, a route that stretches from Patagonia to Alaska. If you want to see waterfowl in the tens of thousands, the Central Valley's wetlands, especially its rice fields, are the perfect place to observe ducks, geese, and swans stopping on their long trip north. There are many feeder birds that use the flyway too—Anna's Hummingbirds, Dark-eyed Junco, Fox Sparrow, Pine Siskin, and Ruby-crowned Kinglet, to name a few. A whole bevy of birds stop in Northern California, all of them needing the equivalent of an ultramarathoner's water and fuel station after thousands of miles in the air. You don't need your own personal wetlands to catch sight of many of them. If you're lucky—or clever, and study what it is the birds like to eat, what they do—you can see them in your own backyard.

Amy Tan has a backyard and she is most certainly clever, curious, and open to finding out what birds like to eat. *The Backyard Bird Chronicles* is an illustrated diary of her obsession with the winged creatures who come right up to her back porch, some of them, seeking sustenance. Culled from thousands of pages of journals, it reads like a set of two-way binoculars—a book that teaches us how to see creatures of the natural world and how to see yourself as a person within it at the same time. The book's power proceeds from its humility. At the age of sixty-four, Tan was one of America's best-known storytellers, a Pulitzer Prize–winning novelist who'd sold millions of books, but she was just restarting her journey as an artist—something she had wanted to be ever since she was a small child. Page by page, we watch as she studies this new craft with rapture and passion by looking at the birds out her window.

The first one is a hummingbird, those "tiny avian helicopters" she had always imagined as a child, part of her dream that she could "win the trust of wild animals and they would willingly come to me." She puts a feeder on the patio of her Sausalito home, and just like that, within minutes, "a hummingbird came to inspect, a male with a flashing red head. He hovered, gave it a cursory glance, and then left. At least he noticed it. A good beginning. Then he returned, inspected it again from different angles, and left. The third time, he did a little dance around the feeder, approached and stuck his bill in the hole and drank. I was astonished. That was fast."

Tan might be unhappy with her drawing at this stage, but her observatory prose beats with a vital pulse. "Feel the bird," her sketching instructor Jack Laws tells her, "be the bird." It sounds absurd, but notice the effects her prose produces. Those short sentences, the diminutive clauses, neatly mimic a hummingbird's darting ways. Within a sentence, she could be describing the bird or herself—"a good beginning" might apply to his first pass of the feeder. There's nothing wasted in her lines, astonishing for something produced originally as a diary. Like the birds around her, everything in her prose is deliberate—concise, like putting a thin beak through a tiny hole to drink nectar and consume enough calories to recover from a long trip north. Moments later, she describes another male coming back, only because she'd left the feeder on the table next to her. This one "landed on my hand, and immediately started feeding. I held my breath and kept my hand with the feeder as still as possible. His feet felt scratchy. He was assessing me the whole time he fed. We stared at each other, eye to eye."

How many of us long for such an encounter? Even if we know it can also be dangerous for wild creatures. *The Backyard Bird Chronicles* swivels between desire and care. Tan is smitten (obsessed, she says), but instantly realizes that her interaction comes with responsibility. The very next diary is about a sick bird—a Pine Siskin—that is behaving strangely. Like the hummingbird, it, too, hops onto her hand. But Pine Siskins don't breed where she lives in Sausalito, and they are not known for being so friendly to humans. Something is wrong with it. She calls US Fish and Wildlife and discovers that there is a salmonellosis outbreak among the breed and that this bird is definitely dying. She takes down her feeders, destroys some, gives away the bird food, so as not to become a breeding ground for disease.

The Backyard Bird Chronicles is a story of wonder and peril. It is dangerous to be a bird. As Tan points out, 70 percent of fledglings don't survive, and of the remaining group, 40 percent don't make it to three weeks old. They need a lot of food to make it, too. Some go overboard, perhaps. Scrub Jays store between thirty-five hundred to six thousand acorns a year in their fever to have enough. Her beloved hummingbirds are not being overcautious. Their hearts pound at 1,000 bpm. Overnight, Anna's Hummingbirds drop into a hibernation-like state called torpor, and their heart rate slows to as low as 50 bpm, a condition from which they take ten to fifteen minutes to awaken. What an easy snack they'd make. In one startling aside, Tan mentions that house cats kill over a billion birds a year.

What do we owe species that live such brief, imperiled lives? And is *owe* the right word? Seeing birds as pollinators and key parts of an ecosystem we all depend on is surely too basic. As Barry Lopez wrote in one of his final essays, "Only an ignoramus can imagine now that pollinating insects, migratory birds, and pelagic fish can depart our company and that we will survive because we know how to make tools." What if what we must devote ourselves too is not simply our own survival but their mystery—since doing so is, in and of itself, meaningful, important.

The Backyard Bird Chronicles doesn't channel these questions directly. Rather, with great dexterity, it builds them right into the frame. There are four big frames, actually, in the book. One of these contains Tan's beginning to learn to look at and identify the birds that come to her backyard. In a second frame we watch Tan's journey as an artist, as she learns to draw the birds by learning to observe them. A third frame centers the melodramas that happen between the birds, which Tan both imagines and chronicles as wars, as challenges, as epic family squabbles, a hundred thousand episodes of *Game of Thrones* in a season. And a fourth frame involves her learning how to lure and take care of the birds, how to present them with the food they want and build feeders that they can use and that protect them from predators. She's not simply just watching the birds; she's making her backyard more suitable to their needs.

The way these frames nestle neatly one inside the other is one of the marvels of this book's design. Read it for more than a few minutes at a time and the coherence of their interlocking concerns—a feeling of being in and among the natural—produces intense delight. Also the calm that Lopez describes of so many when they are around birds. You can feel this sense of deep connection in the drawings Tan reproduces throughout the book. As she progresses, the confidence of her pencil strokes, a steadiness of gaze, lends the renderings a stilling, sometimes even awestruck beauty.

She's in love. She says this early on, and it's hard not to see all the range of the emotion here. Passion, yes, but also desire, possessiveness, intensity, and lots of courtship. While Tan describes the birds wooing each other, she woos them. She sets up and slowly perfects feeders in four locations around her house: the patio, the veranda, the office porch, and on the other side of her bathroom window. Seeds and suet give way to the caviar of bird diet: live mealworms. She escalates until she is buying and refrigerating five thousand mealworms a week—at one point, she contemplates starting her own mealworm farm or getting another refrigerator to store them, "but doing either would be time-consuming and pathological"—after all, she is already providing them with suet cakes, suet balls, sunflower seeds, millet, nyger seeds, safflower seeds, and butter bark.

The birds reward her by appearing in droves: Chestnut-backed Chickadees, Pygmy Nuthatches, Dark-eyed Juncos, a Hermit Thrush, a Fox Sparrow, an American Tree Sparrow, a White-crowned Sparrow, Townsend's Warblers, Goldfinches, crows, and hawks of several kinds—the last of whom are not necessarily wanted since they eat fledglings, but admired nonetheless. Bobo, Tan's four-pound Yorkie, is hustled inside when the hawks appear. When Tan spies something she doesn't recognize, she checks on her eBird app or on a Facebook bird group to log her discovery. Sometimes she even calls an expert friend.

Tan's goal here is not to become a tower of knowledge. She's a happy anthropomorphizing observer. An exuberant amateur. She has always been a supremely gifted describer of people and their habits; this is what made her novel about a dozen people on a trip to China, *Saving Fish from Drowning*, such highbrow comedy, a literary version of *White Lotus* long before that show became such a hit. Here she trains all her skills on portraiture of the birds. Songbirds at the feeder on Thanksgiving are like "black Friday shoppers frantic to snap up good deals on worms." California Towhees strolling across the patio resemble "landlords inspecting the premises for damages," their round tummies like beer bellies.

She is especially interested in birds who do not behave according to their type, and begins to define birds through their ability to behave differently than their type.

"The *why* is essential," she writes at one point, as she tries to figure out what a bird is doing by zooming out to perceive her garden as a whole, to observe the day, the time of year. "That behavior in context enables me to understand the bird." Still, she tilts, and she knows she tilts, the playing field. She deals as best she can with pests—rats, clever squirrels, and yellowjackets (who steal the live mealworms)—without simply killing them. In doing so she learns something about the finches, who she thought were as messy as teenagers. Every time they visited they left behind a hefty pile of discarded seeds, and if she didn't sweep up, the rats descended. Later Tan discovers from a birder friend that they're not throwing their food on the ground; they're testing which seeds have the most oil. They're not slobs—they're picky.

Time passes. How hard it is, while living, to feel this as deeply as one can. To feel, beneath our clocks and our daily to-do lists, an older sense of order requires reservoirs of focus that are hard to tap into in modern life. The best writing about the wild and about the natural world returns us to a different sense of time by encouraging us to rediscover the skills of focus and attention by narrating in prose that rewards this quality. Tan achieves this state of nonfiction nirvana in plainspoken ways. After years of watching birds, for instance, she writes that "my view of the seasons no longer follows the Earth's spin on its axis. Spring, Summer, Fall, and Winter have been replaced by Spring Migration, Nesting Season, Fledgling Season, and Fall Migration. The timelines pertain only to birds in my backyard. When I left in mid September for a month, I knew I might be missing the start of fall migration."

The focus of this book remains in this soft interior space where we calibrate time and memory, our observations of the world. Halfway through the book, though, COVID comes. "Everything seems like a potential transmitter of disease and death," Tan writes, finding herself in a predicament similar to that of the ailing Pine Siskin she introduced us to on the first pages of this diary. She won't give up her bird-watching, though. "The groceries, a door knob, another person. But not the birds. The birds are balm." Weeks into the pandemic, she is out shopping with a mask on, social distancing, to buy bird food and lamenting she cannot buy more than five thousand mealworms at a time. Later that same year, wildfires start up, bringing new birds to her backyard—for example, a Western Bluebird fledgling, maybe driven in Tan's direction by the serial wildfires that have been burning since August. The context that Tan describes earlier in the book as being essential to understanding the *why* does in fact extend far beyond her garden.

By this book's end, a bird's life doesn't seem any less perilous, but Tan's observations have bored one fact of their existence into us: Their supreme—not endless—adaptability is pushed nearly to its limit. We are in the middle of a great extinction event humans have started, and all of us would be wise to figure out how to do our bit to repair our corner of the wild. Tan shows how rewarding it can be, even if such moments are rare. Three years after the Pine Siskin arrived sick and dying, when Tan had to tear down her feeders, a new clutch of siskins turned up again. Daily she watches as fledglings that are left alone try and try again to learn how to feed. Tan is not overly hopeful, nor is she hopeless, about their ability to survive, if we humans change our profligate ways. "It is remarkable what birds can endure," she says at one point, when another sick bird lands in her backyard. "It is tragic what they cannot. I'm hoping this bird is remarkable."

By training her eye so closely on the migrants and locals who wander into her backyard, Tan has evoked something the most enlightened birders experience: an overwhelming sense that *all* the birds are remarkable, whether they have the power to survive illness and terrible fights and choked skies or not. California is their state too, maybe even originally. Whether they spend their whole brief lives there or are passing through, they are citizens. *The Backyard Bird Chronicles* raises this point by reversing the gaze on nature. This is a book that doesn't just stare out the window and imagine what birds are up to; it peers back at the eye itself. "I, too, am part of their curricula," Tan says. "The young birds have always seen me as part of the yard. I am the flightless animal that sits by the big glass doors and sometimes comes out." With this chronicle of care, she invites us all to see ourselves too, to sit still, and to see, to really see, the splendors we live among.

ACKNOWLEDGMENTS

Most of these essays appeared over the last five years in *Alta* magazine. I thank Will Hearst, Blaise Zerega, Beth Spotwood, David Ulin, and Anita Felicelli, for the space, belief, and superb editing. I also thank the panel of the California Book Club—including Paul Yamazaki, Oscar Villalon, Lynell George, Marissa Lopez, and Danzy Senna—for creating a club in which reading these books deeply was possible; and having the conversations these books made possible was a lot of fun. Thank you to everyone who has come and asked questions, commented, read alongside us. Thanks, too, go to the writers for participating, and to all of their special guests for signing on to ask more questions. I am grateful to Steve Wasserman of Heyday for the last lunch I will ever have at Periyali, out of which came this book. Michele Jones gave this book an absolutely superb copyedit; I am so grateful for her hard work. Thank you Chris Carosi for your review of the City Lights essay. Thank you Archie Ferguson for making the book look so beautiful. Writing this book gave me an excuse to spend more and more time in California with my family, which was a joy beyond words. I thank them for their hospitality and endless good cheer, and my partner for putting up with daily yogurt runs. Finally, thanks and much gratitude to Emmerich Anklam, for your diligence, for your astute judgment, for your patience, and most important, for your love and knowledge of California.

APPENDIX

99 More Essential California Books

This book is meant to make it easier to find what shines in literature about California and the West. To study it, explore this literature, and muse on what it says about California and its history. These essays are just a beginning, though. Here is a small, subjective list of 99 other contemporary books that will lead you down fruitful paths into the depths and furthest reaches, into the cities and deserts and history of California and its people.

Damon B. Akins and William J. Bauer Jr., *We Are the Land*
Isabel Allende, *Daughter of Fortune*
Mark Arax, *The Dreamt Land*
Mary Austin, *The Land of Little Rain*
Eve Babitz, *Slow Days, Fast Company*
Lucia Berlin, *A Manual for Cleaning Women*
Frank Bidart, *Half-light*
Richard Brautigan, *A Confederate General from Big Sur*
Thi Bui, *The Best We Could Do*
Rita Bullwinkel, *Headshot*
Octavia E. Butler, *Parable of the Sower*
James M. Cain, *Double Indemnity*

381

Michael Chabon, *Telegraph Avenue*
Raymond Chandler, *The Big Sleep*
Emma Cline, *The Girls*
Wanda Coleman, *Mercurochrome*
Mark Z. Danielewski, *House of Leaves*
Ash Davidson, *Damnation Spring*
Angela Y. Davis, *Are Prisons Obsolete?*
Mike Davis, *City of Quartz*
Diane di Prima, *Revolutionary Letters*
Philip K. Dick, *A Scanner Darkly*
Philip K. Dick, *Do Androids Dream of Electric Sheep?*
Joan Didion, *Where I Was From*
Tongo Eisen-Martin, *Heaven Is All Goodbyes*
Bret Easton Ellis, *Less Than Zero*
Anne Fadiman, *The Spirit Catches You and You Fall Down*
John Fante, *Ask the Dust*
Lawrence Ferlinghetti, *These Are My Rivers*
Sesshu Foster, *City Terrace Field Manual*
Carribean Fragoza, *Eat the Mouth That Feeds You*
Forrest Gander, *Twice Alive*
Allen Ginsberg, *Howl and Other Poems*
William Goldman, *Adventures in the Screen Trade*
Sue Grafton, *A Is for Alibi*
Yaa Gyasi, *Transcendent Kingdom*
Dashiell Hammett, *The Maltese Falcon*
Bret Harte, *The Luck of Roaring Camp and Other Sketches*
Robert Hass, *Praise*
Jaime Hernandez, *Maggie the Mechanic*
Juan Felipe Herrera, *Half of the World in Light*
Jack Hicks, James D. Houston, Maxine Hong Kingston, and Al Young, editors, *The Literature of California, Volume 1*
Chester Himes, *If He Hollers Let Him Go*
Cathy Park Hong, *Minor Feelings*
Jeanne Wakatsuki Houston and James D. Houston, *Farewell to Manzanar*

Appendix

Robinson Jeffers, *The Selected Poetry*
Jack Kerouac, *The Dharma Bums*
Lydia Kiesling, *The Golden State*
Maxine Hong Kingston, *China Men*
Dorothy Lazard, *What You Don't Know Will Make a Whole New World*
Ursula K. Le Guin, *Always Coming Home*
Edan Lepucki, *Time's Mouth*
Jonathan Lethem, *As She Climbed Across the Table*
Jack London, *The Call of the Wild*
Manjula Martin, *The Last Fire Season*
Armistead Maupin, *Tales of the City*
Carey McWilliams, *Factories in the Field*
Cherríe Moraga, *Loving in the War Years*
Walter Mosley, *Little Scarlet*
John Muir, *My First Summer in the Sierra*
Manuel Muñoz, *What You See in the Dark*
Maggie Nelson, *The Argonauts*
Frank Norris, *The Octopus*
Kem Nunn, *Tapping the Source*
Susan Orlean, *The Library Book*
Julie Otsuka, *When the Emperor Was Divine*
Ivy Pochoda, *Sing Her Down*
Michael Pollan, *The Omnivore's Dilemma*
Gary Phillips, *Violent Spring*
D. A. Powell, *Useless Landscape, or A Guide for Boys*
Richard Preston, *The Wild Trees*
Thomas Pynchon, *Inherent Vice*
Ishmael Reed, *Mumbo Jumbo*
Marc Reisner, *Cadillac Desert*
Adrienne Rich, *An Atlas of the Difficult World*
Luis J. Rodriguez, *Always Running*
Ingrid Rojas Contreras, *The Man Who Could Move Clouds*
Greg Sarris, *Grand Avenue*
Carolyn See, *Golden Days*

CALIFORNIA REWRITTEN

Solmaz Sharif, *Look*
Randy Shilts, *And the Band Played On*
Eleni Sikelianos, *The California Poem*
Upton Sinclair, *Oil!*
Rebecca Solnit, *Savage Dreams*
Gary Soto, *New and Selected Poems*
Kevin Starr, *Golden Dreams*
John Steinbeck, *The Grapes of Wrath*
Susan Straight, *Mecca*
Amy Tan, *The Joy Luck Club*
Adrian Tomine, *Shortcomings*
Frederick Jackson Turner, *The Frontier in American History*
Mai Der Vang, *Yellow Rain*
William T. Vollmann, *Imperial*
Alice Waters, *Coming to My Senses*
Nathanael West, *The Day of the Locust*
Tobias Wolff, *This Boy's Life*
Jade Snow Wong, *The Fifth Daughter*
Rosanna Xia, *California Against the Sea*
Al Young, *The Sound of Dreams Remembered*

Appendix

Recommended Reading from California Authors

I reached out to some of the authors featured in this volume, asking for their favorite California books. Here are their responses.

Deborah A. Miranda, author of Bad Indians
- *Earthquake Weather*, by Janice Gould
- *The Woman Warrior*, by Maxine Hong Kingston
- *The Grapes of Wrath*, by John Steinbeck
- Dorothy Allison—poetry, fiction, memoir, essays (she's from the South, but lived in California for most of her adult life)
- *Under the Feet of Jesus*, by Helena María Viramontes
- *Citizen 13660*, by Miné Okubo
- *Mabel McKay: Weaving the Dream*, by Greg Sarris

These are the books I return to again and again. They've taught me much.

Elaine Castillo, author of America Is Not the Heart

Tommy Pico's *Nature Poem* is for me, California's greatest epic poem: It's California's *The Iliad*, California's *The Odyssey*, and moreover it transcends such comparisons entirely, to be California's sweeping, tender, hilarious anti-epic to all that is inherited by we who identify as Californians. *Nature Poem* isn't just in the Californian canon; it is the California canon.

Javier Zamora, author of Solito

I was just talking to my therapist about Dave Eggers and *A Heartbreaking Work of Staggering Genius*. I didn't realize his memoir was the first memoir I ever read (besides Che's *Motorcycle Diaries*), but he was the first prose writer I ever met in person. I will never forget his description of Berkeley (which made me want to go to school there), the Mission District (where I volunteered as a teenager at 826 Valencia and frequented often to buy our Christmas fits and Salvadoran spices), and his description of the yellow-pilon line that used to divide/separate the incoming traffic on the Golden Gate. That description alone showed me the power of prose, thinking: I've had that same thought, woah, I could write/could've written about it. The thought in his memoir was: any car can easily crash into me and end me. You know, teenager things.

Karen Tei Yamashita, author of *I Hotel*
Hard to say there's an essential California book. Some of my list over the years:
- Sesshu Foster, *Atomik Aztex*
- Carey McWilliams, *Southern California: An Island on the Land*
- Ruth Wilson Gilmore, *Golden Gulag: Prisons, Surplus, Crisis, and Opposition in Globalizing California*
- Maxine Hong Kingston, *Tripmaster Monkey: His Fake Book*
- Carlos Bulosan, *America Is in the Heart*
- Mike Davis, *City of Quartz*
- Frank Chin, *Gunga Din Highway*
- Guillermo Gómez-Peña, *The New World Border* and *Codex Espangliensis*
- Theodora Kroeber, *Ishi in Two Worlds* (and the books on the controversy that follows—for example, Karl Kroeber and Clifton Kroeber, editors, *Ishi in Three Centuries*)
- Ursula K. Le Guin, *Always Coming Home*
- Martin Rizzo-Martinez, *We Are Not Animals*
- Angela Davis, *Angela Davis: An Autobiography*
- Fae Myenne Ng, *Bone*

Steph Cha, author of *Your House Will Pay*
Paul Beatty's *The White Boy Shuffle* is a weird, hypnotic, incisive novel that I haven't really stopped thinking about since I read it a decade ago. It's just unlike anything else, the memoir of a "Negro demagogue" who leads his followers to suicide—deeply grim but stylish and funny as hell. The book takes place across Los Angeles, but that's not what makes it an essential California read. The eclectic characters, the sprawling tragedy, the poetry and laughter and cool—Beatty tapped right into the life force of our state.

D. J. Waldie, author of *Holy Land*
It's tough to get a grip on the southern third of California. Everything below the Transverse Ranges is either desert or suburbia, even if some of it is

Hollywood and much of it looks like Los Angeles. There is another way of seeing this place, however, starting locally with *An Architectural Guidebook to Los Angeles: Fully Revised 6th Edition*, by David Gebhard, Robert Winter, and Robert Inman. Drive around (it's LA after all) with this book in hand and the city will be revealed to you.

Rabih Alameddine, author of *The Wrong End of the Telescope*
Anything Claire Vaye Watkins writes is magical in every sense of the word, and this novel re-magics the California dream—a sun ravaged, drought drenched, surreal road trip of a dream. California is phantasmagoric and *Gold Fame Citrus* is its novel.

PERMISSIONS

"I Am Waiting," by Lawrence Ferlinghetti, from *A Coney Island of the Mind*, copyright © 1958 by Lawrence Ferlinghetti. Reprinted by permission of New Directions Publishing Corp.

"Recipe for Happiness in Khabarovsk or Anyplace," by Lawrence Ferlinghetti, from *Endless Life*, copyright © 1981 by Lawrence Ferlinghetti. Reprinted by permission of New Directions Publishing Corp.

Excerpts from *Postcolonial Love Poem* copyright © 2020 by Natalie Diaz. Used by permission of Graywolf Press. All rights reserved. www.graywolfpress.org.

Ada Limón, excerpt from "Forsythia" from *The Hurting Kind* (Minneapolis: Milkweed Editions, 2022). Copyright © 2022 by Ada Limón. Reprinted with the permission of Milkweed Editions, milkweed.org.

Ada Limón, excerpt from "Body of Rivers" from *Sharks in the Rivers* (Minneapolis: Milkweed Editions, 2010). Copyright © 2010 by Ada Limón. Reprinted with the permission of Milkweed Editions, milkweed.org.

Excerpts from *Citizen: An American Lyric* copyright © 2014 by Claudia Rankine. Used by permission of Graywolf Press. All rights reserved. www.graywolfpress.org.

Excerpts from *Just Us: An American Conversation* copyright © 2020 by Claudia Rankine. Used by permissions of Graywolf Press. All rights reserved. www.graywolfpress.org.

Excerpt from *Nothing in Nature is Private* copyright © 1994 by Claudia Rankine. Reproduced by permission of the author.

Excerpts from *The Best of It* copyright © 2010 by Kay Ryan. Used by permission of Grove/Atlantic, Inc.

"The Mothers," "Dog Talk," "On the Road to Sri Bhuvaneshwari," "Frame," and "Plantation" from *Voyage of the Sable Venus: And Other Poems* by Robin Coste Lewis, copyright © 2015 by Robin Coste Lewis. Used by permission of Alfred A. Knopf, an imprint of the Knopf Doubleday Publishing Group, a division of Penguin Random House LLC. All rights reserved.

Han Shan, excerpts from "Cold Mountain Wonders," translated by Gary Snyder and excerpts from "Hay for the Horses" from *Riprap and Cold Mountain Poems* by Gary Snyder. Copyright © 1959 by Gary Snyder. Reprinted with the permission of The Permissions Company, LLC on behalf of Counterpoint Press, counterpointpress.com.

ABOUT THE AUTHOR

John Freeman has hosted *Alta*'s California Book Club since its founding in 2020. He is an executive editor at Alfred A. Knopf, and he edited *Freeman's* (2015–2023), a literary annual of new writing. His books include *How to Read a Novelist* and *Dictionary of the Undoing*, as well as the anthologies *Tales of Two Americas*, *Tales of Two Planets*, *The Penguin Book of the Modern American Short Story*, and *Sacramento Noir*. He is also the author of three poetry collections, *Maps*, *The Park*, and *Wind, Trees*. His work is translated into more than twenty languages and has appeared in the *New Yorker*, the *Paris Review*, and the *New York Times*. He is the former editor of *Granta*.

A NOTE ON TYPE

This book is set in Perpetua. Designed by Eric Gill, hand-cut by Charles Malin, and published with Monotype in 1929, Perpetua was chosen by the author for its friendly, welcoming style. The chapter titles are set in Wood Condensed Grotesk JNL, designed and published by Jeff Levine.